'In a world spinning with uncertainty, Paolo Gallo will help you find your balance. *The Seven Games of Leadership* is an ambitious and achievable guide to leading with resolve and living with purpose.'

Daniel H. Pink, #1 *New York Times* bestselling author of
The Power of Regret, Drive, and *To Sell is Human*

'In his new book, Paolo Gallo offers fresh, human-centred perspectives on leadership, underlining the need for introspection and self-awareness. Every leader who values personal growth and sustainable success will find this book an indispensable guide.'

Dorie Clark, *Wall Street Journal* bestselling author of
The Long Game and Executive Education Faculty,
Columbia Business School

'Paolo starts with a rather simple and personal question: how do I define success? Each of the seven "games" Paolo suggests gives me a personal diagnostic to turn the breath of ideas into a depth of personal understanding. Paolo is an optimist whose ideas helped me not just to cope, but to have hope in a better future.'

Dave Ulrich, Rensis Likbert Professor, Ross School of
Business, University of Michigan and Partner, the RTL Group

'After the impactful *The Compass and The Radar* Paolo Gallo's new book *The Seven Games of Leadership* offers us a precious and practical guide for our personal and professional growth. What do we need to become in order to thrive and evolve as a human being? How could we improve the cooperation with the people around us? What are the most important habits and attitudes to have an impact at every stage of our journey? In his book Paolo Gallo offers us the right questions to empower us to find the right answer to gives us a comprehensive understanding of the necessary steps – games to build a meaningful life.'

Alessandra Losito, Head of Italy, Equity Partner,
Pictet Wealth Management

'The perfect recipe to find out how to become a better leader today is what you will find in Paolo Gallo's newest book, *The Seven Games of Leadership*. The writer not only enlightens the way for our inner journey but also provides sound guidance for our professional and personal growth. For example, the simple concept that Leadership without integrity is not Leadership was an epiphany to me. In a world when everything changes at a frenetic pace, to focus on our positive changes – or even a real transition – is essential, if you know how to do it. The book includes positive energy and wisdom and I had fun reading it too.'

Mirja Cartia d'Asero, CEO Sole24 ore Group

Paolo Gallo

THE SEVEN GAMES OF LEADERSHIP

Navigating the Inner Journey of Leaders

BLOOMSBURY BUSINESS
LONDON • OXFORD • NEW YORK • NEW DELHI • SYDNEY

BLOOMSBURY BUSINESS
Bloomsbury Publishing Plc
50 Bedford Square, London, WC1B 3DP, UK
29 Earlsfort Terrace, Dublin 2, Ireland

BLOOMSBURY, BLOOMSBURY BUSINESS and the Diana logo are trademarks of
Bloomsbury Publishing Plc

First published in Great Britain 2023

A catalogue record for this book is available from the British Library

Library of Congress Cataloguing-in-Publication data has been applied for

ISBN: 978-1-3994-0547-8; eBook: 978-1-3994-0548-5

2 4 6 8 10 9 7 5 3 1

Typeset by Deanta Global Publishing Services, Chennai, India
Printed and bound in Great Britain by CPI Group (UK) Ltd, Croydon CR0 4YY

To find out more about our authors and books visit www.bloomsbury.com and sign up
for our newsletters

Contents

Foreword by Dave Ulrich   6
Introduction   9

1 Remembering Janus   25
2 Spotting differences, challenging assumptions   65
3 Game #1 – Inner   89
4 Game #2 – Better and Game #3 – Caring & Outer   117
5 Game #4 – Crisis   147
6 Game #5 – Reinvent, Game #6 – Revolution and
   Game #7 – Letting Go   177
7 How to increase your professional value   215
8 From, to   245

With Gratitude   267
Index   269

Foreword by Dave Ulrich

Rensis Likert Professor, Ross School of Business, University of Michigan; Partner, The RBL Group

Whenever I read posts, comments, articles or blogs by Paolo, I walk away saying 'wow', I learned something useful.

So, I was excited to probe his latest work, and again awed! Let me share what I learned and how others might use his ideas for personal and professional insights.

It helped me to organize this work by thinking of a diamond shape. At the top, start with a simple question, then diverge into complex and diverse thinking. At the wide angle of the diamond are a host of ideas that are nearly overwhelming. Then the bottom of the diamond filters those ideas into convergent thought and action, leading to a simple (not simplistic because of the divergent and convergent work shown in the diamond) answer to the starting question.

Paolo starts with a rather simple and personal question: how do I define my success? This captures my attention because I (we all) desire 'success' in whatever form, which comes from defining and clarifying 'what do I want most?' This is a seeker's quest and a journey many of us are on. This personal question frames choices, allocates resources and adapts over time. It is THE question that shapes who we are and who we can become and keeps us out of our personal 'hell' of not living up to our expectations, his beginning and ending metaphors for the book.

Then, as promised in his subtitle, he shares *'everything'* that goes into this success definition bucket. We get a glimpse into

Paolo's eclectic mind and diverse experiences over his 30 years of work including:

- Frameworks about the changing work megatrends that set the context for our individual success;
- Insights from Greek philosophers, psychologists, politics, religious leaders, athletes, professors and colleagues;
- Stories from a prescient daughter to senior executive, to sports heroes to leaders in Africa, to legacy leaders past and present.

I captured a few of Paolo's incredibly diverse experiences in the diamond figure. They remind me that the world we live in today has a tsunami of ideas, frameworks, tools and calls for action. We each have our playlist of context, ideas and stories that shape our experience. The wide angle of the diamond is helpful to broaden our thinking and risky to avoid overwhelming us with options. In an information rich world, there is always more to learn and this flood of ideas leaves me seeking but never finding for fear of missing out other options.

The bottom part of the diamond turns divergent ideas into convergent thinking and action. This filtering allows me to distil the range of ideas from so many sources into ideas with impact for me. Each of the seven 'games' Paolo suggests gives me a personal diagnostic to turn the breadth of ideas into a depth of personal understanding. The seven games, questions or filters build on each other (*see* his spiral on page 19) to help me find my personal answer to what I want and what success means for me.

From playing these seven games and answering these questions, the personal peace I seek emerges. This is not a peace 'in the world' but a peace that comes from inside oneself. Knowing what I want and what I define as success becomes my inner peace and my certainty in a world of uncertainty.

Paolo is an optimist whose ideas help me not just cope, but have hope in a better future.

I hope the book helps each of you as a reader as much as it helped me.

Thank you, Paolo.

Dave Ulrich
Alpine, Utah, USA

Introduction

All the world's a stage,
And all the men and women merely players;
They have their exits and their entrances,
And one man in his time plays many parts,
His acts being seven *ages*.[1]

What is your definition of hell?

Mine is: '*On your last day on earth, you will meet the person you could have become*'. Visualizing the difference between our real potential and what we eventually have become is scary. But what if, instead, we think, 'On your last day on earth, you will become who you were meant to be'? Real achievement is fulfilling our potential: we use the treasure hidden inside us, our talents, and offer it to others. And what does it mean, 'On your last day'? It's about the Never-Ending Quest. 'At each stage of human existence, the adult person is off on his quest for the holy grail, the way of life he seeks to live. At every stage, the solution to existence is not the solution he has come to find. The quest is never-ending.'[2]

The purpose of this book is to make sure that you will not have any bad surprises on your last day on earth. On the contrary,

---

[1] William Shakespeare, *As You Like It*, https://www.poetryfoundation.org/poems/56966/speech-all-the-worlds-a-stage
[2] Clare W. Graves, www.clarewgraves.com/theory_content/quotes.html

9

you will have achieved your full potential by mastering your personal and professional development.

Why can this book be helpful to you? Because you will learn to:

1. Open the window, notice what is happening outside and develop contextual intelligence, the capacity to connect the dots. To pay attention to the seven megatrends (*see* Chapter One) that are shaping our new world context and handle the frequent moments of uncertainty and crisis.

2. Challenge and remove outdated assumptions about work, success and personal and professional development.

3. Gain a better understanding of who you are, what your strengths and talents are, what you are good at – and what you are not.

4. Learn, internalize and master the seven phases – I call them Games – of your personal and professional development.

5. Face the necessity of losses and crises, and discover the joy of reinventing yourself.

6. 'Steal' the secret formula for increasing your professional value, to remain relevant and employable, not simply employed.

7. Have fun through reading *The Seven Games of Leadership*, a book focused on supporting you in your personal and professional development. I will not – arrogantly – tell you what you think but will try – humbly – to help you how to think, so you will draw your own conclusions. Yours, not mine.

But wait: what exactly do we mean by development?

Personal development is something we tend to equate with the ageing process, assuming, for example, that a 50-year-old person has gained more wisdom, judgement and experience than a 30-year-old person. Plausibly yes, but we have learned that sometimes this is not the case.

As for professional development, we often confuse it with climbing the corporate ladder: we assume that CEOs or vice presidents have achieved more professional growth than a person lower down in the hierarchy. They may have more power, better salaries and status, but not necessarily real and meaningful development.

Swiss Psychologist Susanne R. Cook-Greuter[3] proposes a framework to define adult development, applicable to both the personal and professional domains. She says we need to distinguish between lateral and vertical development. Lateral development is about providing additional skills and competencies: expanding, enriching and deepening a person's meaning-making. It is the equivalent of filling a suitcase as efficiently as possible. Vertical development is rarer and – the way I see it – more fun and meaningful. In a vertical development, we learn to see the world from different perspectives; we transform our interpretation of reality. Actual development refers to the *transformation of consciousness*, a vivid life experience of gaining new insights and understanding of life.

Personal development is somewhat similar to climbing a mountain: a person who has reached the top is at a later stage and can understand and 'see' the full view, but a person still in an earlier stage cannot yet understand what is in store. The hike to get to the top is tiring but the view and the understanding are truly worth the effort.

The Seven Games is a book that offers a framework and guidelines for personal and professional development because we need to thrive, not just survive. It reflects what I have found and observed, not what I have predicted or assumed. The book you are reading offers you a meaningful and practical path to master the seven phases – I call them the Seven Games – for the most relevant and exciting journey of your life: one of

---

[3] Susanne R. Cook-Greuter, 'Making the Case for a Developmental Perspective', *Industrial and Commercial Training*, volume 36, number 7, 2004, pp. 275–281, Emerald Group Publishing Limited.

self-discovery and self-development. The greatest predictor of growth and happiness is actionable self-knowledge, especially during the times in which we are currently living.

We are not alone in our journey. We need to understand the broader picture, the new context, connect and collaborate with people, and co-create a legacy more significant than ourselves. It is a true Revolution: I am because we are.

What's the best part of my job? Listening to your questions and your stories.

Your questions, stories and reflections are the key to understanding what is in your minds and hearts, what keeps you awake at night, your challenges, doubts, frustrations, pain, expectations, hopes, dreams, pride and your joy. I have received several thousand questions from you: from people attending my keynotes, from executives participating in my workshops, from clients in my coaching practice, from readers of my articles, posts or books, and from university students. Yet, after listening to several thousand questions and stories for many years, I can see specific themes constantly emerging.

Sure, we all would like to get a good job and progress by climbing up a few steps on the corporate ladder. But this is not enough: the recent Great Resignation seems counterintuitive. I would instead call it the Great Realization, coupled with the Great Acceleration, as we identify relevant professional and personal life elements. Are these people crazy to leave paid jobs? No, they are not. They are searching for meaning, not just money. But, unfortunately, organizations that believe that the problem can be solved by tossing out large bonuses have not understood that people are not for sale, that there is something more than just 'getting by': collecting a pay cheque every month is not enough.

From your questions and my own 30-year experience, I understand that there is more to life than racking up accomplishments and working 60 to 70 hours per week with a couple of weeks of holiday a year (if you're lucky), during which you'll check your emails at least 15 times a day. You and I are proud of what we have achieved, but are we equally proud of what we have become? From your questions, I have learned that success is defined not only by results (I became vice president, increased sales, reduced costs) or by running in the rat race, but mainly from the journey and the process of self-improvement and mastery. **Self-Leadership**. Our personal development consists of first understanding the context and then learning how to avoid the wrong games and how to play the Seven Games.

In this book, I will provide you with a clear, meaningful path, tools, insights and more questions to master the Seven Games you have always played, and will continue to play, in your life. The point is that your career is not a stand-alone star: we are part of a fascinating universe, a bigger picture, a complex system. I am sure that we have figured out that we are not dealing with business as usual. We are in an entirely New Context – not a new normal – hence the need to understand it, to see clearly which megatrends are impacting our lives, to connect the dots and develop our contextual intelligence and our system thinking.

We also need to deal with the many destabilizing moments that can derail our journey. I call them 'WTF moments': we've collected many of them recently, haven't we? If we aspire to be a leader, which behaviour do we need to internalize? How can we develop our 'response-ability' rather than merely react to what is happening around us? How can we take care of ourselves as a precondition to taking care of others? How can we be at our best in order to give our best?

Still, something is missing here. What if we define success not as a list of individual accomplishments, but as working in a psychologically safe place with a real mission? What if we offer our families, communities and the world something extraordinary: anyone up for a revolution?

Don't worry: it's not about destroying, criticizing or protesting for the sake of it. There is too much competition in this domain. Building a revolutionary career is about *leaving behind a legacy* that will genuinely improve what we do, why we are doing it and who we are. Ironically, we achieve true happiness when we stop focusing exclusively on ourselves and offer our talents and values to others. Indeed, EGO can be the enemy here. While excellence can be defined by what we achieve, character is who we are, and genuine integrity is what we are NOT prepared to do to accomplish our goals. Frequent and necessary losses and failures are the main ingredients of learning, an integral part of our journey.

I do not doubt that you can become a true champion of the Revolution: I can see it in the sparkle in your eyes. Can you see it yourself? You can get a hint of understanding the essence of a genuine revolutionary by reading four letters of the word revolution backwards, starting from the letter L.

L. O.V. E. It lies at the heart of everything. To love is a verb that implies action: respect, sharing, honesty, gratefulness and time. With special gratitude to the Beatles for their musical reminder: all we need is love, with perhaps some help from our friends, if we care to invest the time for them. We are the others or, if you prefer, I am because we are.

What did you learn so far?

I love Saturday breakfast time with my family. Like everyone, we are born to run during the week until, finally, Saturday morning arrives. We always have exciting and meaningful conversations triggered by powerful questions.

My favourite question to my daughter Sadika for at least a decade is, 'What is the most important thing that you learned this week?' Before she was 12, the answer invariably related to something like the history of Egypt, British literature, or maybe a chemistry formula. But in the last few years, she has started to reflect on the behaviour of other students, teachers and her own. Now her learning is about her, no longer outside her. I guess it is her first significant step towards self-mastery?

One day, she was the one who asked me the first question. 'Dad,' she asked, 'how long have you been working?' My answer was immediate and precise, with a tone of over-confidence. I started back in 1990, so my answer implied 'As I started working 15 years before you were born, please defer to my extensive, amazing experience, young lady.' She was too kind to react, or maybe she was interested in my answer. She continued (with a technique that we call 'probing' in coaching). 'So, what is the most important thing you have learned so far during the last 30 years?' I put down my coffee and then solemnly answered, 'Can you please give me a week to think about it?'

I didn't answer the following week and thought she might have forgotten; but she didn't and she repeated the question two weeks later. I negotiated one more week with the promise that this time I would return with an answer. This book is my answer to Sadika. Bear with me. It is not the memoir of some guy: why would you ever read it if it was? But I trust that, despite all the shortcomings, you will be referring to this book as a helpful guide and a caring pocket-sized coach devoted to you for your personal and professional development.

I have given it a lot of thought and decided to go deeper rather than faster. On reflection, I have started with data, remembering an excellent manager I used to have who began every meeting with his team with the phrase 'In God, we trust'. Our task was to complete the sentence by adding 'don't worry, we will also bring you data'. He often told me that he was not interested in my opinion but only facts; then – and only then – my judgement and my wisdom on a good day. The point is that collecting data is relatively easy while understanding the difference between data and information is not. Connecting the dots – you can call it developing contextual intelligence – starts to get tricky, while translating data into insight is genuinely challenging. But the most challenging leap is transforming data into wisdom, a true ART done with experience, judgement and love. Yes, love.

As I was preparing to answer Sadika, I started collecting some data. What have I really learned by listening to thousands of people? Given my roles – 30 years in Human Resources, 16 as Director at the World Economic Forum, the World Bank and European Bank for Reconstruction and Development and my current role and passion as executive coach, author, speaker and adjunct professor – I am offering and sharing with you experience and respect. Most importantly, I have made at least a million mistakes and got a few essential things right, with a bit of luck and lots of help from my friends, coupled with some bitter lessons. Who hasn't had some of those?

What did I learn by engaging with so many people literally from all over the globe? Suddenly, I realized that I did NOT have thousands of different conversations but similar conversations with similar topics that emerged with regular, chronic frequency. I notice constant patterns of language and behaviour in people. I recall that the same issues and dynamics came up with Angela in London, Dennis in Washington and Igor in Geneva. When Rob told me 'I feel stuck', his words and body language were saying precisely the same thing I observed with Sarita 10 years earlier. I've noticed that successful people have many traits, behaviours and mindsets, regardless of any other variable.

I've seen amazing people with such incredible potential, yet they're stuck somewhere in the quicksand of their own making. I've witnessed extraordinary careers of people who were considered the underdogs, yet they grew exponentially. Not only on climbing the corporate ladder but also as individuals. I have seen, eaten with, listened to, and laughed with so many amazing people who, at times, were too busy or preoccupied to notice that opportunities, family and life were fading away. They were somehow unable to reconsider their life, prisoners of their identity and recurrent *modus operandi*: it seems that some were banging clumsily on the self-destruct button, unable to stop. They confused their jobs with their career: these are two different things. A few fell into depression and some into the abysses of addiction to numb their pain. Some were too busy to notice that the world was changing around them faster than their capacity to pause, ask the right question and adapt. Others blossomed: it was spectacular to watch them.

I have listened to thousands of questions and stories and seen common themes, an unmistakable red line, a clear pattern constantly developing regardless of their seniority, academic qualification, sector, function or job. During the last decade, I've started having a distinct feeling of 'Hey, I've already seen this movie,' as people begin to unpack their issues with me. I have already seen the next scene, the next move and the following line that every actor will do or say. From their body language, voice and posture, I understood which game they were playing, not with me but within themselves. At times the movie I was watching was a feel-good film; at times, it was a horror show or thriller, and more frequently, a comedy or tragedy, a farce or even porn. Good grief!

By rereading one of my favourite books, *Games People Play* by Eric Berne,[4] I got a better understanding of structural and transactional analysis and grasped a powerful concept. People play games, not necessarily as conscious players but as actors in a predetermined role assigned by someone else, e.g. their families, company, communities or by themselves, without them knowing. I noticed the same dynamics, listening to the same conversations, just with different choreography.

A game is defined not as a shallow, mindless activity but rather as a real contest with clear, mostly unwritten rules that every player should understand to master the game and be able to walk away and leave it when necessary. By reflecting on these conversations, I noticed and later understood that, fundamentally, people are playing preset and well-defined games, each with rules of engagement, predictable dynamics and predetermined outcomes.

This realization formed the structure of the book.

Chapter One provides an overview of seven megatrends that are reshaping our lives, and the lives of our families, communities

---

[4] Eric Berne, *Games People Play*, originally published in 1964, updated 40th anniversary edition, Ballantine Books, 1996.

and countries. We will emphasize the need to develop our contextual intelligence, how we connect the dots and our capacity to understand and master transformation without being derailed by frequent WTF moments.

Chapter Two is about remembering what we stand for, our value system, and challenging some assumptions that no longer serve us. We need to develop an *appetite for disruption* to see the world from a brand new, different perspective.

We will then learn to play and understand the Seven Games.

Chapter Three is about unfolding Game One, the Inner Game. The quest to fully understand why you are here, finding your true inner voice. What are you good at?

Chapter Four starts with Game Two, the Better Game: how can we improve, gain credibility and earn a reputation? Game Three, the Caring and Outer Game, occurs when we grow as individuals and we care – responsibly – about others. We 'open the windows' by understanding the bigger picture.

Chapter Five is fully devoted to Game Four, the Crisis Game. How can we avoid the loyal soldier syndrome, the red ball, Peter Pan – by embracing the necessity of a midlife crisis? How can we become brave travellers, to steer our life in the right direction? How can we effectively shape a meaningful life transition?

Chapter Six is about the energy and rebirth of Game Five. Reinvent yourself, because of a conscious personal decision not generated by external life-quakes. Game Six is igniting a Revolution, the joy of giving, being of service, the ultimate sign of wisdom. Last comes Game Seven, Letting Go: it's a process that starts with healing, losing, quitting and then letting go. It's the ultimate success, the supreme sign of fulfilment, it's returning home, it's passing the torch with graciousness.

Chapter Seven tries to provide an answer to the question: how can you increase your professional value? What is leadership in the new context that is unfolding so rapidly in front of us? It is about being relevant and impactful – employable – rather than being employed.

Chapter Eight, 'From, to', offers you reflections but never conclusions. We will learn what Lagom and Ubuntu mean, the difference between ghosts and ancestors, how we move from something toxic to something else, meaningful and impactful. You will also find a table summarizing the main elements of each game and the Development Framework Spiral (see below) to visualize the Seven Games. I trust you will be able to measure and see where you are in your development journey and how to progress and move to the next game. This final chapter gives a sense of the journey of our personal and professional development, in many different ways.

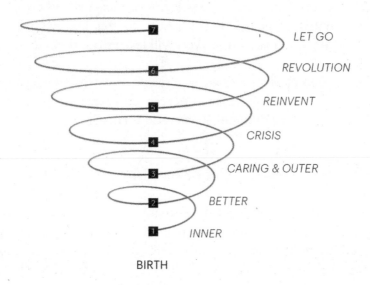

Spiral Development Framework – Paolo Gallo

I would like to make a bet with you: I trust you will recognize yourself or some colleagues, friends or family playing one of these games. Or perhaps you've played one or two of them yourself in the past. So hold on a second – there is more to come.

I have written *The Seven Games* based on three sound principles.

One: we learn from many different sources, disciplines and experiences, and especially from storytelling and emotions. This is the everlasting lesson we learned from Peter Drucker, the founder of Modern Management Theory, who has used several disciplines to build his own theories and ideas. John Muir wrote, 'When we try to pick up anything by itself, we find it hitched to everything else in the universe.'[5]

You will find in this book references and stories related to Greek mythology, sports (mainly tennis and basketball), politics, philosophy, psychology, coaching, biology, history, movies, literature, poetry and music.

Two: we learn from listening and by co-operating with other people. I have invited 15 guests to contribute to this book. They are first-class professionals: I hope you will learn from them as much as I have.

Three: as the Romans used to say 'Repetita Juvant' – repeating helps. So you will find that many concepts and ideas are presented more than once in different shapes and forms.

This I believe

When I rejoined the World Bank, many colleagues were simply delighted but not because of me. They could finally dump on my desk many tasks and responsibilities that, according to them, belonged to me. Saying 'no, thank you' was not an option: it's called the rookie syndrome, even if your title is director. As a result, I had a tsunami of work. One week after starting my new job and I was three months behind schedule.

One of the tasks that I inherited was the famous induction programme: a week of training for all the new people recruited by the World Bank Group. This induction took place almost

---

[5] Andrew Schwartz, *How to Innovate Fearlessly*, Peter Drucker Challenge essay award, 2013, https://www.druckerchallenge.org/uploads/pics/Andrew_Schwartz_Drucker_essay_Schwartz_238830567-1.pdf

every month, and people gathered together from all over the globe. It was wonderful to meet this group, about 120–150 people each time.

My predecessor told me not to worry about the meeting. All I needed to do was ask people's names, roles, positions and reporting lines, and by the time everyone had spoken, the two hours were gone, and voilà, the meeting was over. Easy, isn't it? The problem was that it was a horrible meeting, people were bored and mentally absent, and there were no emotions in the room, like in a classroom where people were only accounted for but not listened to.

So I decided to change the question to: *why are you here?* What do you stand for, believe in? All of a sudden, the positive energy re-emerged and people engaged. I remember three people sitting just in front of me: one was a driver from Mexico, the other was a former minister of education in Eastern Africa and the third was a lawyer from Poland. They all answered the same way: I am here to help, to fight poverty. They had tears in their eyes. They did not take a job; they kept a promise to themselves. They did not have titles like manager or officer or senior economist. They acted like faithful missionaries with a notion deep inside, the burning desire to improve the state of their own country and communities, for real, by being there. They knew what they stood for and they believed in something bigger than themselves. The secret sauce held such a complex, fascinating and diverse organization together: maybe also the magic glue of purpose, connection and motivation?

This I Believe was originally a five-minute programme hosted by journalist Edward R. Murrow from 1951 to 1955 on CBS Radio Network. The show encouraged famous personalities and everyday people to write short essays about their motivation in life and then read them on the air. The US National Public Radio (NPR) resumed this programme from 2005 to 2009. Their archives contain absolute gems from regular people, like you and me, who shared their stories in five minutes. You may consider this radio programme like the father of TED Talks. I listened to dozens of these stories and I always ended up with a smile on my face and restored faith in humankind. For example, a 12-year-old girl lost her dog during a picnic by the lake with her family: she was desperate to find her beloved dog and she remembered that they used to listen to the Beatles in the car. Maybe, if we return to the same spot where we lost the dog and play the same song loudly, the dog will reappear? 'Yellow Submarine' did the trick. These stories are a powerful antidote to depression and sadness. So, if you were a guest on this radio programme, what would you say after, 'This I believe'? *The Seven Games* also offers the answer to this question. This I believe: if you have similar beliefs, this book is worth reading. Let's see if we have a common value system, the same beliefs.

1. I believe in opening the window to see what's happening outside
We need to have the capacity to develop system thinking, to see how one element in the system has an impact on everything, to develop *contextual intelligence.*

You will find seven megatrends that are already impacting our lives. In the first chapter, you will find a concise executive summary for each element. The purpose is to raise awareness of how these megatrends will impact you, your community, your company and your country.

2. I believe in collaboration based on trust.
When you move from independence to interdependence in your journey, you realize that the only way forward is by collaborating with others rather than competing.

3. I believe that integrity and trustworthy leadership matters.
Relativity applies to physics, not ethics, said the great physicist, Albert Einstein. He was right. Ethics starts by having a shared understanding of words and principles. The opposite of the truth is a lie; it is not an alternative fact. Leadership without integrity is not leadership; it is something else.

4. I believe in the necessity of a crisis.
Never miss the opportunity of a crisis, or the pain and the discovery that every moment of transformation brings. What matters most is how well you walk through the fire, wrote poet Charles Bukowski.

5. I believe in helping people.
I frequently ask myself a question: What did I learn in my travels in the favelas in South America, in the slums in India, in meeting the *campesinos* in Guatemala, in listening to the survivors of the horrific regime of Pol Pot in Cambodia or the street vendor in Addis Ababa? People don't want pity or charity: they want and deserve Possibilities, Dignity and Respect.

6. I believe in developing people's potential.
What do you see when you look at people? I always see their potential: I know the gap between who they are now and what they could become tomorrow. It is somewhat similar to what the Italian artist Michelangelo once said: 'Sculpting is easy: you just go down to the skin and stop.' You have to carve out the unnecessary to find the perfect form. It gives me joy to carve out and support people in their journey; it fills my heart to show them their untapped possibilities. Most of the people I work with have a sort of unacknowledged greatness, a hidden treasure inside. I try to help it to resurface.

7. I believe in constant transformation and life-long learning.
We can't be what we have always been, do what we have always done, think what we have always thought, go where we have always been and close the door to change and transformation: playing the same song.

Let me introduce you to Walter Othman, born in 1922. He's been in the Guinness World Records since 2018: the person who has worked the longest in the same company. He works at Reneaux View in Santa Caterina, in Southern Brazil. He joined the company in 1938, so he's been working there for 84 years.

Yes, you read it correctly, 84. Walter noticed that his colleagues became lonely and sad once they retired, so he decided to keep on working. He has been marketing director for 43 years and he gave some advice in a recent interview. Go to bed early, do some exercise and avoid soft drinks and junk food at all costs. Most importantly, keep learning; be ready to transform and adapt every day. He has done it for 30,660 days: *parabéns* (congratulations), Walter!

In short: I believe in you, in us and in people. But, of course, the real challenge is to keep faith in humankind after you lose your innocence. But magic does happen once you give other people possibilities, respect, dignity and caring. I also believe that a story is the shortest distance between two people.

We remember stories much more than numbers or principles: as Ben Zander wrote in *The Art of Possibilities*, 'life is a story we invent'. So in every chapter of this book, you will find several stories – accurate, documented and verifiable. In Chapter Six, we will go to jail and you will find more stories of true revolutionaries, people who have left a legacy behind them that will last forever.

There is also an extra bonus: I believe in walking away from toxic people and situations, walking away from dangerous environments and negative individuals who want to bring you down. A bad system will beat a good person every time, as the great thinker W. Edwards Deming told us. It is an act of self-respect and self-care. My point is that if they're going to get you down, they are already below you. As Former First Lady Michelle Obama once said, 'when they go low, we always go high'. Always. Don't forget to smile when you meet them and then walk away. It drives them crazy, and frankly, it's quite a lot of fun.

Ready? Fasten your seat belt and let's go.

1

Remembering Janus

'In a time of drastic change it is the learners
who inherit the future. The learned usually find
themselves equipped to live in a world that no
longer exists.'

ERIC HOFFER[6]

WTF times

I need to confess something to you. By writing this book,
I have a hidden agenda. I deserve to be nominated as a worthy
candidate for a Nobel Prize. But wait a second, not just any
Nobel. I would appreciate the one in Economic Science.
I know that psychologists and behavioural economists such
as Daniel Kahneman[7] got it in 2002, so why not me? I trust
no one will check my credentials (I'm not a psychologist
myself), but with so many charlatans in charge, I may get away
with it. I have been studying and working for decades, and –
eureka! – I have found the formula that will revolutionize our
understanding of why we feel the way we think. Bear with me
because the sophistication and complexity of my three-part

[6] Eric Hoffer, https://www.britannica.com/biography/Eric-Hoffer
[7] https://www.nobelprize.org/prizes/economic-sciences/2002/summary/

formula require your full attention. The problem is these days I get most of my exercise from shaking my head in disbelief. I wish we were living *only* in VUCA times: we are in the middle of WTF times.

Part One: WTF

Yes, you heard me. For the few unfamiliar with the jargon, sophistication and intricacies of the English language, WTF means *What the F…* a familiar sentiment that we have felt many times in the last two decades, with exponential speed, frequency and intensity in the previous three or four years. The essential components of WTF moments are the following:

- *Total surprise:* we did not see *that* coming, followed by an initial grasping, but not yet a complete understanding, that *that* event will impact our lives in many different ways.
- *Increased anxiety, anger, sadness, fear, rage:* not nice stuff.
- *Feeling stuck,* as we can't answer the fundamental question: Now what? What does this mean to me?

The examples of WTF moments are a dime a dozen and, in retrospect, WTF could have been the title of this book.

We all had many WTF moments, too many. Think about the 9/11 terrorist attack, the tsunami of 2004, the devastating natural disasters affecting the planet or the countless, horrific acts of violence towards innocent people; or visualize the effects of climate change or learning the results of elections that broke our hearts and witnessing in disbelief incompetent clowns elected or promoted to positions of power. But, wait: I'm not done yet. Shall we consider COVID-19, two years of complete hell for the entire planet, or maybe the invasion and the war against Ukraine? We don't know when or how it will end as I write these pages. Good grief! This list could be several pages long and I haven't even added all the events that have personally affected our families and loved ones.

Part Two: Multiply WTF by at least 10; higher numbers are even more credible.

WTF moments of complete and utter disbelief are frequent: how do we feel by witnessing and hearing people, such as Flat Earthers, or climate change, COVID-19 or Holocaust deniers, who reject reality or construct absurd conspiracy theories? What is their golden rule? The more outrageous, the better. This explains why we need to multiply WTF by at least a factor of 10.

Part Three: WTF multiplied by n (at least 10) has to be squared: (WTF × n) ^2.

Charlatans in bad faith are self-promoted to the same level as Nelson Mandela or Martin Luther King: they are freedom fighters of the same category, aren't they? So voilà: here's the formula and a possible explanation about why we feel the way we think. Luckily, we have an antidote to WTF moments. Perhaps, with this formula, I may be considered for a Nobel Prize. Who knows?

The problem with WTF moments (Andrew James collected thousands of them,)[8] is that not only does WTF derail our existence but it also impairs and diverts our attention to focus on and understand what really matters: the megatrends that are already underway. We need to pay attention to megatrends, notice and understand how they are impacting our lives.

Festina Lente

Festina Lente is a classical adage as well as an oxymoron: *make haste, slowly* or *hurry up, but take your time.* The motto became famous in ancient times and was later adopted by Roman emperors such as Titus and Augustus, by the Medici family in

---

[8] Andrew James, *1000 WTF Facts: WOW Facts to Blow Your Mind,* self-published, 2022, written by the creator of Twitter account @mrwtffacts

Florence and quoted by William Shakespeare in one of his first comedies, *Love's Labour's Lost*.

The emblem of the motto is a dolphin (*Festina*) encircled by an anchor (*Lente*). Twenty centuries later, this motto is still relevant. We need to both go fast by understanding the transformation around us (more to come), but at the same time we feel the need to go deeper, not only faster. *Lente* – slowly – implies taking the time to fully understand and internalize what is happening to avoid feeling like a kite in a storm, unable to find meaning or maintain a steady direction in our journey.

In addition to the WTF moments, we also witness many significant events. How do we deal with them? We all have quotes, phrases and lyrics from songs or poetry that have impacted our lives. One of my favourites is from the remarkable book by Viktor Frankl, *Man's Search for Meaning*.[9] Frankl was a Jewish psychiatrist who was tragically taken prisoner with his family and sent to Auschwitz by the Nazis. As soon as they arrived at the concentration camp, all his loved ones were killed – only he was left alive. One day, alone and desperate, he realized that while the Nazis had taken away from him almost everything, he still retained what he called the last of human freedoms: the power to decide how to respond to whatever happened to him. As he wrote, 'Between stimulus and response, there is a space. In this space, our freedom to choose.'

Our freedom to choose: can you believe it? His soul is devastated by the loss of his family; he's barely surviving in the worst possible conditions. Yet, he had this illuminating insight, an intuition that saved him and later served as the basis for his new theory: logotherapy. Frankl quotes the words of Nietzsche, 'He who has a Why to live for, can bear almost any How.'

What can we learn from Frankl? Pretty much everything we need to know in life. There is a space between stimuli – what happens to us – and our response. If we immediately react, we

---

[9] Viktor E. Frankl, *Man's Search for Meaning*, Boston: Beacon Press, 1959.

remove our capacity to respond, our response-ability. Reacting fast is activated by the amygdala, the reptilian part of the brain. The frontal cortex, the most developed by our intellectual and emotional intelligence, drives responding. If we act consciously, we can shape a meaningful response, which is the ultimate proof of our freedom. So, yes, we have a choice, what in Latin is called *libero arbitrio*, free will. We are therefore what we choose, not what others or what situations choose for us.

Last, but not least, we need to take care of ourselves; self-care is a precondition to being a leader. We can give our best only if we are at our best; when all our batteries – emotional, physical, cognitive and spiritual – are fully charged. It is probably the perfect example of cognitive dissonance: we know it well, but we don't do it. Since we have to know the Seven Games of our life, we need to be in great shape to master them all. I know you will.

We make our own choices. We need to be at our best to give our best. *Festina Lente* is a meaningful motto that we need to apply to understand the seven megatrends that impact our lives. Let's take a quick look to see what they are and then we'll visualize them together. WTF moments also derail our attention from what is essential: maybe we don't perceive them as urgent as we are emotionally hijacked by WTF moments and disturbing events.

The point is that we cannot afford to miss what is happening, the systemic change: megatrends that are already impacting our lives, our communities, countries and jobs. Let's see what they are. I have asked recognized, credible, competent top professionals to summarize each of them in two pages. Ready?

1. **Climate Emergency** by Marco Albani
2. **Inequality and Trust** by Carlos Scartascini
3. **Demographics** by Jennifer Blanke and **Diversity** by Sandra-Stella Triebl
4. **Technology AI** by Fred Werner and **Digital Transformation** by Giuseppe Stigliano

5. **Infodemic and Reputation** by Mirja Cartia D'Asero
6. **Geopolitics** by Salvatore Pedulla
7. **What do workers want? The world of work** by Riccardo Barberis

Climate Emergency – by Marco Albani

Planet, we have a situation here. I have asked Marco Albani,[10] former senior executive at McKinsey, World Economic Forum, co-founder and current CEO of Chloris Geospatial, to explain why we are in a climate emergency and what it means for us.

2022 was the year in which the climate emergency, a slow-moving global train wreck since at least the second half of the twentieth century, was becoming fast enough, and throwing enough sparks and debris around, that it would take a particularly strong commitment to denial to ignore it. If you have not been living under a rock, you've noticed that extreme weather events, snowballing since the last decade and fuelled by a warmer climate, reached unprecedented dimensions in the summer of 2022. Severe droughts struck Africa, China, Europe and the Western United States. Pakistan saw unprecedented monsoon floods, killing over a thousand people and displacing millions. From India to Europe extreme heat waves broke records everywhere. While no single extreme event can be exclusively attributed to climate change, all these disasters would have been incredibly less likely in a world that had not warmed by $1.1°$ Celsius over pre-industrial levels. What's worse, we have now added enough greenhouse gases to the atmosphere that even with zero emissions moving forward we are bound to see what the IPCC calls 'irreversible damage'.

[10] https://www.linkedin.com/in/marco-albani/

Your personal climate risk and opportunities assessment
So, what does that mean for you and for your personal and professional development? It depends a lot on your situation. You might find it helpful to carry out a personal assessment of your exposure to climate risks and opportunities, which will come primarily in two areas regarding physical aspects and transition issues.

The first area covers the risks and opportunities presented by the physical reality of climate change. As this continues, extreme weather events become more common; ecosystems respond with subtle and then abrupt changes, and infrastructure is challenged by unprecedented conditions, especially around water management. Understanding your personal resilience, and that of your community, to the impacts of climate change is essential and offers opportunities to mitigate risks and adapt to the unavoidable component of the change.

The second area covers the risks and opportunities created by transitioning to a net-zero economy. All industries will be transformed, but some more than others. Understand how your current or preferred one is exposed to the transition: is it heavily dependent on a future with continued emissions like coal mining or oil and gas exploration? Could it shift to zero-emissions, but with profound transformation, like the automotive sector? Or is it exposed to unsustainable models that are indirect but strong, like a financial institution deeply invested in fossils? Depending on your current studies, professional experience and aspirations, you might be at much greater risk of having your plans and possibly even your financial and job security threatened by the transitions. This will surely colour your perspective on the issue as well. In any case, you should find out.

Finally, you should also consider the political, social and even emotional implications of facing the climate crisis. The worst impact of climate change will largely affect those who have done the least to cause it – the global poor and the future generations – while those who carry the biggest responsibilities, having enjoyed a world of seemingly unlimited opportunities, are largely shielded from the fallout.

As the reality of the crisis settles in, it will undoubtedly add tension to existing fault lines among and within countries, but also inside communities and even families. You might find that you want to completely change the direction and goals of your professional and personal development journey, or at the opposite extreme you may feel more determined about your plans and objectives. Climate change is already here and it will only worsen if we don't take transformative action.

Inequality and Trust – by Carlos Scartascini

We have heard it many times: *we are all in the same boat.* I respectfully disagree.

I believe that we are in the same storm but in different boats. Very few are pampered in luxury yachts in Mykonos or Portofino; many are surviving by floating along in cheap inflatables, trying to escape war and famine, to find a better future somewhere else other than home. Most are somewhere in the middle. At times we wonder if the current system has given us just a few rotten apples we need to remove, or if we have a rotten tree to eradicate. Have we produced a monster system for the benefit of the few at the expense of the many? Do we even care?

My family and I have gone many times to volunteer at a charity organization here in Geneva: the task was giving food and basic goods to people affected by the COVID crisis. Now, Geneva is one of the richest cantons in rich Switzerland, constantly at the top of the rankings for quality of life. We did not expect to see what we saw: long lines of people waiting patiently to get a bag worth 20, maybe 30 Swiss francs, filled with food, soaps, diapers and toothpaste. Hundreds of them, all very kind and grateful: they could hardly look into my eyes when they collected their bag, ashamed to be in this situation. The current system has left too many behind. We have failed them. When did they become invisible to us?

Economies are traditionally assessed by GDP growth. This growth measures the size of the cake but not how the cake is distributed. Instead, the index for determining income distribution is called the Gini Coefficient,[11] which gauges the inequality among values of a frequency distribution, such as the levels of income. So, the real problem is not limited to creating growth but to achieving shared prosperity. Regrettably, the world is going exactly in the opposite direction.

One continent that is suffering from a lack of shared prosperity is Latin America. I cannot think of a more qualified person than Carlos Scartascini,[12] Head of the Development Research Group at the Inter-American Development Bank, to explain why it matters to us.

On the morning of 25 October 2019, Paula woke up, had breakfast and took the bus to downtown Santiago, Chile, to join a protest. In Bogota, Colombia, Pedro left work early on 21 November of the same year and headed downtown, ready to shout and show his discontent. Paula, Pedro and thousands of fellow compatriots and Latin Americans that year asked for, among other things, equal treatment and better opportunities for all. Even in a situation of some prosperity in the region (for example, Chile's income per capita had grown more than 50 per cent since 2000), people were unhappy about the distribution of that income, an understandable feeling, given that Latin America and the Caribbean is the region with the most unequal income distribution in the world.

There are many ways to measure inequality. A simple one is by looking at how much one group in the population earns compared to another. For example, in Latin America and

[11] https://en.wikipedia.org/wiki/Gini_coefficient
[12] https://www.linkedin.com/in/carlos-scartascini/

the Caribbean, on average, the wealthiest 1 per cent takes in 21 per cent of the income of the entire economy. That number is 10 per cent in the case of developed countries. In Latin America and the Caribbean, the wealthiest 10 per cent of the population earns 22 times more than those in the bottom 10 per cent, making the distance between rich and poor more than double the average in developed countries.

In addition to being undesirable in terms of justice, high inequality has many drawbacks. One of them is that it proliferates mistrust. Trust is the belief that others will not act opportunistically; if given a chance, others will not exploit a given situation, when they have more information or power.

Signs of unequal income and wealth naturally breed mistrust, mainly if people believe that those in the upper tiers of distribution are there unfairly and use their riches to amass more power and advantages. Inequality tends to favour segregation, which also engenders mistrust.

Shared prosperity had been lifting everyone's boat. Still, expectations seem to have risen faster than fortunes; perceptions of injustice have too. Individuals tend to misperceive both their country's income and wealth distribution and their own position in that distribution. Instead of using objective data, they take clues from their environment and those around them to estimate their relative position. Choosing a reference group that is not representative makes things worse. Watching the rich parade around the world in yachts through social media gives a sense of being poor to most.

When there is no trust, individuals prefer to stop paying their taxes and tend to walk away from public goods. It is not a coincidence that some of the most extensive private education and health systems are established in less developed countries. It would not be surprising that Paula and Pedro, while enraged about inequality, are also thinking about sending their kids to private schools. And they would rather not pay their taxes, but instead provide their own security and health services.

Paula and Pedro are right that unequal income distribution should be dealt with, particularly when the system is rigged to favour some over others. The key is doing it in a way that enhances trust and social cohesion. Countries can only prosper when their citizens are willing to make individual sacrifices for the common good (from paying taxes and bus fares, to voting and refraining from littering). Social cohesion depends on a common objective, more information and empowerment and lower segregation. Inequality will recede as we find ways to trust each other more.

Gary Stevenson was Citibank's most profitable trader in 2011. He got extremely rich, very fast, and retired when he was 27 (not a typo, yes 27). How? By betting that inequality would destroy the US and the UK.[13] He bet – and he won – that inequality would be the name of the game. He has seen inequality growing: he kept on betting on it so he kept on winning. He's now an inequality economist, somewhat ironic. Gary lives in a luxury penthouse in London. *But in the house down the road the mom doesn't eat and she hopes that the children don't notice. But they do.* His reflection, not mine.

Understanding the rainbow: Demographics and Diversity

The Stanford Center on Longevity has produced an insightful paper called *Map For Life*.[14] The world's population has now reached 8 billion people.[15] What does it mean when today's children will be able to live to 100 years of age?[16] What does it

---

[13] https://fortune.com/2022/09/29/rich-betting-inequality-uk-budget-truss-destroy-us-uk-sorry-finance-economy-politics-international-gary-stevenson/
[14] https://longevity.stanford.edu/the-new-map-of-life-full-report/
[15] https://www.statista.com/chart/28744/world-population-growth-timeline-and-forecast/
[16] Lynda Gratton and Andrew Scott, *The 100-Year Life: Living and Working in an Age of Longevity* Bloomsbury, 2016.

mean to our health, finances, pension, food and energy supply and to our lives? What does it mean to the job market, your career and your life-long learning? I asked Jennifer Blanke,[17] former Vice President of Human Development and Agriculture at the African Development Bank and Chief Economist at the World Economic Forum, to share her insights.

Demographics: a portrait of humanity – by Jennifer Blanke

It is hard to think about any big issue – whether socioeconomic, environmental or political – that is not somehow impacted by demographic trends and shifts. Demographics describe a given population based on selected criteria – usually aspects like age, race, gender and income. When devising strategies and policies, governments make decisions every day based on demographic considerations.

To illustrate the importance of demographics, one trend everyone should be aware of is the diverging age profiles between advanced economies, which are getting old rapidly, and the increasingly youthful developing world. This will affect geopolitical, economic, financial, societal and environmental balances around the world for years to come.

At the aggregate, our world is getting younger and younger. With nearly 2 billion people between the ages of 10 and 24, the world has the largest number of young people ever in history.[18] But they are not distributed evenly, with the great majority in developing countries. For example, the median age in South Asia is a spritely 27.6 years, but much more notably in sub-Saharan Africa it is an incredibly youthful 19, meaning that half of Africans are 19 or younger![19] On the other hand, rich countries are greying rapidly. The median

[17] https://www.linkedin.com/in/jennifer-blanke-b8377b4/
[18] Youth – United Nations Sustainable Development.
[19] Sub-Saharan Africa.pdf (un.org)

age in the United States is 38,[20] in Europe 43[21] and in Japan a categorically ancient 48![22]

Why is this important? For ageing and advanced economies, it means that the working-age population is shrinking compared to the many people society must support (mainly children and retirees). The bottom line is that rich countries will find it harder to pay pensions and cater to the healthcare requirements and other needs of older adults, with fewer and fewer people working.

On the other hand, young developing countries are facing the opposite challenge. Along with their youthfulness, many are still experiencing high population growth, which means they need to deliver good jobs and opportunities in large measure to develop sustainably and foster social cohesion. The bottom line is that the young populations of developing countries represent a huge opportunity for a demographic dividend of energetic new workers, but if they do not find gainful employment it can instead spell demographic disaster and social upheaval.

How can we think about the consequences of a world splitting into an ageing, rich bloc and a young developing bloc? Adding up these two challenges can deliver solutions if the situation is managed well. I will highlight two in particular.

The first is to encourage massively more investment to flow from rich countries to developing ones. It's good economics, given that rich country economies will likely slow along with population shrinkage.

The second is to recognize that immigration is a necessary win-win for both youthful and ageing societies. Advanced economies will need to adopt public policies to make up for their 'missing' workforce, including openness to migration as well as greater participation by women in

[20] Median Age Doesn't Tell the Whole Story (census.gov).
[21] Ageing Europe – statistics on population developments – Statistics Explained (europa.eu).
[22] Japan: Demographic Shift Opens Door to Reforms (imf.org).

THE SEVEN GAMES OF LEADERSHIP

the labour market. Needless to say, changing perceptions around migration is top priority.

No matter where you live on our planet, the global age divide is but one illustration of how – whether directly or indirectly – demographic trends will likely have a bearing on your own life and that of generations to come.

Diversity – by Sandra-Stella Triebl

Eight billion people on the planet: and what about diversity? I asked Sandra-Stella Triebel,[23] one of the top corporate leaders in Switzerland, journalist/author and media entrepreneur, to share her experience on the strategic competitive advantage of diversity.

Diversity & Inclusion (D&I) is part of Risk Strategy and has reached the top executive floors and has made its way onto the public agenda. But in Europe, many leaders think that this is simply another gender debate. Well, it's not. Gender is just one of the variables. If you narrow it down to what's an asset for your business, D&I could be an essential ingredient for success in terms of 1) innovation and 2) risk evaluation.

Mirror your customer base within your company
Why is all this important for innovation and risk evaluation? Let's start connecting the dots. Depending on your industry, innovation can be a technical novelty, a patent or a new service. But sometimes your customers don't even know what they need. So you create the need with the power of your marketing and PR team. Now let me ask you something: would you say that your employees understand the company's

---

[23] https://www.linkedin.com/in/sandrastellatriebl/

purpose and goals? Are they good at what they do? If you said yes, you just agreed that your employees are the most important assets. Your staff knows every single flaw of your organization – ask all of them, from the junior ranks to the top manager – how they would improve the company. Gather this information strategically, on a regular basis.

Access the wisdom of your diverse workforce strategically for better, faster results.

Let me ask you another question: if you plan to build a house from the ground up, do you just talk to the architect? Of course not: you also speak to all the tradespeople who will make your house perfect. If you see diversity and inclusion in your workforce from this perspective, it's a tangible asset for your business. And the same is true for personal relationships. If you have friends who all have the same opinion, and share the same reality, how would you ever hear about anything new in your life? So with two steps, you can transform your company into a highly agile, diverse and talented team.

Technology, AI and Digital Transformation

We have not only understood but also internalized the fact that changes in technology are disrupting how we live as they proceed at exponential speed. I wanted to share two of the most significant changes related to Artificial Intelligence and Digital Transformation.

Fred Werner[24] is the creative mastermind behind Artificial Intelligence for Good[25] organized by ITU: possibly the most impactful and relevant gathering of global experts on Artificial Intelligence on the planet. I asked Fred: is AI actually for good?

[24] https://www.linkedin.com/in/fredericwerner/
[25] https://aiforgood.itu.int

Can AI help power our Seven Games? Fred has written his contribution with the help of Artificial Intelligence (AI).

Is Artificial Intelligence (AI) for Good? – by Fred Werner

I used Open AI's GPT-3 to write a paragraph on AI's impact on the future of work and it generated the following text in under two seconds.

'Artificial intelligence is already starting to impact the future of work, and the trend is only going to continue. With AI becoming more and more sophisticated, it is going to be able to do more and more complex tasks, eventually taking over many jobs that are currently done by humans. This will result in a future where machines will perform many jobs, and humans will be left with only the jobs that require creativity and human interaction. While this may seem like a scary prospect, it will also free up humans to do the things that they are best at, which will ultimately lead to a more prosperous and efficient society.'

The text is rather good and generally representative of the views of many AI thought leaders I have encountered, albeit slightly on the optimistic side. Not to worry though! You can simply use a slider to make the output more pessimistic or change its tone depending on your mood. This tool is a great time saver but the only way of knowing if what it spewed out was useful is because I have been organizing the United Nations AI for Good Global Summit since 2017. Context and understanding are key and a human-in-the-loop will always be necessary when it comes to safe and effective human–machine collaboration.

In my daily work, our team uses AI to generate videos, animations, graphic designs, transcripts and translations and even an AI-generated avatar to introduce our webinars. A video that once took a week to produce now only takes a couple of hours. We can come up with an original poster design in minutes instead of hours, avoiding costly, boring stock images.

And our AI avatar never gets tired or sick, and it could open 200 webinars a day if need be. These AI-powered tools require no coding knowledge and have saved us countless human days, allowing our team to focus their energy on higher-value tasks.

As AI continues to advance, the million-dollar question on everyone's mind is, 'What will AI mean for the future of work?' Research shows that the use of AI in many sectors has grown 270 per cent over the last four years. In fact, 90 per cent of leading businesses are already making ongoing investments in AI technologies and more than half have reported an increase in productivity. On the flip side, studies show that anywhere from 9 per cent to 47 per cent of jobs will be taken over by AI and robots, depending on the relative methodology.[26] This is making a lot of people anxious, especially when Silicon Valley magnates such as Elon Musk claim that 'AI will make jobs kind of pointless'. He sees a future where AI will be able to do most things better than humans.

The three tasks most likely to be automated are collecting data, processing and analysing data, and predictable physical work. While it is true that many repetitive physical tasks will become automated, a common misconception is that AI will primarily affect blue-collar jobs. Actually, even historically safe white-collar jobs such as doctors, accountants, computer programmers, data analysts and lawyers are at risk.

In an optimistic scenario, however, the benefits of human-machine collaboration include higher productivity, increased consistency and predictability, greater autonomy, lower costs, and if managed well, enhanced morale, because augmented teams enable staff to focus on higher-value work. While all this may be true, it doesn't mean we can expect a smooth transition, with truck drivers suddenly becoming knowledge workers. There are likely to be some bumpy roads ahead.

---

[26] McKinsey Technology Trends outlook 2023, at www.mckinsey.com

So, what does this mean for your career and how can you prepare for it? In the future, decisions will be made in three ways:

- By humans alone or with other humans, which we are all very familiar with (i.e. preparing a budget alone, planning a conference with others, etc.);
- By machines alone, which we are becoming familiar with (i.e. Google maps, spam filters, Netflix recommendations, etc.);
- By humans and machines in collaboration, which is unprecedented in history (i.e. diagnosing patients with an AI assistant, having an AI as a board member, etc.).

This could lead to the emergence of three new classes of job based on human–machine collaboration, as outlined by an MIT framework for leveraging AI in business:

- AI trainers (junior to mid-level)
- AI explainers (mid-level to senior level)
- AI sustainers (senior to C level)

AI trainers will use reinforcement learning and a human-in-the-loop to continuously develop and improve readily available AI services such as virtual assistants and robo-investment advisors, and to monitor autonomous systems. AI explainers will be needed to describe the proverbial 'black box' and to be accountable for how AI reaches decisions such as hiring, firing, loans, prison sentences, insurance premiums, etc. Finally, AI sustainers will be needed to ensure that AI is safe, secure and ethical, that it respects privacy and has goals and incentives aligned with our own.

AI is here to stay and will have a profound effect on future careers. In fact, AI and machine learning are at the top of many lists of the most important skills in today's job market. Do you see a future where you might work in one of these categories? How will AI affect or perhaps even enhance your ability to thrive in the Seven Games?

Could AI be a catalyst for a revolution that pushes the limits of human creativity and performance? Maybe it's not so bad if it helps unlock the next Picasso! AI can be the trigger that helps you reinvent yourself and augment your performance and creativity through your own Seven Games.

Digital Transformation – by Giuseppe Stigliano

How many times do you hear *Digital Transformation*? Giuseppe Stigliano[27] is the CEO at Spring Studios in London. I asked him to share a real story: as we both believe that digital transformation does not start from technology, it starts with people. *Technology and capital make it possible, but only people make it happen.* Let's see how.

Passion Eats Skills for Breakfast. 'I just wanted to buy a nice pair of loafers without overspending.' This is how the story of Velasca started in 2012, from a casual conversation between two friends in the back of a taxi. Velasca is a contemporary shoe brand made in Italy which, since that taxi ride, has grown into a global direct-to-consumer company selling hundreds of thousands of shoes in over 30 countries.

Enrico Casati, who co-founded the company with Jacopo Sebastio, was living in Singapore at the time. When his friend and present-day business partner Jacopo went there to visit him, the two ended up debating about how hard it was to find men's shoes with the right mix of design, quality and price. A creative spark was ignited. The two friends, then in their twenties, realized that there was a gap to fill in that specific segment and decided to pursue the opportunity. At that point,

---

[27] https://www.linkedin.com/in/giuseppestigliano/

animated by the desire to see if they were right, they started talking about their idea with all their friends. They also tried to reach out to potential suppliers in the Italian region of Marche, well known for manufacturing leather goods and mapped out the competitive landscape.

Wait a minute. Was at least one of them an expert in the market? Did they belong to a family that had been in that business for a while? Did they have at least a bare minimum of understanding of the world of footwear? No, no and again no. So how is it possible that two young men with backgrounds in economics and no clue about the shoe market could spot such a business opportunity and go as far as building a multinational organization in a few years?

The short answer is: if you combine the right attitude with the right aptitude, and you add perseverance, luck and accessible technologies, you can do magic. But let's try to focus on the critical aspects of the story to infer a causal relationship between ideation and execution, and hopefully distil some guiding principles that everybody can apply to replicate Velasca's success.

In the past, it was virtually impossible for wannabe entrepreneurs with limited means and no understanding of a market to launch and scale a company in such a short time frame. So how did the co-founders of Velasca manage to escape these challenges?

The only way to appreciate what happened is to understand the paradigm shift that has taken place in the last few decades caused by digital transformation: the combined action of the democratization of technology, with the disruption of communication, sales and distribution channels (social media and e-commerce) and the pervasiveness of connected mobile devices. This powerful mix created the conditions for Enrico and Jacopo to bootstrap their business, bypass intermediaries, overcome all barriers and start selling their products to thousands of people all over the world. Once they had found the right suppliers to make the product, they could launch an e-commerce website, create powerful storytelling to engage the right customer profiles and transform them into actual customers.

So, if this shift creates such great conditions for new companies to proliferate, why for every company that succeeds are there hundreds that fail? What is the 'secret sauce' that allows companies to go beyond the basics – idea, team, product, customer, sales and communication platform, and finance?

In my opinion, there is one very critical ingredient that is too often neglected and underestimated, because it's hard to measure: passion. Passion is what makes the difference between the thousands of people with potentially good ideas and those who successfully execute those ideas. Passion is what motivates you to try, and if you fail, to try again, to persevere. Passion is what attracts like-minded talents and convinces them to join your team. It is what galvanizes you during an elevator pitch to a potential investor, making you more credible and determined than you thought you could be. It is what allows you to unlock the full potential of collaboration with your team members, suppliers and with your clients. Passion is the opposite of the 'thank God it's Friday' mentality. It's a 'looking forward to Monday' mentality.

Digital technology is definitely the most powerful means ever, but to achieve a meaningful end, the main ingredient is the apparently obsolete ingredient called passion. You may ask any successful digital entrepreneur, they will all tell you a story of hard work, very long nights, limited social life, deep crisis and moments of demotivation. How did they handle so much pressure? Where did they find their motivation? They all have the same answer: for them, it's not just a job. None of them was working 'for someone on something'. Instead, they were all leveraging the (digital) tools at their disposal to forge their (analogue) passion in the direction of their (business) idea. And if you think about it, the greatest human beings have been doing the same since the dawn of civilization.

THE SEVEN GAMES OF LEADERSHIP

What is at stake here? What is important for humankind and our professional and personal development? *To retain and develop our capacity to use our critical thinking, our capacity to use our judgement and our decision-making rather than delegate crucial decisions to machines.* We need to understand the difference between what is legal and what is ethical. These qualities will be more and more relevant in the future. The real problem is not to find out if computers can think: the real problem is to find out if we – humankind – will *continue to think,* as cleverly pointed out by Fausto Turco.[28]

Infodemic and Reputation – by Mirja Cartia d'Asero[29]

You have probably heard the proverb: 'A lie travels around the globe while the truth is still putting its shoes on.' In the fascinating book *Conspiracy,*[30] Tom Phillips and Jonn Elledge try to answer a vital question: how can we log off from fake news and start trusting hard evidence again? This is not an easy task as we can always fall back on the classic theme of conspiracy: claiming that any evidence against our theory is in fact part of the conspiracy itself. Part of the problem is that conspiracies tend to accumulate evidence, but they do not evaluate nor do they validate. They create a new equation: a hundred ridiculous lies equal one undisputed truth. Really? Here again, we stumble into another WTF moment.

Actor Denzel Washington[31] said, 'If you don't read the news you're uninformed; if you do read it you're misinformed... What is the long-term effect of too much information? One of

---

[28] https://www.linkedin.com/in/turcofausto/
[29] https://www.linkedin.com/in/mirja-cartia-d-asero-8117363a/
[30] Tom Phillips and Jonn Elledge, *Conspiracy: a history of boll*cks theories and how not to fall for them* (USA: Wildfire Publishing, 2022)
[31] https://www.youtube.com/watch?v=bwnNrr9RO2Y

the effects is the need to be first, not even to be true anymore.' It doesn't look good. How can we develop critical thinking? Which questions should a critical thinker ask?[32]

1. What is happening? Gather the basic information and ask the right questions.
2. Why is it important? Ask yourself why it's significant and if you agree.
3. What don't I see? What is missing?
4. How do I know? Where does the information come from? Has it been verified? By whom?
5. Who is saying it? Is there any conflict of interest or hidden agenda?
6. What else? Are there other ideas?
7. What if?

What is the critical role of a national newspaper?

I can't think of a more qualified and credible person than Mirja Cartia d'Asero, the CEO of Il Sole 24 Ore Group.[33] What is the role of Il Sole 24 Ore in a context of fragmentation?

Since May 2022 I've taken up the post of CEO at Il Sole 24 Ore Group. A common thread throughout my career has always been focusing on creating positive change and facing that change in a responsible fashion – values I find in the multimedia group that I have the good fortune and honour to lead. Values that underpin the growth path I'm building in the direction of internationalization, enhancing our brand, technological innovation and building trust.

When I joined the Board of Directors of Il Sole 24 Ore, this newspaper already had 156 years of history, credibility

[32] www.learningcommons.ubc.ca
[33] https://www.gruppo24ore.ilsole24ore.com/en-us/chi-siamo/

and reputation: an extraordinary legacy, exemplified by a tremendous sense of responsibility from everyone who collaborates with the paper.

In a world that is overwhelmed in an infodemic, where it just takes a click to get news on anything from everywhere in the world in real time, where around 4 billion people access the Web through their smartphones, the quality of information is the key to our present and future success. Indeed, it's the foundational value of our brand. The quantity of content published on the Web is astounding: every minute, 571 new websites come online around the world, Facebook publishes 41,000 posts which get nearly 2 million 'likes', not to mention the 2 million people every minute who search the internet. In this inflation of information offerings, Il Sole 24 Ore is the go-to newspaper because of the value and the credibility of the information we publish.

The challenge that we're facing now entails intercepting that share of readers who are looking for authoritative, verified, accurate answers and will settle for nothing less. What you hear people saying is, 'If Il Sole 24 Ore says so, it must be true!' And this is the principle that I'm embracing, where I'm anchoring the drivers of change for Il Sole 24 Ore of the future.

Beyond the negative phenomena that are attracting attention – carefully crafted fake news, bots that comment on social media, post-truth – there is considerable demand for authoritative, in-depth answers to the big questions we're facing today, at a time when uncertainty abounds. The ultimate aim is to respond to the demands of a very attentive readership willing to trust a source that can offer different information centring on readers' needs.

In light of our attention to processes and standards of quality, Il Sole 24 Ore has become a member of the Trust Project, which counts over 100 newspapers the world over which are striving to mitigate disinformation. How? By committing to consistently verifying sources, subjecting all news items to rigorous fact checking, clearly defining the different types of information we offer (transparently distinguishing hard news from opinion and analysis) and interacting continually with readers (which also means apologizing for any errors) – by now all this is an integral part of our way of reporting the news.

Innovation is not only technological. It also has to do with the rules that set the boundaries of our work. To be a vanguard – for us, like for many other publishers – represents a moral duty, which is necessary to embody excellence in a rapidly evolving market, and to be credible interlocutors who are attentive to their readers.

In this multifaceted world, which is undergoing a dramatic transformation, the role that Il Sole 24 Ore plays as a source of information can only be one of knowledge intermediation, to promote individual growth and the collective development of the country.

Geopolitics: Dancing on landmines – by Salvatore Pedulla[34]

Over the last 21 years, I have served in United Nations field missions during active conflict or in the immediate post-conflict environment in countries such as Iraq, Iran, Lebanon, Syria and Jordan. It is common practice for UN HQ to put us through 'survival' courses for UN staff preparing for assignments in hot spots. Learning to identify, avoid and, if ever trapped, be equipped with the tools and methods to safely get out of minefields or areas contaminated by unexploded ordnances devices (UXOs) was, unsurprisingly, one of the skills we had to acquire prior to deployment. If you think

---

[34] https://www.linkedin.com/in/salvatore-pedulla-b8bb0b53/

about it, minefields may well be a good enough metaphor for the rapidly changing geopolitical landscapes we are all confronted with.

Why do I say that? You do not need to be a military expert to know that there are different types of explosive ordnances: landmines, in all their forms, are placed under the terrain to make the advances of enemy forces more arduous and perilous. There are also the infamous cluster bombs, which are forbidden by international humanitarian law, consisting of small bomblets delivered through mortar shells or missiles, which open a few hundred metres from impact, unleashing thousands of explosive capsules across large areas. They impact livelihood, generate profound physical and psychological barriers between and among communities, and kill people, primarily civilians.

During survival training we learn several methods for getting out of a minefield, but the most effective way to stay alive remains the same: do not get lost or stranded in a minefield in the first place. I am sure you would not be surprised when I say that the most critical part of our training is how to look for signals suggesting a certain area may be contaminated.

Does this ring a bell? If we take a critical look at current geopolitical trends, we ought to recognize that many of our models and risk assumptions (the maps of minefields laid by a party to a conflict) may no longer hold, at least not entirely. The euphoria that spread across the Western World at the end of the Cold War period stemmed from the myopic and naïve conviction that the collapse of the Soviet Union was the ultimate validation that liberal political values, free trade and globalization were the only possible way forward for the whole of humanity. Yet, these assumptions and beliefs have been increasingly put into question by the emergence of more politically aggressive regional powers, coupled with the re-emergence of ethno-nationalism.

Just like in the case of landmines and cluster bombs, we perhaps did not and could not account for the impact of shifting sands, winds, rains and floods, basically some of the elements that can only be marginally and partially forecasted and mitigated with the level of knowledge of complex systems and the technology available to us today.

If we still think that the post-COVID world will inevitably return on a path of globalization, let us for a moment reflect on how some national governments and multinational companies will find solutions, for example, to energy dependency on Russia. Is the world going to be more globalized or less so? While we have seen the emergence of global jihadism, we have also been witnessing an even more divided UN Security Council and more fractious and divisive international politics, resulting in conflicts such as Syria, Libya and Yemen, to mention those I have close personal experience with, which are still unresolved. The poorest people, mostly civilians, feel the pain in their lives. So do we still wonder why the number of refugees and internally displaced persons has been rising exponentially over the past 15 years?

Yet, there are other critical issues such as climate change, demographic growth, massive inequalities in terms of access to education, health services and job opportunities, regional tensions (think about Egypt, Sudan and Ethiopia over water from the Nile) and never-ending conflicts. All this will also shape the future geopolitical landscape, which still requires a truly global collaborative effort and a shift in values and priorities. International co-operation on Sustainable Development Goals, climate change, conflict resolution and the realization of fundamental human rights may still provide a safer path forward for all if indeed we accept that the best way of getting out of a minefield is not to get into one in the first place.

Question is then: wow, all these megatrends will affect the job market, jobs and skills?

Jobs of the future and the future of jobs

Climate change, lack of wealth distribution and erosion of trust, demographics, immigration & diversity, the Fourth Industrial Revolution, technological changes such as AI, knowledge and fake news, geopolitical changes, pandemics: all these elements – and many more – have a visible and measurable effect on job markets, our careers and our professional choices. The employment outlook has changed dramatically,[35] and one unique feature of the current job market is unprecedented in history. Since the First Industrial Revolution, employment has been strong during phases of economic expansion, while unemployment has been dramatically high during recessions.

But since mid-2010, this link has broken. We now have massive unemployment among vulnerable workers with obsolete skills, coupled with a high number of job vacancies. Many companies are struggling to recruit and/or retain workers, no matter what salary they offer. Then we have a new category of people who are not unemployed – they are un-employable because they offer market skills that are obsolete, no longer relevant. At the same time, a few professionals are in high demand and command salaries even three or four times higher compared to traditional, rapidly disappearing jobs.

If we want to understand how to share and direct our careers, we need to take these megatrends and the features of the job market into account. For example, trying to become a kindergarten teacher in Japan or Italy is not a great idea with an ageing population. How can we better understand the complexity of the new job market?

I have some questions for Riccardo Barberis,[36] President for Northern Europe at the Manpower Group. He is at the forefront of work and has been on the frontline of the world of work. Now, as work recalibrates in a post-pandemic world, what workers want and how they will work in the future has changed forever.

---

[35] https://go.manpowergroup.com/hubfs/MEOS/2022_Q4/Global_EN_MEOS_Report_4Q22.pdf
[36] https://www.linkedin.com/in/riccardobarberis/

Interview with Riccardo Barberis

What do workers want?[37]

We accepted many things about work pre-COVID. Now, post-pandemic, many people want much more control of their lives. They are looking for some way to have a better impact. Individual choice is now clearer than ever.

Take IT, for example. Today, candidates for IT jobs don't even go to interviews because they are in such high demand. They answer calls from recruiters by saying, 'You have my resume, you see my qualifications, give me your best offer, tell me about your company culture and I'll think about it.' They are in a position of power because they know that with their skill sets, they will always be in demand. They also think about the importance of purpose, and purpose really is the driver for the younger generations. They are working on the 'why' – a sense of purpose – more than previous generations. They see that what worked before (study, work hard and you will be better off than your parents and grandparents) won't work for them. Because of that, the newer generations want to go where they can have a much bigger impact.

Even for a blue-collar job it's important to have at least basic digital skills. That's what employers want. Technology is impacting who can play the game. This is where schools and different types of educational institutions can change that status; the study-work model is dead. We need to think differently. Today, there are too many people moving from unemployed to unemployable because they don't have the minimum requirements to enter the labour market due to the exponential speed of the technological revolution.

[37] https://go.manpowergroup.com/whatworkerswant

How do you see the demand for soft skills changing and how important is it that people develop those skills?

Honestly, I like to call them internal competencies rather than soft skills. Internal competencies are our attitudes, who we are. The first element is knowing yourself. Self-leadership. You can educate someone but you cannot drastically change who that someone is. But we can identify the areas where people are strong, where they can be better, and of course where they best fit in an organization. Also, teamwork is very relevant. The more we talk about differences and inclusion, the more we expect companies to deal with different generations at the same time, so to be able to work with your team in a very efficient way is critical.

What are the younger generation's concerns about the future of work?

It's so difficult to imagine an answer that fits for all of them. Really, one size fits one. From what we're seeing, for them having the opportunity to learn and grow is very important. The challenge for companies and for us as leaders is to make sure that we identify their talents faster. And based on that, we can create a very clear, open career path for them: if there is agreement on a path forward, they will stay. They want to thrive, not only survive.

The younger generation wants to be challenged and do new things, as long as it's something that they can learn from. That is directly connected to the growing freelance market. People are taking more control of their careers and the freelance world gives them more challenges, more opportunities to take on new roles.

What would your advice be to someone who was stepping into a leadership role?

Don't be scared to try. Because we come from a culture of failure, where failure is seen as something definitive for your own life, you should always try. Even in the labour market, you can say, 'I tried, it didn't work and I will try again in a different way.' Don't view a situation in which you are not performing optimally as a failure. Don't be scared by failure, because what you can learn makes you stronger. Second, when you do something, do it with intensity. Prove you can make sacrifices to be better because in that improvement there is a lot that you can bet on. And third, make sure that you offer opportunities to others because this is the only way for a team to grow and this is how we can create talent.

Riccardo Barberis's insights, validated by granular evidence from Manpower's studies and data, are confirmed by another recent study by Velocity Global:[38] as the world has changed, so have the expectations of workers. Talented individuals want to work from anywhere; they demand work-life balance and flexibility. They accept being assessed, but on results, not on the number of hours spent in a cubical. Many of the assumptions about work are now gone, as we will see in detail in the next chapter. Another recent study by Manpower,[39] 'Skills Revolution Reboot: the 3Rs-Renew, Reskills and Redeploy', emphasizes the need to create Human Power by adding human soft skills to technological skills.

WTF moments do derail our attention. Instead, we should focus on impactful megatrends such as climate emergency, inequality, demographic & diversity, technology, geopolitics, infodemic and reputation (the way we get informed) and job markets. These megatrends will have an everlasting effect on your countries, communities, families and jobs. And we need to tackle another question: what does all this mean to me?

[38] https://velocityglobal.com. The Future of Work: What Talent Wants, released in September 2022.
[39] Manpower Group, 'Skills Revolution Reboot: the 3Rs – Renew, Reskills and Redeploy', Skills Revolution Series, 2021.

Remembering the Roman god Janus

I have a question for you: which country created superheroes and heroines?

I imagine you guessed the United States: the birthplace of Superman, Spider-Man, Wonder Woman, Batman, Iron Man, the Hulk and many more. Superhero is a genre of fiction that, since the mid-1930s, has been incredibly popular – and profitable – first in the United States and then in Europe. Japan has also created many superheroes such as Ultraman and Astro Boy Kamen Rider. In addition, they use this genre in comic books and very successful movies (e.g. the Avengers Saga).

But wait a second. Superheroes with superpowers were not invented in the United States or Japan, but around 2,800 years ago in ancient Greece. The Greeks came up with 12 gods, the Olympians. As they were keen on gender parity, they worshipped six male gods and six female goddesses.

The Romans conquered Greece in the defining battle in Asculum (modern-day Ascoli, in central Italy) in 279 BC. The Romans were very pragmatic and somewhat less spiritual compared to the Greeks. They figured out that Greek gods were pretty cool, so they ditched their 2,000 pagan deities and replaced them with Greek gods. They, of course, changed the names from Greek to Latin, so Zeus, the supreme commander-in-chief, became Jupiter, Aphrodite became Venus, Athena became Minerva, Hermes became Mercury and so on. I suppose it was a fascinating case of infringement of intellectual property, but they elegantly called it *Interpretatio Greca*.

The Romans did keep one god they were particularly attached to. The name of the only authentic Roman god was Janus. This god has a unique feature: he has two faces, one face looking behind at the past, representing *Gravitas,* wisdom and the experience accumulated over the years. The other face is looking forward to the future. It is a young face, *Juventus*, representing youth, energy and the optimism needed to face the challenges unfolding. Janus is the god of transition, so the

Romans celebrated Janus in every transitional moment, such as the end of a war, or weddings, births and funerals. If you ever wondered why the first month of the year is called January, it's a tribute to Janus, to celebrate the transition into the New Year.

Is transition the equivalent of change? Not at all, but we tend to confuse the two terms. Change happens 'outside' us; change is situational and occurs when we move house, get married, have a new manager, or when our company enters a new market or launches a new service or product. Change management is undoubtedly challenging, but it's limited to adjusting or adapting to a new situation. Transition is even more challenging to master as it's psychological, as described by William Bridges in his book, *Transitions: Making Sense of Life's Changes.*[40] Change is not under our control, but we need to understand it. Transition is within our control, but we must internalize it and master it.

As the 18th-century French chemist Antoine de Lavoisier wrote: 'In Nature, nothing is destroyed, nothing is created: everything is transformed.'

I believe that the same principle applies to our lives and careers. Everything is transformed. Always.

This book aims to help you understand, master and enjoy the transitions you will face in your personal and professional life. So, yes: as the Romans did, we should worship Janus, as we are in a historic transition: we need both *Gravitas* – judgement and experience – coupled with *Juventus* – energy and optimism to understand and shape transformation.

What's next: The Five Cs

'Dad, when we will go back to Normal?' My daughter Sadika asked me this question a few months into the pandemic when everything seemed frozen in time. She could not go to school,

---

[40] William Bridges, *Transitions: Making Sense of Life's Changes*, Da Capo Press, 2004.

and for her, and for 6 billion people on this planet, it seemed like we were in a movie or a TV series like *Black Mirror*. My watershed moment occurred when Pope Francis celebrated Mass in St Peter's Square on 27 March: he was alone. It was a sobering moment of realization that normality was gone. And it was more than finding a vaccine: I understood that COVID had obliterated our life. So the thought of returning to it was an understandable feeling of quasi-nostalgia for the past that looked quite nice in the rear mirror. Still, many of us are taking for granted the fact that we will eventually find a new normal: the idea of a 'New Normal' is not new.

'New Normal' is a term in business and economics that refers to financial conditions following the financial crisis of 2007–08, the aftermath of the 2008–12 global recession and the COVID-19 pandemic. We understand why this term has been accepted and used globally from a psychological standpoint. It is about the legitimate need that each of us feels in our bones. We desperately desire to return to normality after accepting months of total disruption in our personal and professional lives. Yes, we all would love to return to normal, but it is simply delusional, and as such, this desire won't help us.

What comes next, and how can we deal with it? Let's pause for a second and reflect on the definition of 'normal'. Normal derives from (you'll never guess) a Greek term *Kanonikos*: 'conforming to a type, standard or regular pattern'. 'Average, predictable, ordinary'. But my favourite definition of normal is *what people expect*. Can we then really assume that the new normal is up for grabs, just around the corner, and that we will simply move to a place where we once again come to know what to expect? What can we expect? I guess the unexpected, not the new normal. I suggest renaming 'new normal' to something very different. I believe that we now have five elements, or ingredients, which are constantly present in our lives. I call them the Five Cs and they will bring us NOT to a new normal but to a new context. Bear with me.

The first C stands for **Chaos**, the perfect storm of speed and uncertainty combined. The peculiarity of this moment is that speed is not linear but exponential, and technological changes mainly drive it. Do you remember the prophecy of Gordon Moore, Founder of Intel Group? 'The performances of computers will double every 18 months.' So we can understand *kaos*, a Greek term, by adding the geopolitical changes, climate change and social unrest today.

The second C is **Crisis**, and it also comes from the Greek. A crisis is a difficult or dangerous time when a solution is needed – and fast. It is a term derived from medicine that implies the need to move quickly with a clear decision. We know that a half decision means a squared mess and that crisis does not build character but instead reveals it. If we leave inept and unfit leaders in charge during a crisis, their true colours will shine through, a litmus test of their leadership.

The third C is **Complexity**. He was as famous as Napoleon and admired by Goethe during his lifetime, but not many have heard of Alexander von Humboldt. He was a Prussian naturalist, explorer and geographer (1769–1859) and the first thinker who suggested that the natural world is a web of intricate, inconstant, dynamically and interconnected elements. While it seems an obvious statement now, it wasn't when he wrote it: 'In this great chain of causes and effect, no single fact can be considered in isolation.' He may have been the first system thinker on the planet. We are used to framing problems as merely complicated. A complicated problem requires technical expertise with a disciplinary focus. One example: Geneva is the capital of watches. Possibly the most prestigious watchmaker, Patek Philippe, has named their flagship collection Grand Complication. They have built a reputation for designing, producing and assembling exquisite pieces of art, very complicated and very pricey. Solving complicated problems implies a high degree of expertise in this domain, which requires specialization. If we need to fix a broken laptop, we need to call a computer technician, correct?

A complicated problem is seen and interpreted as a standalone element that needs to be 'repaired'.

Complexity is different: the magnitude of the issues we face today forces us to de-code complexity by constantly learning, adapting, sense-making and leveraging interdisciplinary as the norm. Everything is connected. From the cognitive standpoint, complexity requires contextual intelligence, the ability to connect the dots and see the correlations between different elements in the system. Peter Senge called it *The Fifth Discipline*,[41] another book that you can't afford to miss. Complexity requires trust and co-operation to solve problems rather than authority to impose someone's views upon others.

The fourth C is **Confusion** or Ambiguity. Nothing will be clear-cut or easily distinguishable from a distance. Ambiguity means that concepts, ideas and situations have different meanings for different people, hence the need to reconcile these differences by including everyone in the conversation, provided that people who are sitting at the table have at least some competence and credibility on the subject matter.

The last C stands for Change – actually, let me scale that up to **Constant Change**. Do you remember the book *Who Moved my Cheese?* by Spencer Johnson?[42] It's more than 20 years old and still relevant, as it says that change is not the exception but the constant in our lives. We were all amazed to see our capacity to adapt rapidly during COVID-19, for example, when we started working from home. Ironically the only standard and stable component in our lives is constant change.

Let's reflect for a moment on what that means for us. There are four levels of intensity and complexity to frame our decision-making process.

[41] Peter Senge, *The Fifth Discipline*, Doubleday Business, 1995.
[42] Spencer Johnson, *Who Moved My Cheese?*, G.P. Putnam & Sons, 8th Edition, January 1999.

Level One: Linear. This happens when the correlation between cause and effect is evident. Example: It's raining, so I need an umbrella. A typical case of easy, low-effort decision-making.

Level Two: Complicated. We have lots of data; we need to select the relevant information and build a clear cause and effect. Example: You need to go to the airport and catch a flight. You have to consider the traffic and the weather conditions, the time and day of the flight, if you'll go by car or public transport, if you're checking in before getting there, if you have heavy luggage and so on – medium level of decision-making.

Level Three: Complex. We have lots of scattered data from different disciplines; we need to connect the dots to find a cohesive framework and create a new understanding of the issue. Example: How can we nudge and influence the electorate? We need to consider demographics, history, political climate, the available budget, social media, etc. and this requires a high level of decision-making.

Level Four: Chaotic. There is NO cause and effect, and the current situation is unprecedented. We have several independent variables that collide. Therefore, we need to invest extraordinary effort in sense-making and decision-making. Example (you know it already): the times we live in.

Reflect for a moment: What level is your thinking process usually? If you are oscillating between levels two and three and sporadically at four but rarely at level one, you are in a thinking overdrive mode. By definition, your mental energy is depleted. Later in the book, we'll discuss the need for self-care and the urgent necessity to preserve our energy to deal with the intense, chaotic situation we are living in.

We are now focusing on understanding what the new context requires from us. What's waiting for us around the corner is not a new normal, nor a perfect storm, because flagging these dramatic scenarios does not help us reflect but only frantically react. Sorry to say, another thing it's not is *Andrà tutto bene,* meaning everything will be fine, a lovely Italian phrase that can momentarily reassure us but does not help us to reframe and act. The sum of these **Five Cs – *Chaos, Crisis, Complexity, Confusion and Constant Change* – is creating a New Context**, not a new normal. If we accept this new context as part of our future, we will see opportunities and learn new perspectives and insights that will allow us to reset the system. The new context is about transformation, not change. The difference between these two terms is substantial.

Change means that the external situation is not what it used to be. Transformation means that we are different and there is no going back like a caterpillar that has become a butterfly. If we internalize that we are in the midst of a historical transformation, we realize that 'predictable' and 'ordinary' are not waiting for us around the corner. Transition is the process that takes us there, transformed.

Context is a neutral term that does not trigger fear (like a perfect storm) or false hope (such as 'everything will be fine'). Instead, it's like an empty home we need to rebuild and decorate. It's about taking the responsibility to reconsider what's happening and reset our understanding. It's called a paradigm shift, a term introduced by Thomas Kuhn in *The Structure of Scientific Revolutions*.[43] Kuhn demonstrates that progress occurs when we break with traditional thinking by embracing a new approach and understanding. He challenged the prevailing view of scientific progress: it's not advancement via the accumulation of accepted facts, which he considered normal science. Example: electric light did not come from the continuous improvement of candles. Instead, periods of normal science are interrupted by revolutionary science created by anomalies that lead to new paradigms. New paradigms force us to frame completely new questions; they don't just rearrange the furniture. Paradigm shifts

[43] Thomas Kuhn, *The Structure of Scientific Revolution: 50th anniversary edition*, University of Chicago Press, 4th edition, 30 April 2021.

change the game and the same rules and lead us to a revolutionary way of thinking.

Using the expression 'the New Context' is not just a semantic exercise because context sounds more elegant than 'normal'. Instead, the new context is a paradigm shift that will allow us to reset the system, to understand and frame transformation. The genuine opportunity of a lifetime to recreate a revolutionary life by reflecting on a simple question: what do we stand for? So, a new context is unfolding right now, right in front of us.

Now what?

2

Spotting differences, challenging assumptions

'What assumption am I making, that I am not aware that I am making, that gives me what I see?'

BEN ZANDER

How can we anchor our professional journey to our principles?

'Who will represent the Human Resources Team in the working group tasked to provide a set of recommendations to the President on improving diversity at the World Bank Group?' I got this message during my second week at the World Bank. But the last thing I wanted was to have more responsibilities. I was still dazed and confused, if not overwhelmed. One colleague raised his hand at the meeting to decide who would be the lucky volunteer. I was safe. I thought he was the self-sacrificial lamb, ready to put the team's interest above his own: what a great guy. He said that while he would have personally been honoured to accept this opportunity, he did not want it for himself and preferred to leave it to a new recruit – for example, Paolo. We had never spoken before and when he pronounced my name, I noticed a grin on his face. The team voted and – guess what? – everyone enthusiastically approved my candidacy. Ironically, I also needed to thank my dear colleagues for the gift; they were so happy that the monkey was on my back, not on theirs. When

I left the meeting, I felt even more confused and frustrated: I anticipated wasting tons of time on a useless topic. I was wrong: I will tell you why after this story.

A few days later, I went to the task force's first meeting, co-chaired by two highly influential vice presidents, several levels above me on the corporate ladder. From the choreography and the number of senior people in the room, I noticed that it was not a Mickey Mouse meeting: it was a serious one. I was the most junior person, the youngest, at the lowest level among senior managers and directors with at least 25 years of seniority, the average age in the mid-fifties. Ouch! The meeting started with the question, 'How can we improve diversity at the World Bank?' Simple question, isn't it? Although it isn't. The floodgates opened. What followed were contributions from a large number of employees at the meeting championing a huge variety of ethnicities, religions, disabilities, genders and everything in between. This meeting lasted two hours. Near the end, the vice president said, 'Everyone spoke except the representative from Human Resources. Paolo, do you have any practical suggestions or recommendations?' The wise words of my father resonated in my mind: it's better to shut up if you don't have anything helpful to add. 'Thank you for the opportunity: I will reply after consulting with my team.' I was safe: until the following meeting, of course. After a few intense meetings, the working group first decided to address diversity in terms of nationality. Based on the data, in fact, it was evident that certain countries were severely underrepresented.

So now let's see how we can tackle a complex problem. We need to look at these issues:

- Can people contribute to the solution of the problem by working in a *psychologically safe environment*? Is each opinion counted and listened to? Do you have credible data, granular evidence and facts, or just personal opinions?
- Do we have a *shared understanding of the problem* we are trying to solve? Do we have the exact definition of the

problem? What mental models are we using? Colleagues were sharing a passion for solving the problem, but each had a legitimate yet different interpretation of it.

- *Which assumptions are we making* about possible solutions? Can we look at the problem with different lenses, from different perspectives, see the connections and open new possibilities we didn't see before?

About point one, the answer was positive. We had plenty of data and each person was free to speak and raise their concerns and opinions. Although some meetings were at times frustrating, I realized the complexity and beauty of diversity by working with a truly diverse group of people.

As far as points two and three are concerned, I have learned that we can solve a problem only if we have correctly defined which problem we are trying to solve. We need to ask the right questions and share the same understanding of the meaning of words and concepts. We need to challenge our assumptions. Albert Einstein was even more emphatic about the importance of the definition of the problem. He was once asked: 'If you had one hour to save the world, how would you spend that hour?' He replied, 'I would spend fifty-five minutes defining the problem and then five minutes solving it.' Actually, he didn't say that, yet we always assume he did.[44]

I told you I was wrong: at the beginning of the project, I thought it would be a waste of time. But instead, I learned to value data and diversity, the importance of finding a standard definition and understanding the problem, agreeing on what success will look like and above all the need to challenge the assumptions we always make without paying attention. The same logic applies to our careers. We need to anchor our professional journey on sound principles.

[44] https://quoteinvestigator.com/2014/05/22/solve/

Spotting Differences

In the next pages, we will follow this path: first, we will look at the meaning and significance of some words and concepts that will shape your career and we will play the Seven Games. Second, we will look at some assumptions we have always made about work. In the new context, it is time to revise these assumptions. *The combined effect of coming up with new definitions and removing outdated assumptions will clear the path and will open new understanding and new possibilities never explored before.*

Special Military Operation. Really?

Words matter. Language counts. Intellectual honesty is critical. Let's see how and why. Would you like to work for an international information technology organization, specializing in websites with more than 120 million visitors per day? They have elegant headquarters in Canada and Luxembourg, and the annual revenues were close to $460 million, with a profit margin close to 40 per cent. Stunning returns. So how do they describe themselves?

> MindGeek continues to drive the state of technology forward, developing industry-leading solutions enabling faster, more efficient delivery of content every second to millions of customers worldwide. The company is committed to enhancing its technological capabilities and thrives on a sustainable growth trajectory built on innovation and excellence. MindGeek Holding is a global industry-leading information technology firm headquartered in Canada and Luxembourg, with offices in Nicosia, London, Bucharest and Los Angeles.

What a terrific company to work for: the name is also captivating, MindGeek, maybe a start-up in neuroscience or machine learning or AI? Before you get too excited – sorry to disappoint you – MindGeek is the group that has created and manages the most visited porn sites on the planet, such as Pornhub. However, you will NEVER EVER find the word *porn* anywhere on the institutional website of MindGeek or on the balance sheets, which are regularly audited. Perhaps you will be less enthusiastic about applying by clicking on 'open positions'. Words matter, *including the ones you haven't spoken.* You may say they are generous in self-celebrating but economical with the truth. By the way: the CEO of MindGeek, Feras Antoon, and the COO, David Tassillo, resigned from their positions in June 2022.[45] The reasons for their resignations are unclear: probably we will never find a word about it. They also had to deal with activist Laila Mickelwait, who started a movement and campaign to shut Pornhub down with #traffickinhub. The article 'Children of Pornhub'[46] by *New York Times* columnist Nicholas Kristof also contributed to expose the shameful 'business model' of MindGeek.

Words matters. Since late January 2022, the world has been hearing disturbing news about Ukraine. We all feared the invasion of Ukraine by Russia, but in our heart of hearts, we all hoped that it was only propaganda or maybe another dirty political trick by Vladimir Putin. Then, on 24 February, when we woke up, we got the terrible news. The war had started; watching in disbelief, the 64-kilometre tank column and an estimated 150,000 soldiers invading Ukraine stunned us. It was war. Yet it wasn't, according to Russia; it was *only a special military operation.* Interesting, if we opt to use a British understatement; infuriating and shocking if we choose more appropriate terms. We will remember 24 February 2022 as the day we lost our innocence and the illusion that Europe is protected from direct military attack. We felt sadness, anxiety and rage: how can Russia call it a special military operation? I couldn't sleep for

---

[45] https://www.theguardian.com/society/2022/jun/22/pornhub-executives-resign-mindgeek-underage-videos
[46] https://www.nytimes.com/2020/12/04/opinion/sunday/pornhub-rape-trafficking.html, *NYT*, 4 December 2020.

days, outraged by the invasion and the devilish manipulation of the truth. How can we negotiate peace if one side denies starting a war? In the meantime, 6 million Ukrainian refugees left their country, as the Syrians had done before them, because of another senseless, cruel war.

'Facts are stubborn things; and whatever may be our wishes, our inclinations, or the dictates of our passions, they cannot alter the state of facts and evidence,' wrote John Adams, the second president of the United States. I share two examples to make a point: we need to clearly understand the meaning of words. What is the opposite of a measurable, evident fact, which is clear to everyone? It is a lie, not an alternative fact.[47] Words matter. The issue is not to craft a perfect academic definition, but to link behaviour – including words – to values and clarify our life's principles. The difference between what is true – supported by facts, granular evidence, science – and lies – supported by obscure theories and viral posts on social media – is the same difference between democracy vs. dictatorship. By accepting that truth is negotiable, that the opposite of truth can be also true, we contribute to demolish our value system: words, therefore, matter.

Clarity is the foundation to play the Seven Games intelligently and in complete alignment with who we are and what we stand for. Happiness happens when what we think, say and do is in the same place.

We start from here.

Success: according to whom?

Who is in charge of defining your success? You or someone else?

You – and only you – define what real success looks like. It starts inside you and it's not up to someone else to decide. It's up

---

[47] 'Alternative facts' was a phrase used by U.S. Counselor to the President, Kellyanne Conway, during on 22 January 2017. https://www.youtube.com/watch?v=VSrEEDQgFc8

to you. I shared this story at the beginning of my last book, *The Compass and the Radar.* I define success based on three criteria: Do I love what I do? Am I learning something new? Have I helped other people? Whatever I do, I need to answer yes to these three questions.

Credibility vs. Visibility

Fyre Festival, 2017:[48] it was supposed to be the festival and the party of the decade. Three full days and nights in the beautiful Bahamas, live music with bands like Blink-182, exquisite food and plenty of drinks, dancing on the beach, supermodels and celebrities: according to the promotional video 'an experience beyond your wildest dreams'. The VIP package was $50,000 per person and more – much more – if you wanted to enjoy a cruise with a personal chef added to the package. But, as the opening of the festival dawned, the reality was very different. An almost complete lack of infrastructure – accommodation, food, toilet facilities, catering, you name it – to cope with the 6,000 visiting patrons. The whole enterprise was fraudulent, a mirage.

So what is real and what is only glittering visibility, appearances and a fraudulent narrative? You will be pleased to know that Billy McFarland,[49] the organizer of Fyre Festival, is now a convicted felon. He's trying to repay 26 million dollars to his creditors. But according to his lawyers, it looks like he's planning new entertainment ventures after prison.[50] We can't wait.

Is visibility something to avoid at all costs, a bad thing? No, as long as it's not the only thing you have to offer. Visibility is like the icing on the cake. First, we need to prepare a delicious cake, viable and meaningful value for the people, the communities

---

[48] Please refer to Netflix documentary *Fyre: The Greatest Party That Never Happened.* Scary.
[49] https://en.wikipedia.org/wiki/Billy_McFarland_(fraudster)
[50] https://www.theguardian.com/us-news/2022/may/19/billy-mcfarland-prison-release-fyre-festival-new-entertainment-ventures

and the purpose we serve. The icing is only a nice extra to have, visually appealing, but not to be confused with substance. We have seen a similar approach in politics and modern organizations: CEOs become rock stars; communication is about the external image of the CEO, not about the purpose of the organization, and success is defined based on number of followers rather than the real impact on society.

The difference between purpose, goals and a wish

Shall we do a brief coaching exercise? Here we go. Write down what you would like to achieve in your professional life. Before reading the following pages, please pause for a minute and read what you have written.

Let's see.

You still don't know.

Keep on reading. I'll give you some prompts.

A Wish

Example: I wish I could work less.

However, it will always remain wishful thinking until you lay down some guidelines and rules. Working less? OK, let me start by leaving the office at 6 p.m., not working during the weekend and being able to say no to unreasonable requests. Sound like a good start?

A Goal

Example: I want to get promoted by the end of the year.

This is a reasonable and ambitious goal, but the problem is simple: it does not depend on you. There are too many variables you can't control, such as the available budget and the other candidates vying for that promotion. When the achievement of a goal depends on someone else coupled with the expectation of a properly functioning process that you don't control, disappointment is almost always inevitable.

A Purpose
Example: I want to become a better leader and improve my skills.

Oh, yes! This depends on you. You decide that you are in the driver's seat; you are in control. I trust that your purpose will reflect your hopes and not your fears.

More than IQ

In the late 1800s, Sir Francis Galton, considered the founder of differential psychology, published his first studies about human intelligence. He believed that he could measure intelligence and that intelligence was mainly hereditary. His work set up a foundation to develop the very first IQ test. A few years later, Alfred Binet,[51] a French psychologist, focused his studies on measuring mental processes and human intelligence. He started to find a way to identify kids who needed extra help in school by developing questions to measure attention, problem-solving and memory. With the help of a colleague, Theodore Simon, they created a test with 30 questions, later recognized as the first-ever IQ test. It became the basis for measuring intelligence and many believe that the Simon-Binet Intelligence Scale[52] is still the most accurate way to do so. The good news: it is accurate. The bad news: it measures only one type of intelligence: the use of logic. More good news: decades of progress, studies and empirical evidence in psychology have demonstrated that there are many kinds of intelligence.

How would you rate the intelligence and chances of success of Amadeus Mozart as a chemistry teacher, Michael Jordan as a sculptor, Winston Churchill as a flamenco dancer, Nelson Mandela as a physicist, Pablo Picasso as a basketball player, Mahatma Gandhi as a jazz guitarist, Donald Trump as President

---

[51] Alfred Binet, France 1857-1911, psychologist, https://www.britannica.com/biography/Alfred-Binet
[52] https://www.britannica.com/science/Stanford-Binet-Intelligence-Scale

of the United States, Frida Kahlo as a tax advisor, Jimi Hendrix as a dentist or Pablo Neruda as a Web developer? You get the point: 90 per cent of these people were indeed geniuses but in their respective fields. One of them a little bit less. By associating them with the wrong discipline, we smile at the absurdity of this correlation. The point is, there are several kinds of intelligence, not only the logical-mathematical kind measured by IQ.

Psychologist Howard Gardner[53] identified the following seven distinct types of intelligence:

1. Linguistic
You enjoy writing, reading, telling stories or doing crossword puzzles.

2. Logical–Mathematical
You're interested in patterns, categories and relationships, and drawn to arithmetic problems, strategy games and experiments. This is measured by IQ.

3. Bodily-kinaesthetic
You process knowledge you gain through bodily sensations; people with this kind of intelligence are often athletic, dancers, or good at crafts such as sewing or woodworking.

4. Spatial
You think in images and pictures; you may be fascinated with mazes or jigsaw puzzles, or spend free time drawing, building things, or daydreaming.

5. Musical
You love singing or composing music. You're usually quite aware of sounds others may miss; you're excellent at learning new languages.

6. Interpersonal
You're good at communicating and understand others' feelings and motives, with high empathy and capacity to relate to others.

[53] https://www.howardgardner.com

7. Intrapersonal

You may be shy, but you are very aware of your feelings; you're self-motivated and have a well-developed self-awareness. While interpersonal skills are labelled as 'soft skills', Josh Bersin[54] called them, more appropriately, Power Skills.

How do you rate yourself in each category when you do a self-assessment? Which habits do you have? What do you naturally enjoy doing? Answering will give you a hint of your professional journey.

We indeed have many kinds of intelligence: from the work of Edward de Bono and Roger von Oech, we've learned something new. How can we use our intelligence and creativity to solve problems?

Edward de Bono built his reputation by inventing the concept of lateral thinking – that is, 'seeking to solve problems by unorthodox or illogical methods'. The purpose of lateral thinking, says de Bono in *Lateral Thinking for Management* (1971), is 'to generate new ideas and to escape from old ones'. Therefore, creativity is breaking established patterns to look at things from a different angle. He suggests using discontinuity techniques and summarizes the lateral thinking process in five steps:

1. Escape from fixed patterns
2. Challenge assumptions
3. Conceptualize valid alternatives
4. Try new ideas and see what happens
5. Move forward.

He later wrote *Six Thinking Hats*.[55] 'The main difficulty of thinking is confusion: we try to do too much at once; emotions, information, logic, hope, creativity. It's like juggling too many

---

[54] https://joshbersin.com/wp-content/uploads/2020/05/POWERSKILLS2.jpg
[55] Edward de Bono, *Six Thinking Hats*, first edition 1985, Little, Brown and Company.

balls at once.' The solution is using all six hats, but not all of them at once. The principle behind his book is simple and convincing: we need different kinds of intelligence to deal effectively with complex problem solving.

The white hat: Look at the situation factually; the approach is neutral and objective, focused on data, facts and figures.

The red hat: Look at the situation emotionally. What is your gut feeling telling you?

The black hat: The cautious approach; this involves critical thinking, what-can-go-wrong? thinking.

The yellow hat: Look at the situation positively, optimistically; have a can-do attitude.

The green hat: Creativity, generate new ideas and connections; lateral thinking.

The blue hat: This is the organizing hat, the thinking about thinking. What is the best overall solution?

We tend to wear one particular hat: which one is your favourite? Which one do you use the least? Where are you particularly strong?

Roger von Oech[56] went one step further by breaking down the process of creativity. We need to be an explorer by evaluating options, an artist by assembling different pieces, a judge by assessing the validity of your ideas and a warrior by fighting to make it happen. Everyone can be creative. More good news: we can develop our intelligence. This is called growth mindset vs. fixed mindset.

The question is not new: can we develop our intelligence, or are we – like Lady Gaga would sing – born this way? Carol Dweck[57] discovered a simple and impactful idea: the power of mindset. She demonstrates that we can develop our intelligence only if we have internalized a genuine growth mindset and the attitude to learn, evolve and grow as human beings. Those with a

---

[56] Roger von Oech, *A Whack on the Side of the Head: How You Can be More Creative*, first published in 1983, Hachette Book Group.
[57] Carol S. Dweck, *Mindset: The New Psychology of Success*, first edition 2006, Ballantine Books USA.

growth mindset find success in doing the best they can, day after day, keeping on learning and raising their personal bar every day. They do not compete against anyone as they are striving for continuous self-improvement.

A fixed mindset means the opposite: we are born this way and there is nothing we can do. A fixed mindset is a rather depressing framing of our life, as we are giving up the most meaningful journey of our existence: self-development. Can I count on you to be part of the growth mindset fan club? With the growth mindset, we can keep growing, and we have a different kind of intelligence.

What else? For some reason, most people believe that passion, talent and strength have the same meaning. They don't.

Passion is something that YOU love doing. We all have passion; the beautiful moments of our lives are when we can dedicate quality time to what we love doing. You may love playing guitar, painting, gardening, taking Thai cooking classes, learning a new language, or cycling. I love playing tennis, but relatively early in my life, I realized that God was generous with Roger Federer but not with me as I have zero talent on the court. The quintessential element of a passion is that YOU love doing it. I love playing tennis, but please go elsewhere if you want to see any talent. Your passion is NOT necessarily your talent, when it costs you more effort than the average person to perform the same task and to get worse results.

Talent: OTHER people will notice what you are good at. The essential thing here is to see what others are noticing. You start getting compliments; you hear people say that you are pretty good at doing something (you get referrals, repeat clients). You start enjoying what you're doing. It takes less effort for you to get to the same level as everyone else: in only three lessons, you are already middle level when it usually takes two years.

Strength: Talent multiplied by sweat: this is about determination, grit, obsession, effort and the relentless pursuit of improvement, an impeccable work ethic and discipline. You need to pass the marshmallow test,[58] demonstrate the capacity for self-control and delay gratification. The video of the kids trying to resist devouring the marshmallow immediately or waiting a few minutes to get a second one is hilarious.

Team: which one to choose?

When you get upwards of six and a half billion results in 0.67 seconds by searching 'Definition of Team', you understand it all. So, let's skip the definition, as I'm trying to provide the essential elements that I have seen emerging in three typologies of a team:

The Dysfunctional Team
The Ghost Team
The Effective Team

The Dysfunctional Team

You know it when you're on one. Do you remember when you went to a restaurant with your family, you ordered the food and it took almost two hours to get served? The fish was served cold, the pasta greasy, the meat chewy and – horror! – your beer was warm? Do you remember calling the waiter three times to get a clean napkin and that they charged for something you didn't order when you got the bill? Yep: this is an example of a dysfunctional team. Nothing seems to work, you are frustrated and you suspect they are cheating you.

How do you recognize a dysfunctional team? What are the features to pay attention to? High turnover[59] and absenteeism, team members suffering burnout, everybody always seeming to be in a bad mood, no clear accountability and people running

[58] https://psycnet.apa.org/record/2014-43233-000
https://www.vox.com/science-and-health/2018/6/6/17413000/marshmallow-test-replication-mischel-psychology
[59] https://www.brookings.edu/research/tracking-turnover-in-the-trump-administration

around like chickens with their heads cut off. Anxiety, stress, people get sick. When a problem occurs, a dysfunctional team punishes a plausible perpetrator. The team does not even try to find a permanent solution. So, another victim is appointed, and – voilà – the blame game can continue and the illusion of action permeates the team. Gossiping prevails over honest and transparent factual information; the rumour mill is more effective than the production line.

The person in charge is the only one who can talk; others can be no more than colourful parrots. This kind of toxic leadership does not want mere loyalty but demands total blind obedience. The management team seems to confuse unity with conformity. The new staff is 'harmonized' more than trained.[60] Appointments of senior leaders are based on their capacity to obey, to follow orders; there is a premium on branding and image at the expense of competence and integrity. Visibility matters more than credibility: it is more about casting actors than staffing.[61] The leader's image is frequently broadcast internally and externally as a sign of power. Pictures of the person in charge are everywhere, to remind everyone who has the power. The people on this team and in this organization believe that George's Orwell's *1984* is not a book but an instruction manual.

Policies are interpreted loosely for friends and applied mechanically to non-friends. You experience WTF moments almost daily; you almost feel like you are in a video game, not as a player but as a target. There is zero trust and no psychological safety; you think that only obedience can save you. It's fun only if you're writing the script of a horror movie or seeking endless inspiration for a book. Avoid dysfunctional teams at all costs. You may get paid a salary, but you will pay a much higher price.

---

[60] Kai Strittmatter, *We have been Harmonized: Like in China's Surveillance State,* Old Street Publishing, 2019.
[61] Philip Rucker & Carol Learning, *A Very Stable Genius: Donald J. Trump's Testing of America,* Bloomsbury Publishing, 2020.

The Ghost Team

This type of team exists on paper, maybe in some elegant organization charts or corporate webpage. Still, in reality, it is only a group of people who are individually focused on performing but tend to ignore each other, not necessarily with malicious intent. Sadly, COVID-19 has increased the number of ghost teams as many teams have simply never met in person and don't know each other. Features to pay attention to? A silo mentality, focus on individual and functional responsibilities rather than corporate objectives, compliance to internal rules rather than collaboration, planning rather than adaptability, a mechanical approach to decision making, attention to cost without understating the actual value. Technical experience is valued more than personal expertise.

The focus is limited to what is legal, with remarkable disregard for ethical standards, or what makes sense. In these teams, innovation is lacking: improving what the team does is more relevant than imagining a different future and people are seen as mechanics rather than gardeners.[62] Communication is mainly top-down. Relationships among the team members are purely transactional. What is the general mindset on problem solving? Gathering more data or setting up working groups are preferable to tackling real problems as they may generate conflicts. The leader is rarely accessible but highly replaceable, with a marked emphasis on titles and hierarchical levels and long working hours.

Being part of a ghost team is not traumatic, but it is somewhat dull, repetitive and suffocating. The thought that you will be there in five years terrifies you. By Tuesday afternoon you start fantasizing about the coming weekend, and on Monday morning, you are tempted to call in sick for a day, better two. And you experience more of the same every day: the same

---

[62] Gary Lloyd, *Gardeners Not Mechanics: How to Cultivate Change at Work,* Double Loop Limited Publishing, 2021.

meat and potatoes. It is not fun and you don't even know if it will ever get better. But you're getting by, hoping that things will eventually change. Eventually. One day. Sound familiar?

The Effective Team – by Bruno Bianchini

It doesn't need to be dysfunctional or suffocating. You can be part of – and contribute to or even lead – an effective team. It sounds exciting, but the question is: what makes an effective team? If you google 'effective team' you'll get 5 billion hits. It's a bit time-consuming. So, my guess is that Google, rather than providing us with 5 billion answers, wanted to find the answer themselves. Not the ultimate answer, but a concrete, practical, credible one. Needless to say, they leveraged a healthy amount of internal data to identify what differentiates effective teams from the rest. They are Google, after all – they're quite good at it.

Bruno Bianchini[63] is a talented manager at Google, based in Dubai. I've asked him to share with us the findings of one of the most impressive surveys I've ever seen. Google wanted to understand what makes an effective team. This is what they found:

Much of the work we carry out at Google is the result of collaboration between teams and team members. So, what makes an effective team? Our researchers at Google tried to answer that question by running more than 35 statistical models on data collected from more than 200 interviews and including over 250 items from existing survey data.[64] With the objective to reflect the diversity of all of Google, our research included 180 teams located all around the world and working in different functions, such as engineering and sales.[65] We called this study Project Aristotle, a tribute to the

[63] https://www.linkedin.com/in/bruno-bianchini/
[64] Bock, Z. (2014), 'Google's Scientific Approach to Work-Life Balance (and Much More)', *Harvard Business Review*.
[65] https://hbr.org/2014/03/googles-scientific-approach-to-work-life-balance-and-much-more. To learn more about the data collection and measurement of effectiveness, refer to this link.

philosopher's quote, 'The whole is greater than the sum of its parts.' We studied elements in two separate categories. First, we looked at team members' **characteristics**, such as skills, background and personality traits. We wanted to figure out if these characteristics, either singly or in combination, could impact how teams perform. Second, we studied **team dynamics** and how teams interacted. For example, how teams set up their norms and their goals, how they resolve conflict, if they socialize inside or outside of work and so forth. What we discovered is that **how a team works together is much more important than who is on the team**. We learned that five team dynamics are responsible for differentiating effective teams from the rest: psychological safety, dependability, structure and clarity, meaning and impact.

Psychological safety

Psychological safety is defined as a 'shared belief held by members of a team that the team is safe for interpersonal risk taking' (Edmondson, 1999, p. 354).[66] It refers to the perception

[66] Edmondson, A. (1999), 'Psychological Safety and Learning Behavior in Work Teams', *Administrative Science Quarterly*, *44*(2), 350–383. https://doi.org/10.2307/2666999

of the consequences of taking interpersonal risks, or a belief that a team is safe for risk taking in the face of being seen as ignorant, incompetent, negative or disruptive. Team members feel confident that no one will embarrass or punish anyone for admitting a mistake, asking a question, or offering a new idea. Teams can work on this dynamic by soliciting inputs and opinions from the team, focusing on solutions rather than searching for someone to blame for mistakes, or being vulnerable.[67]

Out of all the five dynamics, psychological safety is the most important one. It is the necessary condition to build an effective team. It is the foundation of the pyramid. Without psychological safety, the entire structure crumbles, even if the other layers are solid.

Dependability
Dependability is the 'quality of being able to be relied on to do what somebody wants or needs' (Oxford Dictionaries, n.d.).[68] This implies that team members complete high-quality work on time and can depend on each other to get work done. One of the main causes of low dependability is the diffusion of responsibilities and lack of clear ownership for tasks.

Structure and Clarity
Structure and clarity refer to understanding job expectations, the process for fulfilling these expectations and the consequences of performance. To foster this dimension, teams can regularly communicate team strategies, objectives and goals, and ensure that team members understand the plan for achieving them.

---

[67] For a deep dive into the concept of psychological safety, refer to *The Fearless Organization*, a book by Professor Amy C. Edmondson of Harvard Business School. https://fearlessorganization.com/the-fearless-organization
[68] https://www.oxfordlearnersdictionaries.com/definition/english/dependability

Meaning

The phrase 'meaning at work' refers to the experience of a team member to do something of value that work provides (Hansen & Keltner, 2012).[69] Finding a sense of purpose in either the work itself or the output is important for team effectiveness. The meaning of work is personal and can vary: financial security, supporting family, helping the team succeed, or self-expression for each individual, and so on. Teams can foster meaning by providing positive feedback on outstanding work, offering help with something some team members struggle with, publicly expressing gratitude for someone who helped you out, and so on.

Impact

This dimension ties into the results of work and the subjective judgement that work is making a difference. When team members see that their work is contributing to the goals of the organization, they feel that their work matters and creates change. But too many goals can also limit the ability to make meaningful progress and be effective.

Challenging assumptions

Is it time to reconsider our assumptions?

What assumption am I making that I am not aware I'm making? A powerful question from one of my favourite books of all time, one I frequently quote: *The Art of Possibility*.

Assumptions are neither good nor bad, but it is essential to know we all have them. They are our operating system, our internal framework to enable us to understand the world around us. At times we get upset when our beliefs and assumptions are questioned. In fact, when we reconsider assumptions, we

---

[69] Hansen, M. and Keltner, D. (2012), 'Finding Meaning at Work, Even When Your Job Is Dull', *Harvard Business Review*. https://hbr.org/2012/12/finding-meaning-at-work-even-w

frequently experience cognitive dissonance: a mental conflict occurs when our beliefs are challenged or contradicted by new information or evidence.

A domain still regulated by old assumptions: this is today's work environment. We are still operating based on a framework that was developed during the First Industrial Revolution. Take, for example, working hours. At that time, people used to work at least 10 hours a day, six days a week. Since then, working conditions have improved (regrettably not in the sweatshops in many countries) and working hours are now reduced to 35–40 hours a week. Still, no one has challenged the assumption that our work needs to be regulated by a timetable.

Shall we look at some of the assumptions we've always made? It's time to reconsider them.

Employed vs. employable

'Employed' is a desirable condition: who wouldn't like a regular monthly deposit in their bank account? Still, I remember the prophetic goodbye of my professor at university. He told me there are two categories of employees: the ones who have been fired and the ones who will get fired. Interesting choice of an encouraging wish for a young graduate: I referred to it 30 years ago, but I believe it is even more valid today.

In 2018, the Trump Administration trumpeted to American citizens that the US was great again as there were 6.7 million job openings on the market: isn't that a sign of a prosperous economy? It depends. Yes, at that time, the US job market had close to 7 million available jobs, but a similar number of unemployed people were looking for a job. Based on conventional economics, the challenge was to improve the efficiency of the job market, the supply of qualified candidates vs. the demand from industries and corporations. However, reality proved to be quite different as most of the workers searching for a job remained unemployed for more than 18 months, a threshold that suggests that these workers were not unemployed but, sadly, no longer employable. The skills they were offering were no longer relevant in the job market; Yuval Noah Harari calls this the rise of the useless class.

If there is something that I have learned as an HR director, it is that the combined effect of corporate restructuring, mergers and acquisitions, cost reductions, reorganizations, or simply a new boss who doesn't appreciate your value has put many out of work. I don't know a single person over 40 who hasn't experienced the brutality of being *let go* and the list includes the person I look at in the mirror. So, the objective is not to remain employed but to be employable, as you bring value regardless of your contractual status.

Companies need to locate where the talent is
Silicon Valley is one of the most fertile lands for talent: many organizations and start-ups moved there, assuming it would be easier to get the talent they needed. But is this assumption still valid? A survey in the US revealed that 71 per cent of the people with a salary above $180,000 could work remotely, but the same is true for only 41 per cent of the people with a wage below $24,000. The increased number of people working in the gig economy is another factor. The assumption that when employees are working for you, they are not working for somebody else applies only to full-time staff, but does not pertain to the new context.

Work is a place to go
Work is the activity of the mind, not the presence of the body. However, working remotely is an option for highly skilled knowledge professionals, but not for blue-collar workers. A professor can do his job (prepare his lecture) anywhere; a cashier at Wal-Mart can't. COVID-19 has demonstrated that people's productivity does not decrease while working from home.

Therefore, the assumption that if employees aren't in the office, they are not productive is not valid. But the opposite belief is also not true: being at the office does not automatically make you effective. What's happening is that we are becoming like mangroves, trees that grow in brackish waters. We are surfing, suspended between work and personal life, enjoying *bleisure* time, a mix of business and leisure, coupled with *workations,* another combination that's something like a vacation while working or, more plausibly, vice-versa.

In-person is always better than digital, or vice-versa

You need to buy a ticket for a concert. Which experience – buying the ticket or going to the concert – do you want to have online, and which one in-person? The assumption that digital or in-person is always preferable overlooks one key element: we prefer in-person when there is an emotional component. We opt for digital when it's a transaction and/or purchase but not when there is an experience attached to it.

Still, at times we desperately need to keep the personal experience rather than the digital, as we have learned from Margaret McCollum, who spends her days seated at the Embankment Tube Station in London. If you've ever been to London and taken the tube, as the train is approaching, you have heard: Mind the Gap, Mind the Gap. To remind passengers to – guess what? – mind the gap between the platform and the train. The voice of Mind the Gap was Margaret's late husband, Oswald. A few years ago, London Underground replaced Oswald's voice with a pre-recorded, computer-generated, mechanical voice. Margaret wrote to the London Underground: they agreed to keep Oswald's voice, but only in the tube station close to where she lives, Embankment, so she can continue to listen to her husband. Mind the Gap.

9 to 5, Monday to Friday

Do you remember when you used to take a flight and the same movie started at the same time for everyone? But then the airlines figured out that people want to have choices; they choose their movie and start watching it when they wish. The same will apply to working hours. Companies will begin measuring output and contribution rather than working hours. Paying people based on time is an assumption forged during the

First Industrial Revolution and is no longer valid. For example, say you want to buy an apartment, so you hire two different real estate agents. Agent A will show you 50 apartments, none of them of your choosing. Agent B will show you three apartments and you'll find the one you want. Do you reward time invested or results achieved? Who would you pay?

Control System vs. Trust Ecosystem

The assumption is that the main task of leadership is to enforce a control system. Perhaps it's time to develop an ecosystem of trust? It's about *psychological safety,* the belief that you will not be punished or humiliated for speaking up with ideas or concerns, or for making a mistake; the belief that the team is a safe space for personal risk-taking.

You need a Boss

Really? Perhaps you need a mentor, a coach, a sparring partner, a critical eye, a supporter or simply someone who cares about your professional and personal development. But a boss is not always what we need to grow.

The Wealth of Nations vs. Health of Nations

If Adam Smith were alive today, I bet he would change the title of his book to *The Health of Nations.* The combined effects of the new context have again made us realize the importance of wellbeing, to wake up happy rather than loaded with anxieties, fear and diseases. The evidence is overwhelming.

The list above is not exhaustive: how many other assumptions about work are we still making that we don't realize we're making?

This chapter looked at two key aspects to clear the path for a meaningful seven-game journey. We first discussed anchoring our career to our principles, we then reconsidered and removed assumptions that no longer serve us. It is time to continue on to a new set of learning.

Future mindedness is rooted in our past and in self-knowledge: we start from here.

3

GAME#1 – *Inner*

'Who looks outside dreams, who looks inside awakes.'

CARL JUNG

Games people play

We can find an early description of phases in human life in a Chinese proverb: *'Human life consists of three stages: twenty years for learning, twenty years for fighting and twenty years for attaining wisdom.'*

Carl Jung is one of the fathers of psychoanalysis, together with Sigmund Freud, and the founder of the psychology of adult development and ageing. Jung believed that significant psychological changes occur throughout the entire spectrum of our existence, not only during the first half, which is divided into four distinct phases: **the Athlete, the Warrior, the Statement and the Spirit**. These are correlated to the level of maturity and personal growth we have achieved in our lives. Becoming psychologically mature is a life journey; it takes time and we can't skip over or artificially accelerate any single stage.

The **Athlete** is the stage in the development of our ego when we gain a sense of personal identity, usually during adolescence. We have to find the sweet spot. If we don't develop our ego, we will spend our life conforming to others and confirming what they say. However, the danger is when our ego becomes too strong.

When we are self-absorbed, we fall into narcissistic tendencies, the world rotates around us and we interpret everything as what it means to us, ego could become our enemy.[70] It's about me, me and still me.

At this point we need to ask for some help from our ancient Greek ancestors: the word 'idiot' comes from *Idiotes*, a person who elevates his agenda above everybody else's.[71] So *Idiotes* are exclusively interested in themselves; they are convinced they are the centre of the universe. On the other end of the spectrum, wise men and women are the ones who work for the benefit of others and for the community. In any case, the Athlete phase is essential to develop our personality and a *balanced sense of identity*: it is a challenging period to navigate.

The next stage is the **Warrior**: when we create ourselves, when we become achievers. In this phase, 'deficiency motivators' (what we don't have, from Latin *deficere,* to fall short, missing) drive us as we are focused on becoming who we want to be. We are building our reputation; we are goal-orientated and working hard. This phase coincides with early adulthood until the early to mid-forties. By the end of this phase, we are confronted with the difference between self-perception and reality. It could be a bitter moment when we realize that our dreams were too optimistic or just unrealistic.

For example, Steve wanted to become a partner in his law firm; he worked 70 to 80 hours per week for 20 years but it did not happen. At that point, his attitude changed completely and he became bitter and cynical: 'They crushed my dreams.' Steve believed he had only one identity, his professional one, and this was the reason for his profound resentment. A healthier attitude is to develop several identities (e.g. father, husband and professional) and a mature sense of responsibility and accountability. It's crucial not to cut corners; we need to preserve our integrity. We no longer

---

[70] Ryan Holiday, *Ego is the Enemy*, Portfolio Publishing, first edition, June 2014.
[71] Paolo Fallai, *Corriere della Sera*, 15 December 2021.

expect that someone else will come along and solve our problems like in the Athlete phase; this is a sign of maturity, *gravitas* in Latin. The secret to a successful Warrior stage is to keep working hard to improve ourselves as individuals, not only as technical experts in our professional domain.

The following stage, the **Statement**, occurs when we become more empathic, we grow our spirituality and we focus more on our family and close friends; this coincides with the beginning of the second part of our life. We also encounter our midlife crisis (more in the following chapters), when we take stock of our life and we start to imagine something different. It's a time when we stop considering only the salary or financial rewards; instead, we begin reflecting on the price we pay. This usually happens when we are eating a sandwich alone at the airport and we realize that we've missed our son's birthday. If we don't handle this stage in a balanced way, we neglect ourselves and often our families and our relationships too. During this phase we also start to think about legacy: we realize that life is not only about results, goals and financial gains.

We then move to the final phase, the **Spirit**. During the sunset phase, there are still amazing opportunities. It's another transformational phase before becoming a spirit, returning to our authentic self or, like Ulysses, returning home to Ithaca after a life of travelling. It's about closing a circle where meaning and significance prevail over money and fame.

I have always been fascinated by adult development and wanted to use this framework in professional growth. Can we see a pattern in development in the professional sphere linked to our personal one? *Can we correlate personal with professional development?* Yes, we can.

Bernard Lievegoed, a Dutch physician, framed a powerful question. *What can we do now to lay the foundations for the future, so we can solve the problems in later life creatively?*[72] Indeed, it's more

---

[72] Bernard Lievegoed, *Phases: The Spiritual Rhythms in Adult Life*, Sophia Books, first edition, 1979.

helpful to support a person – or an intellectually curious reader like you – to anticipate, shape and define a new future rather than lingering on a past that can't be changed anymore.

When we think of our professional life, we visualize steps going upward or a ladder we need to climb. This image implies that we are facing a linear sequence and that the ultimate goal is to get to the top. Let's reconsider whether this assumption is valid. Is a career a straight and predictable line? For example, my daughter is exploring many academic avenues: she has not yet decided which path to take. Even if she chose to become, let's say, a doctor, by the time she is active in the job market, many currently available jobs will be extinct. But wait; it gets better. Many jobs that today do not yet exist will be opening up. So, I wonder if it still makes sense to prepare the journey for our children, *or is it more helpful to prepare our children for the journey?* We are delusional if we believe that our careers will be a straight line, always going upward. It is more complicated and more fascinating than that.

Something that I have learned in my 30-year journey is that our careers and our professional development are in permanent evolution and transformation. Maintaining the status quo is not an option: *stability is a liability.* We often feel like kites in a storm, directionless, or held hostages by external factors: a reorganization, a merger, a toxic manager, you name it. It doesn't need to be that way if only we stay in the driver's seat of our lives. We can't delegate the task of driving to someone else. It's our job; our core identity. In my coaching practice, many clients share the same opening line: 'Paolo, I do not know what I want but I know it's not this'.[73] Helping them to find the answer to this dilemma is at the core of what I love to do.

Being able to stay in charge of our lives implies that we need to know how to drive, where we are going and who our

[73] Julie Jansen, *I Don't Know What I Want, But I Know It's Not This: A Step by Step Guide to Finding Gratifying Work*, Penguin Books, first edition, 2003.

supporting and caring companions are on our journey. We need people we trust, where the direction is more important than speed: going nowhere fast is meaningless. We need a compass. It is important to surround ourselves with people who want us to grow. We need people who want the best for us, not from us.

More than climbing the rungs on the corporate ladder, I believe we are going through different phases. I call them games. There isn't an automatic process that will magically propel us from one stage to the next. There are stairs, not an elevator. Physical development is pre-programmed by biology and genetics, while we are in charge of planning and building our personal growth. We can't take any credit for our wisdom teeth, but we must work hard on attaining wisdom. We make it happen: we do, no one else. We need to understand the rules of each game and learn how to play; we need to know the advantages and the pitfalls of spending too much time in one game or another. Observing and working with thousands of people over the years, I have noticed that we are all playing the same seven games.

The Seven Games shape and define our professional development. This is why we need to understand each of them and learn how to move from one to another. Chapter Three will explain Game One, the **Inner Game**. You can refer to the inner game as *the self-discovery channel*. Chapter Four focuses on Game Two, the **Better Game** and Game Three, the **Caring & Outer Game**. Chapter Five is devoted to Game Four, the **Crisis Game**, a challenging and necessary transition. Chapter Six will cover Game Five, the **Reinvent Game**; and Game Six, the **Revolution Game**; before closing with Game Seven, the **Letting Go Game**.

Start with questions

'Doubt' is a masculine word in most languages except in Portuguese, *duvida*. So *duvida* is the *mother* of all questions. We can find the correct answers only if we ask the right questions. We'll start from here.

What is the most critical and complex question you have to answer in your life? I've asked this a thousand times. In my professional roles, I've interviewed thousands of candidates, coached hundreds of executives and listened to many more people globally. When answering, some refer to complex technical matters, like an exam at university or a project at work. OK. Some refer to family problems or spiritual or political issues such as the existence of God or the value of democracy. Fair. Surprisingly, only a small number of people decide to search inside themselves. When they do, they start to explore and eventually come up against THE ultimate question: *What should I do with my life?*

Mark Twain said it all: '*The two most important days of your life are when you are born, and the day you find out why.*' For uplifting storytelling about real people who have found their answers to this question, check out Po Bronson's book.[74] You will find true stories of people who had the courage to search and find the answer to the ultimate question. No one finds a solution by applying a mathematical formula or an algorithm or by pure analysis. They find it by using their hearts, by looking inside themselves (most in a very unpredictable fashion) and genuinely believing in a better, different future.

Sorry, Simon Sinek,[75] but the idea of *starting with why* is not yours, nor is it a very original idea, not even close. It comes from Greek mythology. Here's the story. Zeus decided to punish Sisyphus for his many crimes and blasphemies, not with a death sentence but by obliging him to push a heavy stone up to the top of a hill, only to watch the boulder roll back down again,

---

[74] Po Bronson, *What Should I Do With My Life? The true Story of People Who Answered the Ultimate Question*, Random House, first edition, 2004.
[75] Simon Sinek, *Start With Why*, Penguin Books, 2017.

for eternity. So the real torture is not death but performing a senseless activity, the real tragedy of life.

After framing the question, *what should I do with my life?,* some people may continue with the wrong follow-up questions such as 'where should I go?' (e.g. London or Paris), 'how much?' (money) and 'which sector?' (e.g. banking or academia), 'which role or position?' These are legitimate questions, but they come well after a crucial query to clarify your self-understanding. I believe the logical and meaningful next question is: *What do I stand for?*

It's not relevant what you do but *why* you are doing it. I believe that we all are potentially missionaries, not in a religious sense but with a spiritual approach. By finding our *raison d'être,* our purpose, our 'why', we will not perform an activity delimited by a job description on a rigid organizational chart. Instead, we will *be* what we do: finding magic, meaningful alignment and congruence of ourselves with our heart and brain, a key component of genuine happiness through meaning, not via careless amusement or – worse – dangerous addictions. If we don't search for this alignment, or we fail to find it, we will delegate external motivators to find the solution on our behalf.

I have always found negativity, cynicism, aggression and greed as the main components of this misalignment. I call people who suffer from it mercenaries; I feel their pain, gloominess and joylessness. Indeed, they may be intellectually bright and competent; they may be in charge of some large company. But they are also chronically unhappy, constantly comparing themselves with somebody else. They spend their life accumulating money, trophies, poison. Actor Jim Carrey said 'I think everybody should get rich and do everything they ever want, so they can see that it's not the answer'. Something joyful is missing in their lives. Their real job is rolling their personal boulder up the hill, the same as it ever was. We can continue celebrating birthdays, but we should also celebrate the day we discover why we are here on this planet. What do we stand for? Why are we doing what we're doing? One story came from a tennis player.

> 'My name is Andre Agassi: I play tennis for a living even though I hate tennis, hate it with a dark and secret passion, and I always have.'[76]

I had to read this passage again. Did Andre Agassi, one of the best tennis players ever, really hate tennis? According to *Time* magazine, his autobiography – cleverly titled *Open* – is one of the better memoirs out there. Oh yes. His book is sincere and authentic, and it helped me to crystallize one idea. You can be ranked number one in tennis or any game you decide to play, which is excellent. Agassi held the world's top ranking for a total of 101 non-consecutive weeks, from 1995 to 2003. Still, you can be deeply miserable with serious problems and Agassi had many to cope with. Even if you are number one, sometimes you can't find your purpose.

We all need to look at the person in the mirror and find the answers to these questions:

1. Why am I doing what I'm doing?
2. What do I stand for?

Spoiler alert: Andre Agassi eventually found his answers with the support of a caring, intelligent and amazing wife, Steffi Graf, also a fantastic tennis player, ranked number one for 377 weeks, widely referred to as one of the greatest tennis players of all time. So, to excel in your game – whatever game you play, whatever profession or role you choose – it does NOT start with improving your backhand or any of your technical skills. It begins by finding out why you are doing it and what you stand for. The magnificent beauty of finding your 'why' will give you positive energy forever and propel you in the direction of your

[76] Andre Agassi, *Open: An Autobiography,* Vintage, 2009.

dreams. It's about waking up with a smile, a purpose, and the person you love beside you.

Whatever you are doing in life, ask yourself *why* you are doing it. If you are doing something to achieve something else, you will never excel at it: at best, you can become quite good, most probably just average if not mediocre. But, on the other hand, if you have decided to do something because you genuinely love performing this activity, you are walking in the direction of excellence. If the only reason you are showing up at the office – whatever role/company/sector you are in – is to collect a pay cheque at the end of the month, think again. You can't start a fire without a spark.

You may want to read the inspirational poem *So: you want to be a writer*[77] by Charles Bukowski: 'Don't do it, unless it comes out of your soul like a rocket'.

Is that all? Not yet – there are a few extra self-discovery and awareness elements to consider. For example, on a scale from zero to 10, how motivated are you? Even if my sample is limited to 50 people, the average is 7.9, quite a nice number. Too bad that's the wrong question. The real question is, *Are you able to delay gratification to achieve something meaningful?* In fact, one of the most accurate predictions of success in life is linked to our capacity to delay short-term gratifications to achieve long-term objectives. It's about self-discipline.

The marshmallow test[78] is a landmark psychological experiment summarized in a fun-to-watch TED Talk by Joachim de Posada.[79] Stanford University scientists gave children aged four to six a marshmallow and were told, 'if you can resist and not eat it, you will get another one in 15 minutes.' Two-thirds of the kids couldn't resist and ate it immediately. One-third did not eat the first one and got the second one. Fifteen years later, they correlated the

[77] https://poets.org/poem/so-you-want-be-writer
[78] Walter Mischel, *The Marshmallow Test: Why Self-Control is the Engine of Success*, Little, Brown and Company, 2014.
[79] https://www.ted.com/talks/joachim_de_posada_don_t_eat_the_marshmallow

results of this experiment with the students' success. All of the kids who resisted were successful – 100 per cent! The opposite, with few exceptions, was true for those who did not resist.

A straightforward litmus test of our capacity to delay gratification is linked to our ability to save money. As Morgan Housel noted in *The Psychology of Money*,[80] past a certain income level, you need just what sits below your ego: savings are the gap between your ego and your income.

My real birthday

'What is necessary to change a person is to change his awareness of himself.'

ABRAHAM H. MASLOW

Do you mind if I take a moment to share a personal story? First: which one of these three statements do you think is true about me?

At age 15, after getting my report card from school, I suddenly realized I was:

1. An excellent student, an absolute genius in the making.
2. An average student: I was merely languishing, doing as little as possible.
3. A teenager – but not a student at all – forced by an obscure global conspiracy and malicious family members to attend school. Even worse, they expected me to show up every day, early in the morning.

Difficult question, I know. To help you to select the correct answer, let me share the following written feedback from

---

[80] Morgan Housel, *The Psychology of Money: Timeless Lessons on Wealth, Greed and Happiness*, Harriman House, 2020.

my teacher: 'Dearest Paolo, the world is full of plumbers and carpenters; would you consider joining them?' Funny: recently, I thought of her. Maybe I should have listened to her advice after paying a heart-attack-inducing invoice to the plumber who fixed my shower.

The rest of secondary school continued in this direction: I was excellent in a few subjects, such as philosophy and history. The keyword in this phrase is *few*, by the way. I survived and did as little as possible in many subjects: the keyword this time is *many*. I refused to use my super-nova brain for lessons that did not interest me; for some reason, chemistry was always at the bottom of my list. Miraculously, I made it to the final exams at the end of secondary school. They're called the *Maturità* in Italy – translatable as wisdom – still an elusive concept at age 18.

Before the exam, I got the written assessment from my professors. 'Paolo is a brilliant young man who tends to get easily bored. Paolo is intellectually curious and has many hobbies and interests. Regrettably, *none* is about school. None.' I thought the second *none* was unnecessary. I later understood it as a hint of the frustration I copiously generated in each of them. It did not help that my twin sister Francesca was doing extraordinarily well in every subject: comparisons were frequently a source of embarrassment for me. The idiot was often used as my family nickname: I always suspected it was not linked to Dostoyevsky's masterpiece but I have never asked, preferring to live with this doubt.

Honestly, I had a point. Why should I waste my time in school when I could (in this order): play basketball, chase girls, go to parties, listen to rock music, drive my motorbike, play the drums, sleep until late morning and eat ice cream while watching basketball and soccer? Really, why? Like my favourite philosophers, I selected one crucial existential question: Why should I study Latin when I could be with Annabelle, especially when her parents were travelling and her brother was so easy to bribe? The little problem with this majestic and mature attitude was also contending with my mother; her rainbow of punishments I still remember and cherish after decades as true pinnacles of human creativity.

I was chronically directionless and penniless to boot: a difficult spot to be in when you have to take your girlfriend to an expensive dinner, buy the latest Pink Floyd album and repair your broken Vespa. I was lost and my inner voice convinced me that no, I was not at all a brilliant young man, quite the opposite. I was not yet able to find my path, So I started university, mainly by default. Medicine? How can I possibly become a doctor when I faint when I see a drop of blood? Soon I realized, to my complete dismay, that when you choose Business and Economics, you had to study maths and statistics. How regrettable.

So, I went to the first maths class and statistics lesson with the same enthusiasm you feel before a root canal. Armed with this attitude, I failed both exams: remarkably, four times in a row. At least I was consistent. The more I tried, the more the failures became evident and epic in their proportions. My inner voice was getting louder and louder. Maybe university wasn't my thing; my supposed brilliance was a joke, and not a funny one.

I could not and did not find my path. First, Annabelle dumped me for a rich, 30-year-old guy with a villa by the sea and a Yamaha 900. Next, I broke my ankle by playing basketball (badly). Last, but not least, someone stole my old motorbike. 'Heaven Knows I'm Miserable Now' by the Smiths became my anthem. It was game over at 17? I thought it was the time of dancing queens (and kings) but maybe Abba had deceived me. And then the tsunami hit my family.

My father, Renzo, whom I deeply loved, passed away way too soon: he had some pain in his chest, went to the hospital to get it checked and never returned. When his tired heart stopped beating, our hearts started bleeding. Renzo was 57 years old and my sister and I were 17. He worked for Olivetti, more than 80 hours per week, for 38 years. So, I found myself dealing with something bigger than me: chronic grief. And I had to pretend I had none, as it wasn't cool to cry, so

I didn't — a genuine big mistake. Like my mother and my sister, I was devastated, shattered, ashamed and utterly lost. I just did not know what to do.

When I returned to school the day after the funeral, my professor told me that it was OK and understandable not to study and to take a few months off. I would have been *bocciato,* meaning that I needed to repeat the same year. A stigma of dishonour you carry inside you for life. I took her condescending tone and words as an affront I never forgot. I felt rage. I thought about what my father would have wanted me to do, so I started studying like never before. I didn't fail, as my professor predicted.

Recently, I looked up my father's name. According to Google, Renzo Gallo did not exist; you can't find him anywhere. Yet, when I look in my heart, he's there, he peacefully and beautifully occupies a large part of it. I know he's there. Do we exist, live and love only when Google says we do? If you Google Lady Gaga, you get about 187,000,000 hits, but my father zero. Really?

One day, I calmly reread my old school reports. I wanted to learn something about myself that I didn't know. Several questions were floating around in my mind. Did I miss something? Who am I, what do I want, what am I capable of? Perhaps it was the first moment of conscious self-awareness in my life. I noticed the high grades in a few — always few — subjects and the low ones in many others — always many. I thought: I could not possibly be bright, hard-working and intelligent in philosophy and a lazy moron one hour later during chemistry. I knew I was pretty good when I was doing what I loved. I was happy and in the zone. I got an insight.

Then, something started to make sense. What if I were to imagine and design my life doing only what I genuinely love doing? Studying and working should not be a valley of tears, but can it be one of meaning and joy? What if I see options and possibilities to embrace rather than obstacles to avoid? Perhaps, maybe, one day I could find what I wanted to do. I also noticed I used to hate physics. However, I changed my mind when I got a new professor who was enthusiastic and capable of explaining physics rather than forcing students to memorize formulas like parrots. I realized the importance of having the right mentor, teacher, the right friends and the right partner.

Maybe the Annabelles of this world were not what I needed. Maybe my selection criteria for girlfriends should change from attractiveness and casual availability to something deeper and more meaningful. Should I choose brainy, interesting conversation, hobbies in common and caring for each other over high heels, lipstick and discotheques? Uhmm. After avoiding books all my life, I started to read. My curiosity shifted into permanent overdrive.

I recall the joy of studying and reading for pleasure, not because I had to. I couldn't stop! Forty years later, I still haven't and I guess I never will. I fell in love with Fyodor Dostoyevsky, Honoré de Balzac, Leo Tolstoy, Albert Camus, Bruce Chatwin, Ernest Hemingway, George Orwell, Primo Levi and many more. I still have many books I have not read yet: a sober daily reminder of how much I don't know. After watching the movie *Amadeus* three times, I discovered classical music. I used to reject it because there were neither electric guitars nor drums. Mozart. Bach. Chopin. Schubert. And please don't even get me started on movies.

I also had to control my inner voice, which almost convinced me I was a spineless loser, unable to find my purpose. So I began focusing on discovering my real vocation rather than organizing my next vacation. I understood that the main business of an adolescent is to stop being one. Shortly after that, I had a dream where I was an acrobat in a circus without any safety net. People were watching me, shouting: 'Jump, Paolo, jump!' I was shaking, scared to death. But, I needed to jump and could not postpone it any longer. Then, I saw my father in the crowd; he wasn't shouting. He was there with his reassuring, caring, compassionate eyes. I internalized that he was – and always is – with me, beside me, protecting me. Then, finally, I could jump: it wasn't as bad as I thought. I had invisible wings, I was flying; it felt so good.

I still have frequent imaginary conversations with my dad. As Seneca wrote, *we suffer more in our minds than in reality.* When I woke up, I thought I was a different person. It was my real birthday, early spring of 1983: I was 19.

The time for blaming others, careless living, having no discipline and finding excuses was over. It was time to grow up and run, even if I was still recovering from a broken ankle. At university, I enjoyed almost every class. I became interested in politics when I had to vote in national elections and elect the student representative on the board of my university. In the mid-eighties in Italy, you could only choose between extreme left or right and ultra-conservative Catholic. None of them was my cup of tea, so I created a new party inspired by liberal democrats and the Scandinavian social democracies. A few thousand students voted for me and I won the election. It was fun, except when I decided against everyone's advice to wear jeans and sneakers to attend my first board meeting at Bocconi. In retrospect, it was not my best decision.

When I graduated, several former high school classmates came to make sure it wasn't a joke. As we have learned from Ben Zander,[81] *Life is a story we invent.* So I decided to invent and create a story that made sense *to me*: to me only. I wanted an exciting story, energizing and meaningful. And I still try to follow that script: it's not always easy but it's often fun. Along the way, you realize that you are never a finished product and this is part of the adventure rather than a source of frustration.

I became obsessed with finding my voice and avoiding becoming like the character of the unforgettable movie *Zelig*, a person-chameleon who took on the appearance of other people just to be accepted. One day I read this quote from Margaret Young:[82] '*Often people attempt to live their lives backwards, they try to*

---

[81] Rosamund Stone Zander & Benjamin Zander, *The Art of Possibility,* Penguin Books, first edition, 2000.
[82] Margaret Young, American singer and comedienne, 1891–1969.

have more things or more money in order to do more of what they want so that they will be happier. The way it actually works is the reverse. **You must first be who you really are** *and then do what you need to do in order to have what you want.'* Got it. We must first be who we really are. Mindset is what we need to pay attention to. With this in mind, I framed three questions.

The Inner Game

1. Which conditions will allow me to be at my best to give my best?
2. What am I good at?
3. How can I collaborate with my inner voice?

This chapter will provide the tools, insights and self-reflection to find your answer to these questions. There is only one path to success: to be able to spend your life in your own way. I need your permission to be your coach, as you'll be doing some serious work to find the answer to your Inner Game. So let's get started with the first question:

1. Which conditions will allow me to be at my best to give my best?

This is a fun and valuable exercise. Take a sheet of paper and a pen and write.

In my coaching session, I call this exercise the Ode to Joy. I recommend listening to Beethoven's *Ode to Joy* from Symphony No. 9 in D minor, Op. 125 before completing this exercise. It will make you smile.

When were you genuinely happy in your life? Please don't refer to a once-in-a-lifetime event (such as getting married) but to something that you have experienced in daily life.

Ode to Joy

Take your time to provide your answers.

1. ....
....

2. ....
....

3. ....
....

4. ....
....

5. ....
....

6. ....
....

7. ....
....

8. ....
....

9. ....
....

10. ....
....

As I completed my list, I recalled my epic trip on a Ciao, a miniature 48cc motorbike, travelling from Milan to Rapallo, a beautiful coastal town near Genoa (180 kilometres). It took me 14 hours; I got lost several times, fell twice, and it was pouring with rain most of the trip. But I just loved that journey. I also felt pure joy when I moved alone to a small apartment in Milan, when I left Italy to go to my dream city, London, or whenever I went skiing on a cold winter's day. I trust you see my point. My constant theme in whatever event brought me joy has always been a complete sense of freedom, autonomy and independence. What is yours?

When Roy did this coaching exercise, he said: 'Celebrating Christmas with my family, as we only get together once a year; buying an apartment next door to my ageing parents; a permanent job in a bank and returning to the same hotel every year for vacation.' Roy found joy in predictability, order and structure. He's a bright, analytical person with a low propensity for risk, defined by him half-jokingly as 'anything I haven't done or eaten before.'

Very different results for Sarah: she's a natural-born entrepreneur. She recalls 'setting up my first company at age 22, scuba diving, parachuting, running the marathon, getting three million from investors, creating new companies and moving on: no boyfriend has ever lasted more than six months.' She broke a few bones in her life journey, a fair price to pay when you have an insatiable passion for new experiences. Contrary to Roy, Sarah loves taking risks, venturing into the unknown and testing her limits, even physically.

Read your list out loud. Can you see that you're smiling right now? There are no right or wrong answers in the Ode to Joy exercise: you can see your typical behaviour, your personality traits and what conditions will make you happy. It's a meaningful exercise that helps you reflect on what brings you joy in whatever you do. You would not expect Roy to jump out of a plane with a parachute, or Sarah to become the head of compliance in a bank, right?

What is the common theme that's emerging from *your* stories? I offer three additional reflections for you. First, what do you see by reading your list? Second, which narrative do you see unfolding? Third, which traits are common in your stories?

You can give your best only if you have the right conditions to be at your best. This insight explains why I went from hating to enjoying subjects such as maths and statistics, once I had the autonomy to study at my own pace. At university, professors treated us like responsible adults: I appreciate this approach.

When you look at your 'Ode to Joy', do you see *alignment and consistency* between what gives you joy and what you currently do? If not, a salary increase or a promotion will not substitute the joy and the pleasure of doing a job that you love, one of the critical components of shaping and leading a meaningful life.

How do you respond to inner and outer expectations?

I believe that one of the most accurate predictors of personal growth and pure happiness is actionable self-knowledge. So, let us continue on this path to improve our **Inner Game**.

I went to a ski camp once to improve my skills. The ski instructor was a tough guy, abusive in his language. Ten of us went for the first lesson; we spent the whole day on the slopes with no lunch break, up and down all day. His approach galvanized some; he challenged us as if we were in a military camp, like that Stanley Kubrick film, *Full Metal Jacket*. Others chose to quit, offended and disgruntled by his, let's call it, sub-optimal approach. I thought: hold on a second. Everyone is motivated to become a better skier, so we are all here, waking up at 6 a.m. Yet how people respond to expectations is different. Why? The real issue relates not only to our motivations but also to *how we react to expectations*.

Years later, I stumbled upon a book called *The Four Tendencies,* by Gretchen Rubin.[83] She framed a question brilliantly: 'I constantly search for patterns to identify what we do and why we do it: *how do we respond to inner and outer expectations?'* While others define outer expectations, we define our inner expectations. So how do we individually respond to these expectations? You can find out your answer by doing this assessment (she calls it a quiz). It takes 15 minutes and it's worth it.

https://gretchenrubin.com/take-the-quiz

Once you get your result, you will be in one of these categories:

1. *Upholder*: You respond to both outer and inner expectations.
2. *Questioner*: You will meet an expectation only if you believe it makes sense to you.
3. *Obliger*: You respond to outer expectations but you struggle to keep yours.
4. *Rebel*: You resist all expectations. You are determined to find your own way. You break the rules.[84]

The value and the validity of coaching assessments are several: they are not carved in stone as the absolute truth. Instead, they are only tools that allow you to increase your self-awareness by reducing your blind spots. It is not about ranking people but about supporting them in their self-discovery, the **Inner Game**.

What motivates you? This question deserves your attention. In his book, *Drive*,[85] Daniel Pink provides us with the surprising truth of what motivates us. For knowledge workers, it is not about carrots and sticks. It is about *mastery*, the capacity to

---

[83] Gretchen Rubin, *The Four Tendencies: The Indispensable Personality Profiles*, Harmony Publishing, 2017.
[84] Francesca Gino, *Rebel Talent: Why it Pays to Break the Rules at Work and in Life*, Macmillan, 2018.
[85] Daniel Pink, *Drive: The Surprising Truth About What Motivates Us*, Riverhead Books, 2009.

improve in what we do, *autonomy and purpose.* I am convinced we must include one extra element, a sense of fairness. Fairness is part of our DNA and can also be found in capuchin monkeys. Bear with me for a moment.

Dr Frans de Waal shared the impactful experiments in his TEDx Talk.[86] He demonstrates what happens when two capuchin monkeys are 'paid' unequally. Quite simply, one doesn't appreciate getting 'paid' with watery cucumber when the other monkey gets sweet grapes. So I assume you won't like getting paid considerably less compared to your colleagues either, a devastating experience of unfairness and injustice for most women and minorities on this planet. Therefore, understanding what motivates you is key to your Inner Game.

I have one more question for you. *What do you do when you don't know what to do?* Our days are always organized around schedules, calls and work, with very little space for us. So what do you do when you don't have to do anything? How do you use your free time? *What gives you energy?* I found it interesting that some people went back to pick up hobbies they had neglected when they were younger and some started something new to rebalance their lives. Like Phil, an experienced senior banker who at age 50 became a skateboard champion. I asked him why he loved this sport so much. His reply struck me: *'Everyone's the same on their skateboard'*, the opposite of banks and corporations. While removing his necktie to run to the park to skate, I noticed a sparkle in his eyes. He's a rebel, like me.

2. What am I good at?

'I always wanted to be somebody, but I should have been more specific.' This quote from US comedian Lily Tomlin still cracks me up

[86] https://www.ted.com/talks/frans_de_waal_moral_behavior_in_animals

after years. It does contain a gem. We can support our dreams and ambition, provided that we know what we want and what we can offer, how we contribute. Let me offer you three exercises to help you answer the million-dollar question: What are you good at?

There is more to discover inside ourselves than we will ever find by looking outside. But to increase your self-awareness, you need to understand your personality and the main features of your behaviour and character. It is the self-narrative of who you are. It is your story. It is understanding who you are, well before you understand what you do for a living.

Many valid and credible assessments are available: I frequently use one developed by Red Bull, the beverage company. According to the Red Bull psychometric test (bear with me as there is a gift for you here), regardless of our job/role/sector, we all have four different areas of success, which make us unique.

1. **Thinking**: how good we are at problem-solving, connecting the dots, learning ability;
2. **Drive**: our motivation, focus and grit;
3. **Connections**: how well (not how many) we manage and nurture relationships;
4. **Creativity**: how innovative, original and out-of-the-box we are. It's not about replicating a new Picasso, it's about understanding how originals and non-conformists can change the world.[87]

Here's the gift for you. It's free, easily accessible and most importantly, helpful and revealing. Take one solid hour and do this test, ideally when you are rested and without interruptions: you can find it at www.wingfinder.com. You'll end up getting two documents. First, the Wingfinder Report will provide

---

[87] Adam Grant, *Originals: How Non-conformists Move the World*, Viking Publishing, 2016.

insights into your drive, thinking, creativity and connection. You will find relevant the part 'on a good day – on a bad day' that will highlight the most and least helpful traits of a given behaviour. Let me share one example from my report: 'On a good day, you respond well to new environments, while on a bad day, you can take on too many tasks at once.' This is really me and it's so true: I got very practical insight to learn how to say no. The second is called the Talent Passport: it will tell you the main traits of your personality and your top strengths. The question for you is, 'Which environment, role and manager will leverage your strengths the most?'

What am I NOT good at?

I have a fantastic career proposal for you. Let me be candid: I know you are excellent at doing a), b) and c). But I also know that you are rather incompetent in d). So, I promise you that if you work hard, I will upgrade your d) from incompetent to mediocre, or if you work extremely hard, you may get your d) to average. Isn't that exciting?

Not really, I suppose. This approach is exactly what schools, universities and companies do, for example, with performance appraisals and training. They find out – mostly in an unreliable or arbitrary way – what you are NOT good at and they ask you to work hard on your deficiencies and weak points to improve. To improve what? Is this modality motivating? Does it make sense? To me, it doesn't. First, we need to find out what we are not good at; it's not difficult. It happens when you're bored, you make mistakes; your energy is low, or when you have to put in enormous effort just to be average. A more pragmatic and sensible approach is:

1. Know what you are NOT good at.
2. Choose a profession that leverages your true skills: constantly work to improve what you are good at.

3. Work with people who are better than you in the area where you are not strong. Ask for help or, if possible, delegate to them or recruit them to your team.

In my former role as chief human resources officer, I consistently recruited or collaborated with people way more competent than me in many aspects of my job.

I have always worked with many people more qualified than me. I have learned a lot from each of them. First, you don't need to invest enormous energy in something you are unfit, unqualified, disinterested or incompetent to do. Instead, use your heart, mind and soul to upgrade your skills from good to great and then put all your efforts into mastering them: they will become your natural strengths.

When I was at the World Bank, I noticed that many qualified economists were the best on the planet at doing economic analysis. Then some got promoted to managers. Their jobs changed to managing people, reducing budgets and surviving politics. Most hated it: why should you do something you detest 70 per cent of your time for a 10 per cent raise? Would you eat a meal where you can't stomach 70 per cent of what has been served for a 10 per cent discount? It's better that you don't get a job where you can't use your skills as you will become – at best – average.

Four words and a question

The responsibility to find your vocation and what you are good at is 100 per cent yours; still, friends and colleagues can help. How? Here's a simple and effective way to find out more about you. Send a WhatsApp or SMS to at least 30, at most 40 people and politely ask, 'Dear ..., which four words come to mind when you think of me? Please add at least one word about something I need to improve or start or stop doing.' That's it. Prepare an Excel file and add every word you receive. What themes are emerging?

Are you learning or discovering something you didn't know about yourself, increasing your self-awareness? What do you see after reading the list?

Take Bob, for example. In his list, he noticed three themes kept coming up. He was considered 1) caring, generous and compassionate; 2) motivating, inspirational and full of energy; 3) curious, a learner, stimulating; and also 4) impatient, tired and stressed. Bob recognized these traits and behaviours as accurate and decided to work on his ability to say no, to negotiate requests and demands. Improving in these areas made him calmer and less stressed, and he regained time for himself and his family; a great exercise.

One question: Peter Drucker is the father of modern management; his influence can't be overstated. He wrote one of the most impactful pieces ever published by the *Harvard Business Review*, entitled 'Managing Oneself'.[88] In this article, Drucker proposes feedback analysis as a way to discover your strengths: 'Whenever you make a key decision or take a key action, write down what you expect will happen. Then in nine to twelve months compare results with expectations.' It is a simple yet powerful exercise to increase your self-awareness and your ability to evaluate and assess how you are doing in any specific situation. There is nothing more practical than a strong theory, right?

3. How can I collaborate with my inner voice?

Luca was so annoying that I stopped playing tennis and went over to him. I had never met him before, but I knew his name. He was playing on the court next to mine and kept shouting, 'Luca, you are a @*&! Luca, how can you miss that shot? Luca, faster, you're too slow!' His language was much more colourful

[88] Peter Drucker, 'Managing Oneself', from *The Best of HBR*, 1999.

than that, to be honest. Finally, I asked him to stop because he was distracting me with all his shouting and cursing. He replied, 'What do you want from me? I'm just talking to myself. Leave me alone.' His reply was more colourful than that too. A question popped up in my mind. Who are the 'I' and the 'myself' when I am talking to myself? Are they two different people?

To find an answer, Timothy Gallwey came to my rescue with *The Inner Game of Tennis*.[89] It's a phenomenal book, almost a holy one for me. Here's why: Gallwey tells us that every game is made up of two parts, an outer game and an inner game. The outer game is played against an opponent. But the premise of the book is that neither mastery nor gratification can be found in playing any game without giving some attention to the neglected inner game. What can I say? Game, Set, Match! Bravo, Timothy, you nailed it.

At the very beginning of his career, Roger Federer was a mercurial player; at times his mood swung faster than his racket. Finally, he understood an imperative: he needed to control his emotions. He became a master of the inner game. One journalist recently asked Federer, 'What are you most proud of?' He could have talked about winning eight Wimbledons, but no, he didn't even refer to his 20 Grand Slams.

Instead, he said, 'Mental strength is one of the most important factors for a successful career. I achieved it, one of the things I am most proud of. I have to deal with fire and ice situations. The fire is myself wanting to win; the ice is myself accepting losses and difficult circumstances. I was able to find the right balance after two, maybe three years on tour. I decided to act that way and behave that way on the tennis court. That moment I started to win games.' The rest is history. Federer, the master,[90] played tennis 'like Michelangelo painted: every stroke was perfection,

[89] Timothy Gallwey, *The Inner Game of Tennis: The Classic Guide to the Mental Side of Peak Performance*, Random House, 2008.
[90] Christopher Clarey, *The Master: The Brilliant Career of Roger Federer*, John Murray Publishing, 2021.

and the result was a masterpiece.' And you can trust these words as they are from the all-time great, Martina Navratilova.

The incapacity to understand or master the inner game explains why I could hardly speak the first time I gave a presentation, even though I had prepared so carefully. Or why Steve, a fantastic candidate with a PhD and relevant experience, could not answer my questions during an interview we will both always remember. He was paralysed with fear. We understand why a player misses an easy point or why at times, we sabotage ourselves when the decisive moment comes. According to *The Inner Game of Tennis*, we have two selves: the conscious thinker and the unconscious doer. But we need to master the Inner Game, if we let go of judgement ('Luca, you are an idiot!') and start trusting ourselves. Letting go of judgement doesn't mean ignoring mistakes but rather seeing them for what they are and correcting them. We must ensure that our two selves work in a mutually trusting fashion, in harmony, a word frequently used in the Inner Game. Harmony is the ability to reconcile the opposite.

We can master our Inner Game by:

1. Observing our current behaviour non-judgementally.
2. Picturing and then visualizing the desired outcome.
3. Letting it happen within the natural learning process, the same thing we see in children when they're learning how to walk.

We can master the Inner Game, the inner voice that can be our most impactful ally or our worst enemy. So if you can, please read *The Inner Game of Tennis* even if you don't like this sport: it applies to any game, trust me.

The Inner Game is similar to the solid foundations of your house. You know and internalize the answer to powerful questions. What do you stand for? What should you do with your life? Which conditions allow you to be at your best? How do you respond to inner and outer expectations? What are you good at? Can you delay gratification? What do others say about you and how can you reduce your blind spots? Can you control the inner voice and work in harmony with your inner self?

You don't see the foundations when the house is finally built, but you know it will not stand without them. This is because you create your foundations by going deeper, not faster. This solidity and your roots will be able to protect you from the many WTF moments and toxic people you will encounter in your life. After understanding and mastering your Inner Game, you can move to game two, the Better Game.

A journalist once asked business magnate Warren Buffet what advice he would give to people to succeed in business. 'By far the best investment is the one you make in yourself – for example, communication skills. If you invest in yourself, nobody can take that away from you.' Find, improve and then master your Better Game: this is the core message of the next chapter. So how do you do that? Turn the page and find out.

4

GAME #2 – Better and GAME #3 – Caring & Outer

'The fight is won or lost far away from witnesses –
behind the lines, in the gym, and out there on the
road, long before I dance under those lights.'

MUHAMMAD ALI

The Better Game

How do you play Game Two, the Better Game? How do you improve and master what you do? I have invited three guests: an iconic guitar player, a divine swimmer and a legendary basketball player.

'Paolo, would you like to come with me to Eric Clapton's press conference?' Oh yes! My friend, a music journalist, gave me a great gift. Clapton was playing a sold-out concert in Milan; the press conference was organized in an elegant hotel. He arrived on time, was very polite and responded to several questions. Near the end, one journalist asked: 'Eric, it's been a while since your last record. What have you been doing the past few years?' 'Well, I've been practising playing the guitar most of the time.' One person added, 'You, practising playing the guitar? But, Eric, you're the best guitar player in the world!' Clapton then replied, 'This is WHY I'm the best guitar player in the world.'

Underwater is a powerful documentary about Federica Pellegrini, *La Divina,* (the divine), and she surely deserves her nickname. During her stellar 20-year career as a professional swimmer, she has won everything and broken every possible record many times. In the documentary, Federica said, '*I swim at least 6 kilometres per workout, every single day. Every 50 metres, I do about 30 strokes: for each workout, my shoulders rotate 3,600 times, 25,000 per week, 110,000 per month. I have been training for 20 years. Total strokes: more than 26 million.*'

After the humiliating defeat at the 2004 Olympic in Greece against Argentina, the US basketball team wanted to redeem themselves.[91] US Olympic basketball assembled what is considered the strongest team ever, at the same level as the Dream Team of 1992, the one with Michael Jordan, Larry Bird and Magic Johnson. In the 2008 US Olympic team, you find players such as LeBron James, Dwyane Wade and Carmelo Anthony. The head coach Mike Krzyzewski also selected superstar Kobe Bryant, the most popular player and the best in the country. But he also had a reputation for being a bit difficult, a prima donna, and a selfish player.

The US team before heading to Beijing trained in Las Vegas. One day after practice the players decided to go clubbing: everyone went except Kobe. The players thought that Kobe didn't want to mix with them: further proof that he was an arrogant jerk. When the team returned at 6 a.m. to the hotel after a fun night at the disco, Kobe was also returning but from an intense workout at the gym, drenched in sweat after lifting weights. The message he sent to his teammates was clear. In a few days' time, all the players had joined Kobe at the gym early in the morning, and after breakfast, they all went together for the intense training day. The two superstar alpha men, Kobe and LeBron, bonded, pushing the team to play better defence and to win the gold against Spain in what is considered the most intense

[91] https://www.netflix.com/ch-en/title/81452996

Olympic basketball final ever. Kobe was not a prima donna, he was only ferociously determined to win. We miss Black Mamba and his beautiful daughter, Gianna.[92]

So the first rule of mastering the Better Game is sweat: your talent multiplied by your effort equals your strengths. As Estée Lauder[93] famously said, '*I never dreamed about success. I worked for it.*'

I had the good fortune to work alongside fantastic professionals and (you may have guessed by now) I admire people in sports, music, art, science and literature who have left a legacy, a gift to humanity with their work. What do they have in common? They have the determination and obsession to excel in what they do: satisfied, maybe, but never really happy. Being professional will make you good or even extremely good, but only an unwavering obsession will make you great.

If you visit the Ferrari Museum at Maranello, Italy, you will read this quote from Enzo Ferrari, founder of the most recognized car brand in the world: '*The best Ferrari ever built is yet to come.*' Self-improvement is not only a continuous process but also a mindset; it is part of your DNA if you want to win the Better Game.

What do Eric Clapton, Federica Pellegrini and Kobe Bryant have in common? No doubt, talent and determination, but most notably, the habit of improving themselves. *Atomic Habits*[94] sold 1 million copies for a reason: it provides a practical, helpful framework, aside from relying mainly on motivation, which the author considers overrated. Instead, James Clear advocates that we need to adopt atomic habits – in other words, constant habits that will shape who we are and what we do. The author offers four laws that will take us from being

---

[92] https://www.espn.com/nba/story/_/id/28569438/kobe-bryant-daughter-gianna-die-helicopter-crash
[93] https://www.britannica.com/biography/Estee-Lauder
[94] James Clear, *Atomic Habits: An Easy & Proven Way to Build Good Habits & Break Bad Ones*, Penguin, 2018.

merely good to truly great: make it obvious, make it attractive, make it easy and make it satisfying.

Developing habits starts with redefining your identity. One example from the book: let's assume you are trying to quit smoking and someone offers you a cigarette. You can give two responses: a) No, thank you. I am trying to quit, or b) No, thank you, I am not a smoker. With the first answer, you are on shaky ground; with the second one, you are on solid rock as it overlaps with your identity.

So the Better Game is based on:

- *A combination of inner motivation and habits: the relentless focus on improving yourself.*
- *Learning from others: the good, the great and the ugly.*
- *Learning from mistakes.*

I'll share a habit I've had since I was in my twenties. First, I make a list of activities that I love, e.g. listening to music, savouring my espresso in the morning and going to the movies and a list of activities I try to avoid, such as waking up before 5 a.m. or taking a cold shower or doing push-ups. Then, every month I select something that I love and I don't do it, or something that I dislike – and I do it. By developing this approach, I have trained my mind to be in control. One word of caution: don't assume that your job is your career. I have frequently met people who were so concentrated in doing their job that they forgot to invest in their career. We will tackle this issue later, when we describe how to increase your professional value.

Habit first, right? So, what's the second way to improve our Better Game?

Learning from the good, the great and the ugly

Start by asking who are the good people or professionals that you can learn from. If you work in a company, try to find out who's the best, e.g., at getting new clients, conducting an analysis, giving a presentation, or providing advice. Invite them for coffee or lunch, ask questions and seek their guidance. I have always found that 98 per cent of people are proud to share what they are good at and willing to help you. You can learn by asking the same questions to colleagues working in other organizations or sectors, and also learn from the greatest minds such as Leonardo da Vinci. How? Read the biographies and memoirs of the people you admire the most. It is a fabulous experience to get to know and understand them.

My favourite author is Walter Isaacson: he wrote the biographies of Albert Einstein, Leonardo da Vinci, Steve Jobs, innovators in technology, and Benjamin Franklin. You will find *A Long Walk to Freedom* about Nelson Mandela on my list. JFK, Andre Agassi, Bruce Springsteen, Roger Federer, Winston Churchill, Ruth Bader Ginsburg, Rosa Luxemburg, Primo Levi, Rosa Parks, Che Guevara, Barack and Michelle Obama, Mary Shelley, Bob Dylan and Madame Clicquot,[95] the story of the champagne empire and the woman who ruled it.

After reading about their incredible lives, you start thinking a bit like them; you can even 'steal' their secrets, learn from their acumen, wisdom, genius and courage. What would Bob Dylan do? What did Nelson Mandela do? Oh, I remember what Rosa Parks said or what Churchill decided not to do or what Mary Shelley was thinking while she was writing *Frankenstein*. They are beside you, helping you in your life decisions. I have always found reading their stories an antidote to loneliness, a joyful learning experience. It may be a different way to meet imaginary friends, a source of inspiration and a refreshing immersion in their genius to balance the depressing shallowness of many individuals.

[95] Tilar J. Mazzeo, *The Widow Clicquot: The Story of a Champagne Empire and the Woman Who Ruled It*, HarperCollins Publishers, 2008.

Speaking of which, we can learn from ugly, despicable people as well. I am not personally grateful to them and I have not read biographies of Adolf Hitler, Stalin, Pol Pot or Mussolini. Still, there is a massive opportunity for learning by working with – let's be kind – not-so-great individuals we meet in our lives. In my professional life, I have had 18 different supervisors, with a range of 15 nationalities: five were wonderful, most of them were OK, and three were quite bad, one of them a simply despicable, repugnant person: he fully met all the criteria of the narcissistic psychopath. By understanding our reactions and discomfort with the ugly individuals we meet, we also internalize what not to do and not to say if we reflect on the negative impact they have on others. We should, therefore, be *almost* grateful to the villains we have all met in our lives: like in a James Bond movie, villains can spice up our life and push us to be better. Proving them wrong is priceless.

The mistake of denying mistakes – by Francesca Corrado

Since childhood, I have always supported the same soccer team. This season is awfully painful to watch as the number of losses piles up. A few days ago the coach, after another humiliating defeat, said, 'I asked the players to forget about it and move on.' Hold on a second: should you and the players really forget the lesson learned after a defeat, after a failure? Interestingly, the coach has already said this four times since the beginning of the season. I guess that's why they keep on losing. *'If you could kick in the pants the person responsible for most of your trouble, you wouldn't sit for a month,'* said Theodore Roosevelt.[96] The point is: we (should) learn from mistakes. With this in mind, I've

---

[96] https://www.whitehouse.gov/about-the-white-house/presidents/theodore-roosevelt/

asked Francesca Corrado,[97] author and founder of the School of Failure, to explain to us why failing is essential in learning and in improving on the Better Game.

'Errare humanum est' and 'Learning from your mistakes' are two old adages that contain two truths. The first is that making mistakes is human: it's a fact of life and absolutely natural. The second is that making mistakes is a factor in the growth and adaptation of our learning process. But these are two truths that we, as individuals and as organizations, struggle to accept. Otherwise, how do we explain our fear of making mistakes, our reactions of embarrassment and frustration when we realize we've slipped up and our difficulty in tolerating mistakes made by others?

All this is paradoxical because our brain learns through trial and error. In fact, according to neuroscientists, our brains have actually evolved to make mistakes. When this happens, in fact, an initial error detection system is activated in a part of our brain within 80 thousandths of a second. Now this negative stimulus is not sufficient to allow us to effectively remedy the error. But it's a warning signal that something doesn't add up and is causing our response, action or reasoning to slow down.

We humans are not good at listening to our bodies and our emotions. We tend rather to keep them in check. So, it's easy to make a mistake despite the warning signals. What's more, in most cases, we don't realize what's happening as it's happening; we discover our mistakes when we've finished whatever we were doing. It's only afterwards, when we receive an outside sign or feedback (a low grade or a rejection), that our brain tells us our decision was wrong or that we failed to achieve a certain goal. If the outcome falls short of our expectations or desires, another region of the brain reacts within 250 thousandths of

[97] https://www.linkedin.com/in/francescacorrado/

a second after the signal and triggers learning mechanisms to help us avoid making the same mistake in the future.

This positive stimulus could be the key mechanism for re-evaluating what happened and for adapting strategies and behaviours to remedy the situation. It's the conscious phase of error detection. In addition, we learn more from failures than from successes because the element of surprise triggered by the mistake facilitates and reinforces learning. So, when we are faced with a situation like one in which we've made a mistake in the past, an alarm is triggered from the temporal lobe of the brain; it takes just a few seconds to warn us that we are about to fall into the same error again, enabling us to make the necessary adjustments. Let me share a practical exercise to learn from mistakes.

Take a blank sheet of paper and divide it into two parts by drawing a line across the middle of the sheet. In the top half, list your successes and in the bottom half, list events you consider failures or non-successes related to your personal or professional life.

For each failure, think about the following questions and write your answers next to each event.

Why do you define this event as a failure or non-success?
What could you have done differently?

What does success mean for you?
How do you think you'll achieve it?

Now try to find elements that are common to all the events.
What is your recurrent mistake?
What mistakes depend only on you?
In what context (personal, relational, professional) do they occur?
Do you have recurrent patterns of thinking before the event occurs?
What were your expectations?

Who is around you when you need to make an important decision?

It's also important to understand your state of mind when you make a decision. Are you calm or under stress? What emotions do you feel? Now reread everything you've written, look at your ups and downs and then ask yourself:

Does what I once considered a priority still carry the same weight now?

Making the right choice is easier when you know what's most important to you. Is there a failure that has led me to reach a goal I never imagined or hoped to achieve? Yesterday's mistake could in fact prove to be the right choice tomorrow.

After you've answered all the questions, share your answers with another person you trust and value (a family member, a friend, a colleague). It will help you see things from a new or different perspective.

Listening to our body and the subtle signals from our brain, embracing our mistakes with kind eyes and analysing them: these are the three key actions allowing us to understand ourselves, our decision-making processes and enabling us to exploit the opportunities underlying all mistakes. So denial is an epic fail because it reinforces our inability to listen to the signals our brain sends us; it conceals useful information about us and others and it slows down our ability to learn. The risk is therefore making the same mistakes, reiterating the same patterns of behaviour.

For the future, I'd like to invite you to create your own book of mistakes: a diary or notebook in which you can write down not only mistakes and oversights but also patterns of thinking and systematic error. Please note that doubts may also be part of this creative step. Use Post-its, coloured pens and highlighter markers. Customize your notebook. As Leonardo da Vinci suggested, don't erase anything, even what you think might be wrong. Making mistakes is a great teacher and can be fun too.

In the 1500s, Portugal used the spice route to trade spices and accumulate amazing fortunes by circumnavigating the entire African Continent, bypassing the Islamic Merchants. It was a long, dangerous journey and merchants tried to stay close to the land while navigating. Profits, however, were huge: investors earned 1,000 per cent in returns, so even if they lost nine ships out of 10, they were still making an incredible profit.

In 1500, Pedro Alvares Cabral[98] embarked on the same journey with an impressive fleet of 15 ships attempting to retrace the route of Vasco da Gama to India. When the fleet approached the horn of West Africa, somewhere along the coast of Senegal, unusually strong winds pushed the fleet away from the coast. So Cabral decided to sail south. After a few weeks (and after losing some ships), the fleet arrived in a strange and unknown land, covered by wild jungle. We call this land Brazil. For centuries, the wealth of Brazil made tiny Portugal rich, with the same rampant and ruthless colonialism that later depleted the African continent as well.

At times, like Pedro Alvares Cabral, we end up in places we did not know existed, pushed by a mysterious wind we did not expect. Mistakes in our navigation can be opportunities as well. We master the Better Game when by leveraging our motivation and skills (the lessons from the Inner Game) we develop habits, and we learn from others and from our mistakes. We can now further upgrade our personal and professional development with Game Three.

The Caring Game

'Nobody cares how much you know until they know how much you care.'

Theodore Roosevelt

---

[98] Bill Fawcett, *100 Mistakes that Changed History*, Berkeley Books, New York, 2010, pp. 136–37.

Even if you haven't heard of them or you only vaguely remember their names from school, I know that you are a fan of one of the two but not both. So let me reintroduce two philosophers, the Englishman Thomas Hobbes (1588–1679)[99] and the Swiss-French Jean-Jacques Rousseau (1712–78).[100]

Thomas Hobbes was born prematurely, at a moment in time when his mother was deeply concerned about the imminent invasion of England by the Spanish Armada. He later wrote, '*My mother gave birth to twins: fear and myself*'.[101] That may explain why he had a pessimistic vision of human nature. The state of nature, he claimed, is a constant state of war and violence, characterized by fear. *Homo homini lupus:* man is a wolf to man. So you can't trust any men. The only way to avoid chaos is to have a strong State, represented by a ruler called Leviathan, also the name of his masterpiece published in 1651. If you look at the frontispiece of the first edition, you will see the representation of the Leviathan: a giant supreme ruler who alone can counterbalance chaos. Three hundred (small) people make up the torso of this ruler, who holds the symbols of power: a sword and a crozier. Beneath, there is a quote from the Book of Job; *Nos est potestas Super Terram que Comparetur ei*: there is no power on earth comparable to Him. According to Hobbes, man is a dangerous machine that needs to be controlled, guided and ruled by a strong state, headed by a ruler who cannot be deposed. I suppose many dictators around the globe use his book as a playbook and not only heads of state but also political leaders and even some CEOs, clinging to power by their fingernails.

Anton Chekhov wrote: '*You must trust and believe in people or life becomes impossible*': possibly a good introduction to our next guest?

Jean-Jacques Rousseau was born in Geneva in 1712, started his career as a composer and was posted to Venice as a civil servant,

[99] https://www.britannica.com/biography/Thomas-Hobbes
[100] https://www.britannica.com/biography/Jean-Jacques-Rousseau
[101] Thomas Hobbes, *Opera Latina,* published in 1679.

where he fell in love with Italian opera. One day, a question changed his life: the academy of Dijon organized a competition, asking candidates to answer the question, 'Has the restoration of the sciences and the arts contributed to refining moral practices?' Rousseau won the first prize in 1750 by submitting *Discourse on the Sciences and Arts*. He controversially argued that arts and science corrupt and erode morals.

However, Rousseau wanted to take one step further and in 1755, he wrote, *Discourse on the Origin and Foundations of Inequality among Men*. Inequality was a problem at that time too. He was on writing overdrive when, in 1762, he published his two most relevant books: *Emile, on Education* (a treatise on the nature of men and pedagogy) and *The Social Contract*. The first sentence of this second work is stunning: *'Man is born free but everywhere is in chains.'*

Rousseau earned an impressive reputation but also ruffled a few feathers, so he fled Geneva and accepted an invitation from say who he was to move to the UK. Contrary to Hobbes, Rousseau believed that man is fundamentally good. He proposed a new *Social Contract* and an alternative to the mighty ruler Leviathan. The State, he argued, should not be ruled by the monarchy, aristocrats or the Church but by all citizens. The *Social Contract* became the guiding light for the French Revolution.

Liberté, Egalité, Fraternité – freedom, equality, fraternity – the idea of these principles came from Rousseau. He advocated giving legislative power to the people. Democracy, anyone? He trusted human beings. He planted the seeds of the French Revolution, which started 11 years after his death.

Rutger Bregman, in his book *Human Kind*,[102] a refreshing read and an antidote to depression, writes, *'To this day, the influence of Hobbes and Rousseau is staggering (...) whenever an idealist advocates more freedom and equality Rousseau beams down approvingly. Whenever the cynic grumbles that this will spark more violence, Hobbes nods in*

---

[102] Rutger Bregman, *Human Kind: A Hopeful History*, p.49, Bloomsbury Publishing, 2020.

agreement.' I assume you've figured out which camp I belong to and – if you are reading this book – I guess you're a bit of an idealist as well. If deep in your heart of hearts you share an optimistic view of life, you believe that you can trust people, that we need to collaborate, engage and care not only for ourselves but also for others, the following few pages may be helpful.

By mastering the Inner Game, you understand who you are and what you want to be and do with your life. With Game Two, the Better Game, you have learned to improve and excel in your profession. Well done! You are ready to move to Game Three when you become a manager and you are no longer a technical expert or contributor. Your job as a manager is mainly to think, not only to do, but it can be a difficult transition for super-doers. Marshall Goldsmith explained it brilliantly in his book, *What Got You Here Won't Get You There.*[103]

You can upgrade to Game Three – the Caring Game and the Outer Game – when you internalize the need to let go of the technical aspects of your role, adding value by managing people, achieving consensus, defining strategy and becoming responsible for work done by others. You are not a solo player anymore, you've become the conductor of an orchestra. Your objective is to ensure that your team can give their best, not to prove that you are better than they are.

I suggest watching Itay Talgam's TED Talk entitled *Lead Like the Great Conductors.*[104] It's a delightful speech delivered with graciousness, explaining different leadership styles. Which leadership style resonates the most *for* you and *in* you?

Becoming a manager starts with caring about others. Instead, sadly, most people interpret this role as a mere display of power. I won't even get into toxic leadership. Perhaps this will be the topic of my next book or, even better, the script of a horror movie, as I have seen several psychopathic leaders damage

---

[103] Marshall Goldsmith, *What Got You Here Won't Get You There*, Hyperion, New York, 2007.
[104] https://www.ted.com/talks/itay_talgam_lead_like_the_great_conductors

people's lives. Instead, I'm interested in flagging the necessary personal transformation to become first a manager and then – ideally – a leader.

Do you care?

That quote by Theodore Roosevelt genuinely struck me: *'Nobody cares how much you know until they know how much you care.'* Another source of inspiration – and practical application – came a few weeks before starting my first managerial role, when I read *Becoming a Manager* by Linda Hill:[105] true stories of the psychological transformation of several managers in their professional journeys. I would call it a psychological thriller more than a management book: you almost touch and smell their struggles, pain, skills, good faith and hard work to make their transition work.

I found Hill's book remarkable and it teaches a lesson I have since then internalized: becoming a manager is about mastering a new identity, not just getting a new title, ideally more money and surely more work. It is a transformation, to be celebrated with the Roman god Janus. When you become a manager, you work for your team to succeed, not the other way around, even if most miss the point.

Professional growth starts from personal development, self-awareness, humility and listening. First, you improve who you are before you can improve what you do. As the French would say: *savoir être avant savoir faire* – first, we all are human being, not human doing. We are defined by what we are – e.g. I am a decent person; not by what we do – e.g. I am a doctor.

Caring starts with empathy: I never would have imagined learning this so well from a professional clown and storyteller. Her name is Sabine Choucair,[106] Founder and Artistic Director of Clown Me In and the International Institute of Very, Very

[105] Linda Hill, *Becoming a Manager: Mastery of a New Identity*, HBS first edition, 1992.
[106] https://www.linkedin.com/in/sabinechoucair/

Serious Studies. She's a wonderful human being from Lebanon, a country I am fond of, with more than its fair share of serious problems, to put it mildly. The motto at Clown Me In?[107] 'Send us where love is needed.' Their mission? 'To spread laughter, fight inequality and heal through the power of performing arts. Our artistic relief work aims to help people overcome the traumas caused by Lebanon's hard social and financial conditions. We reach people in remote areas, refugee camps, and underprivileged suburbs.'

Sabine Choucair knows that caring starts with empathy and understanding what others feel, not only with our brain (cognitively) but also with our heart (emotionally). Understanding is necessary, but it's not enough. Can we also connect and act? Connecting with people is NOT adding a friend or a 'like' on social media. It is a human, real connection followed by concrete action to remove or at least alleviate pain and suffering. At times it's just listening. Being there. Empathy, explains Sabine, is something we are all born with: it is not a technical skill you need to learn but a human quality you need to use.

Are caring and empathy beneficial only to other people? Interestingly, empathy and caring benefit us as well by building social connections, reducing anxiety, curbing loneliness, decreasing depression and improving self-esteem. Caring, I suppose, is about being interested *in* others rather than appearing interesting *to* others.

Empathy is expected from you when you become a manager, so how do you create it at work? By being vulnerable and accepting other people's vulnerability, by asking questions, listening, accepting people as they are and working in teams in a psychologically safe environment. Most importantly, you need to demonstrate, with actions, that you are interested in people's lives because you care. Start by learning something important

[107] https://clownmein.com

about them, their names and their family situation. Empathy means providing people with support – with respectful care – when they need it. Care is not a noun or just a momentary feeling: it is a verb, an action.

I can almost hear what you're thinking: this is a great story, Paolo. But with all due respect to Sabine Choucair, I am running a business here.

Well, recently the CEO of Microsoft, Satya Nadella, said that caring is the new currency.[108] Managers with coaching mindsets will be key to the new way of working and empathy in managers is probably in highest-ever demand today. Care has become everything. Care is the new currency. Take his word for it, not mine.

Mastering the Caring Game means understanding: How can you collaborate? How can you be creative? How can you build your network?

Collaboration and its contribution to success – by Tobias Degsell

Let me take you to Stockholm, Sweden: get ready, as you are about to visit the Nobel Museum,[109] the Temple of Human Creativity and Knowledge, a joyful, impactful and emotional experience where you can learn about the stunning achievements of humankind. The museum and the Nobel Prize reflect the vision to work 'for the greatest benefit to humankind', as Alfred Nobel expressed in his will.

In his speech at the 1986 ceremony, Wole Soyinka,[110] recipient of the Prize in Literature, with his usual humour, made a surprising statement. The Nigerian author claimed that the origin of the Prize could be found not somewhere in Scandinavia but in Africa's culture. He refers to Ogun, the god of Creativity. According to Yoruban mythology, the world is divided into three

---

[108] https://www.siliconrepublic.com/careers/microsoft-linkedin-hybrid-working-trends
[109] https://nobelprizemuseum.se/en/
[110] https://www.nobelprize.org/prizes/literature/1986/soyinka/biographical/

realms: the world of ancestors, the world of the living and the world of the not-yet-born. Then there is a level above them: the world of constant change, where creativity takes place.

How can we achieve creativity? Is it the sporadic spark from a genius who gets a eureka moment like Archimedes? Or is it about the environment where work is done? Or maybe creativity comes from the collaboration between people who share their ideas openly for the sake of advancing science rather than getting the credit for themselves?

Let me introduce you to Tobias Degsell,[111] former Curator of the Nobel Museum, to answer these questions. He's the perfect person to write about collaboration and creativity because he's the quintessential creative person: he does things differently.

For several years I held a position as a curator at the Nobel Prize Museum, located in Stockholm, Sweden. This museum illustrates a century of creativity, where visitors can follow the changes of the twentieth century through the Nobel Prize and the Nobel Prize laureates. Here are a couple of things about collaboration I personally learned by working there.

A person or organization awarded the Nobel Prize is called a Nobel Prize laureate. The word 'laureate' refers to being signified by the laurel wreath. In ancient Greece, laurel wreaths were awarded to victors as a sign of honour. This may seem trivial or unimportant, but for me, it is not. Because by calling them Nobel Prize winners instead of Nobel laureates you might get the impression that the Nobel Prize is all about competition. This is not just another game with winners and losers. As the founder of the Nobel Prize, Mr Alfred Nobel, so very elegantly wrote in his will, this is for the benefit of mankind. Things were not better in the past. If we compare the world today with the world in 1901, when the first Nobel Prize Award Ceremony was held, the world today is clearly a

[111] https://www.linkedin.com/in/tobias-degsell/

much better place. The Nobel laureates have, together, created a better world.

Between 1901 and 2021, the Nobel Prizes and the Sveriges Riksbank Prize in Economic Sciences in Memory of Alfred Nobel were awarded 609 times to 975 people and organizations.[112] With some receiving the Nobel Prize more than once, this makes a total of 943 individuals and 25 organizations.

Like athletes, we often put the Nobel laureates on a pedestal, but it's not always about being super smart or having the best ideas. Personally, I think it's more about being able to collaborate with people who were different from you. In many cases, the Nobel Prize is awarded jointly.

If we want to increase our chances of success, collaboration is the key. This might sound easy, but it's not. Most collaborations fail. The problem can be boiled down to a couple of critical points. One of them is about diversity; another is about trust.

Diversity isn't just the right thing to do. It's also good business. We need diversity to solve more complex problems. It was a great advantage that James Watson and Francis Crick (Nobel Prize in Chemistry 1962) came from different backgrounds: Watson in biology and Crick in physics. This is not a unique thing if you look closely at different Nobel Prizes.

Trust is the most important business and brand asset you manage, especially in relationships with customers, clients, employees and stakeholders. Our economy works because people trust each other and the businesses they support. The banking system is based on trust: we have seen the consequences when trust evaporates.

Trust requires a relationship between two people and all relationships are complex. Despite the whole 'opposites

[112] https://www.nobelprize.org/prizes/facts/nobel-prize-facts/

attract' thing, most people tend to like people who are similar to themselves. We tend to trust people we like. As the saying goes, 'great minds think alike'.

However, that great minds think alike is often a problem. What we need today is as many good – yet different – ideas as possible, so we can pick the best one. And that means coming up with various perspectives and multiple ways of approaching and meeting particular needs. Building collaborative spaces and cross-functional teams probably feels doable, at face value, for most organizations. But ensuring that people like or trust one another? That doesn't seem as easy, does it? Make no mistake: it can be done. It comes down to understanding and encouraging behaviours that build trust – things such as active listening, transparency, authenticity, empathy, helpfulness, recognition – and discouraging ones that break trust. For me, I've boiled it down to this: trust is created when your actions mirror your words.

Speaking about words and collaboration, sometimes when I talk to people about the importance of collaboration, they tell me that they can follow my thinking when it comes to science but what about the Nobel Prize in literature? Don't authors work alone? Well, collaboration doesn't mean that we always sit and work together. These words from John Donne have always been an inspiration for me.

'No man is an island, entire of itself; every man is a piece of the continent, a part of the main. If a clod be washed away by the sea, Europe is the less, as well as if a promontory were, as well as if a manor of thy friend's or of thine own were. Any man's death diminishes me because I am involved in mankind, and therefore never send to know for whom the bell tolls; it tolls for thee.'

These words have served as a source of inspiration, not only for me. Ernest Hemingway, who was awarded the Nobel Prize in Literature in 1954, was also inspired by this poem when he wrote *For Whom the Bell Tolls* in 1940.

Tobias Degsell makes several valid points: let me validate them even further.

Between 1901 and 2022, the Nobel Prize has been awarded 615 times: shared by two laureates 146 times and shared by three laureates 114 times. That means 42 per cent of the Nobel Prizes went to scientists who wanted to collaborate: they ignited new discoveries and they really made the world a better place. Education should foster the idea that humanity is a family with common interest: hence collaboration is more important than competition, wrote Bertrand Russell.[113]

One of my most treasured possessions is an autographed copy of the masterpiece *Thinking Fast and Slow*[114] by the Nobel Laureate Daniel Kahneman.[115] At the World Bank, we invited him to meet with the Senior Leadership team to explore decision-making and possible bias in selecting and promoting people to senior management positions. I recall this meeting and conversation as one of the most impactful and relevant experiences in my professional life.

Daniel Kahneman is the father of a relatively new discipline, Behavioural Economics. How did it start? Over 40 years ago, two Israeli psychologists, Daniel Kahneman and Amos Tversky, wrote an impressive series of academic papers challenging our assumptions about human decision-making. Their work created Behavioural Economics: before them, we assumed that *homo economicus* always made rational decisions.

Kahneman and Tversky could not be more different in their personalities: the first is an introverted fugitive from the Nazis, the second an extrovert, self-confident and always the centre of attention. Yet both of them are geniuses in their respective disciplines. They decided to collaborate to develop meaningful content. So, they started working together, exchanging ideas and challenging each other in never-ending intellectual debates

[113] Bertrand Russell, *The Conquest of Happiness*, first edition 1930, Liveright UK, 2013.
[114] Daniel Kahneman, *Thinking Fast and Slow*, Ferrar, Strauss and Giroux, New York, 2011.
[115] https://www.nobelprize.org/prizes/economic-sciences/2002/kahneman/facts/

that gave rise to significant paradigm shifts in economics and psychology. Finally, they got to the point when they couldn't recall whose brain originated which ideas. Rather than quarrel in unpleasant, never-ending arguments (as many academics tend to do), they decided to flip a coin to determine the lead author of the first paper. After that, they alternated. Daniel Kahneman dedicated *Thinking Fast and Slow* to the memory of Amos Tversky. You can read the story of their authentic collaboration and friendship in *The Undoing Project* by Michael Lewis.[116]

Let me ask you a question. What is the opposite of collaboration? Most people respond with *competition*. Time to pause and reflect if this is the correct answer. If so, competition should be avoided at all costs, right? To me, the opposite of collaboration is something different. It is envy, sabotaging other people's efforts or taking credit for their work, backstabbing.

One of my favourite movies is *Amadeus*.[117] It's about the life, triumphs, genius and troubles of Wolfgang Amadeus Mozart, seen from the perspective of Antonio Salieri, a composer and contemporary of Mozart. Salieri was consumed and insanely jealous of Mozart's immense talent. He probably even poisoned him, although this has not been historically proven. One scene demonstrates brilliantly what envy is:[118] the opposite of collaboration.

Salieri composes a short musical piece in honour of the King, who decides to play it in front of everyone at his royal court. Salieri is visibly flattered. Mozart, meanwhile, is entering the room to meet the King for the first time. He listens to the music composed by Salieri that the King is playing on the piano. At the request of the King, and without even glancing at Salieri's score, Mozart replicates it, improves it and plays it beautifully, demonstrating his brilliance and consequently Salieri's

[116] Michael Lewis, *The Undoing Project: A Friendship That Changed our Minds*, W.W. Norton & Company, 2017.
[117] https://www.imdb.com/title/tt0086879/
[118] https://www.youtube.com/watch?v=9jlQiHHMlkA&t=14s

mediocrity. The rest of the movie is a crescendo of envy and resentment until the death of Mozart.

So, if the opposite of collaboration is not competition, should we compete at all? The answer for me is based on *who your competitor is*. Let me give you a hint: *look in the mirror and you will find your competition*. You compete against yourself: the goal is constant self-improvement, not being better than John.

Let me move from one genius – Mozart – to another one – Roger Federer. When the legendary tennis player played his last match at the Laver Cup on 23 September 2022 in London, he lost his final game and sat down. He held hands with another legendary player, Rafael Nadal. They cried together. I cried too. Their fierce – and always respectful and challenging – competition was the secret sauce of their individual successes. Along with Novak Djokovic, they have been the dominant players for the past 20 years, racking up a total of 63 Grand Slams among them. Federer always strived to be a better player – and thrived. Winning against his opponents did not motivate this tennis legend; rather, he kept his focus for 20 years on improving himself. So, competition is a welcome friend in our game, provided that you are competing to improve yourself, not to win against someone else. Look in the mirror.

Creativity and Innovation – by Alessandro Bogliari

Does co-operation improve creativity and innovation? I wanted to hear, and to share with you, the perspective of a start-up entrepreneur, Alessandro Bogliari,[119] Co-Founder and CEO of The Influencer Marketing Factory, based in New York. How important is creativity in his role? How can he generate creative solutions for his clients?

[119] https://www.linkedin.com/in/alessandrobogliari/

After spending three years in Copenhagen, Denmark, I made the decision to move to the United States, first to Miami, and then to New York City. The energy of New York helped me a lot, even through a devastating pandemic. I dedicated myself and my team grew from two people to 50 in less than four years, completely bootstrapped. Our team, with 60 per cent of our members who are female, includes people of 15-plus nationalities, who speak many different languages. The company is co-owned and co-led by a brilliant woman named Nicla Bartoli. Collaboration is amazing. It helps me see things from different viewpoints and learn more about other cultures. Each person can bring crucial feedback and distinct experiences that can make a difference in terms of creativity, problem-solving and interpersonal skills.

The company name is The Influencer Marketing Factory, a marketing agency. We help brands and companies, from Fortune 500s to SMEs, to execute their influencer marketing campaigns. This process combines analytical work, media planning, negotiation, trends analysis and, of course, creativity. But don't think of creativity as the result of an artist's work, at least as we know it historically speaking. What I mean are out-of-the-box ideas and a lateral thinking approach.

How can we help these companies get a better organic reach, spending way less than a 30-second commercial during the Super Bowl? What's the best way to drive a message from a brand to a specific demographic? How can we use influencers and content creators to convert passive social media users into actual buyers? Creativity in 2023, at least in our industry, also means understanding the latest demands and trends, always recreating effective ways to capture people's attention.

Creativity, and understanding certain trends ahead of the rest of the competition, allowed us to bring to the table new solutions for our clients. In fact, being one of the first to offer something new helped us become top of mind for TikTok influencer marketing, beating bigger competitors that have been in our industry for a long time. For the brands that trusted our new ideas, we were able to maximize their organic reach. This has taught me that in life you have to be lucky, and in the right place with the right structure at the right time, using creativity to stand out from the competition and overcome new challenges.

Paris, 1874: avant-garde painters Monet, Pissarro, Degas, Renoir, Sisley and Morisot struggled to have their works accepted by the traditional establishment.[120] They challenged the monopoly of the Paris Salon by organizing an independent exhibition that displayed 165 paintings from 30 different artists.

It was a failure: most of the 3,500 people who went to the exhibition ridiculed and sneered at the work on display. Most art critics were hostile. One of them, Luis Leroy, wrote an article 'Exhibition of the Impressionists': *'Impression! Of course. There must be an impression somewhere in it. What freedom ... what flexibility of style! Wallpaper in its early stages is much more refined than that.'*[121]

Ironically, it was reviews such as this that coined the term Impressionism. Monet was able to sell his painting *Impression Sunrise* and four other paintings. Sadly, he was the only artist who managed to sell anything at all; the other 29 did not. Still they didn't give up. They organized a second exhibition in 1876 with the financial support of a collector, patron, organizer and painter, Gustave Caillebotte, who played a number of key roles in the Impressionist movement. The group became larger and the Impressionists organized six additional exhibitions in Paris during the following decade.

They changed art forever: before them, painting was supposed to be an exact and meticulous representation of reality. After them, an impression, reimagined, reshaped, an individual interpretation of reality.

[120] https://www.worldhistory.org/article/2000/the-paris-impressionist-exhibitions-1874-86/
[121] https://impressionistarts.com/first-impressionist-exhibition#4

Picasso once said that the chief enemy of creativity is good sense. '*The creative impulse is a key part of what distinguishes humans from other animals,*' writes Marcus du Sautoy in *The Creativity Code*.[122] Creativity can be *exploratory,* meaning reimagining what already exists in original and newly defined fashion, e.g. the Impressionists. Creativity can also be a *combination* of elements never assembled before: think, for example, of the bullhead by Picasso, made with two bicycle parts. Creativity can be *transformational* too: think about listening to music with digital devices or attending a concert in the metaverse. Creativity is what makes us human. Everything that cannot be digitalized or automated is becoming more and more valuable: creativity, empathy, collaboration, compassion, integrity and imagination. In the past, jobs were about muscles; right now jobs are about brains. I am convinced that in the future jobs will be about our hearts and souls. It is possibly a hint for your future professional choices.

Networks and Networking

Caring. Collaboration. Creativity. How can I create a network? How important is networking? Let me start with a question. What is one of the most valuable assets you have in your life? No, it's not money, it's your relationship capital. Marissa King's book *Social Chemistry*[123] provides a constructive and practical way to assess our networks or groups of interconnected people. The author shares a powerful metaphor. Both graphite and diamonds are made of carbon: graphite is soft, dark and ordinary, while diamonds are hard, transparent and rare to find, and the most expensive status symbol on the planet. What distinguishes the two is how carbon molecules are arranged.

[122] Marcus du Sautoy, *The Creativity Code: How AI is Learning to Write, Paint and Think*, Fourth Estate Publishing, London, 2019.
[123] Marissa King, *Social Chemistry: Decoding the Patterns of Human Connection*, Dutton Publishing, 2021.

The same rule applies to our networks. Are you an *expansionist,* a *broker* or a *convener*? Expansionists have extensive networks; they are well-known and find it easy to meet strangers. However, they have little time to keep up or invest in their relationships because they have too many. Brokers generate value by bringing together disconnected parties: they are bees flying from flower to flower, disseminating innovation and ideas. Conveners instead build smaller but more intense networks based on friendship and trust. I recommend taking the survey by Marissa King at assessyournetwork.com to evaluate your network.

Let me share a few essential rules to strengthen the ties that bind:

- Investing in our relationship capital means investing quality time, face-to-face. Without face-to-face interaction, our emotional attachment quickly evaporates after 150 days without seeing a person and our feeling of closeness drops by 80 per cent.

- Building relationships *is about giving, not taking.* Most people approach relationships by asking first (for time, favours, connections, jobs, pro-bono work). Last year I got 7 million views on my posts on LinkedIn and – quite honestly – I was stunned to read some of the requests I got,[124] mostly from people I have never met. Asking first is the wrong starting point. Relationships are like bank accounts. First, you need to deposit before you make a withdrawal: there is no credit line. The experience has to be mutually transformational, not individually transactional. Both parties need to benefit from the exchange at least on an emotional level.

- *Quality – more than quantity – is critical.* A few relationships in several different networks are better than countless relationships in only one extensive network. Here's an

---

[124] https://irishtechnews.ie/what-happens-3-million-views-on-linkedin/

example: I recently coached a lawyer, possibly one of the best in his field in the world. He knows every colleague in his domain, but no one else outside this narrowly defined network. How do you get new ideas, innovation and creativity if you only get more of the same?

- How many people should we have in our networks? The magic number is 150, known as the Dunbar number.[125] In a 1993 study, Robin Dunbar, a British anthropologist, theorized that humans could have no more than about 150 meaningful relationships, the optimal number of stable relationships we can maintain and nurture.

Being part of a network means that people in that network trust you. The entry fees to a network are not merely qualifications and titles. It is about who you are as a person: your reputation. I have a confession to make. I have never been offered a job because I applied – not once. All the jobs and opportunities came from referrals and people recommending me. The magic of trust is that it unlocks a wealth of opportunities.[126] Interestingly, trust is also reciprocal. It's challenging to trust somebody who does not trust you and vice-versa. Trust is the sum of Credibility + Reliability + Proximity.

So how can we network in a meaningful, productive and mutually beneficial fashion?

The Outer Game

Chapter One, after describing WTF moments, provided a summary of the seven leading megatrends that are already impacting our lives. WTF moments are dangerous as they constantly derail our attention, turning it towards something

[125] https://www.newscientist.com/definition/dunbars-number/
[126] Sandra Sucher & Shalene Gupta, 'The Power of Trust: How Companies Build It, Lose It, Retain It,' *Public Affairs*, New York, 2021.

irrelevant, irritating or simply crazy, while we should keep our focus on essential and significant issues. We should be paying attention and noticing what matters.

I thought it helpful to summarize the Outer Game with Figure 1: it is about developing system awareness and system thinking. It is about connecting the dots.

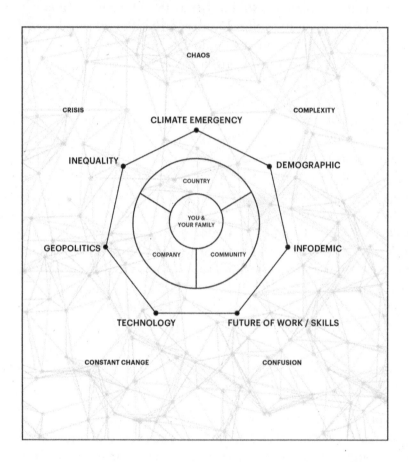

At the very centre are you and your family; the outer circle is about 3 Cs: your Community, your Company and professional life, and your Country.

Around you, notice all the megatrends impacting our existence, as we discussed at the beginning of the book, such as climate change, demography and diversity, inequality, geopolitics, technology, job markets and information. The first point: all megatrends are interconnected. None is a standalone issue; together they are an ecosystem. COVID-19 and the war against Ukraine are only two of the latest examples that have had a lasting and unforgettable impact on the 3 Cs, our communities, companies and countries and, of course, you and your family.

Developing a systemic approach does not mean that we should aim to be experts in every domain: it means that we can see the links, connect the dots and develop contextual intelligence. Then, we can start framing questions without worrying (yet) about finding the answer by understanding and visualizing links and relationships. While knowledge is finding the correct answer, wisdom is framing the right question. If you think about it, statements turn your mind off, while questions make your mind spark.

Let's give it a try. Just as an example.

If you want to be a recruiter, what is the impact of Artificial Intelligence in the process of recruiting candidates? If you want to be a teacher, what is the effect of demography in your country? Where and how can you create an impact if you wish to decrease inequality? How will your job change because of digital transformation? If you work in tourism, how will climate change impact travelling? How will the war in Ukraine impact supply chains and transportation? The list could be a thousand pages long. How do you connect the dots and how can you read what seems unreadable? Questions are the answers if you care to explore to find the right one.

With Game Two, we learned how to excel in whatever role we play. We have grown exponentially with Game Three, the Caring Game and the Outer Game. Now fasten your seat belts as we're starting down a bumpy road, the crucial moment to deal with a personal and necessary crisis.

5

GAME #4 – Crisis

'Our greatest glory is not in never falling, but in rising every time we fall.'

Confucius

'It matters not how strait the gate,
How charged with punishments the scroll,
I am the master of my fate,
I am the captain of my soul'

Invictus by William Ernest Henley[127]

Let's recap the journey we've taken so far.

With Game One, the self-discovery **Inner Game**, we learn who we are, our identity. We find the answer to a simple and powerful question: what do we want to do in life? Our job is not a mere list of tasks and responsibilities; it's anchored to our compass, what we stand for. We don't do a job – we *are* the job we're doing.

With Game Two, the **Better Game**, we move from being naïve amateurs to mastering our role, avoiding the pitfall of becoming bitter or depleted with no energy left. Many people stop at this level of personal and professional development.

---

[127] William Ernest Henley (1849–1903) *Invictus* https://www.poetryfoundation.org/poems/51642/invictus

Not you.

We continue growing by caring and by opening the window, internalizing the need to collaborate and building bridges with people and ideas. Game Three has two parts: the first is the **Caring Game**. We learn it by working with others, cultivating trust and collaboration. This development occurs when we become managers of others and we're constantly asking ourselves if our way of behaving works with them. It's a litmus test to see how we impact others. The second part of Game Three, the **Outer Game**, starts when we acquire contextual intelligence; we think ahead, formulate strategies; we become thought leaders and independent thinkers.

These three games, this significant portion of our professional life, can last up to two decades. Then, one day, something happens we did not anticipate: we are stumbling in the **Crisis Game**: we will see *the long-term benefit of a midlife crisis.*

A walk in the park

The Executive Committee (EC) made an important decision: to increase the headcount to cope with impressive business growth. However, there was also a need to rethink and reshape the organization and upgrade skills. The EC also expected the overall staff cost to remain the same and, of course, to improve diversity while decentralizing operations. That was my job. A piece of cake when you are the HR director of a company with thousands of people in 20 different countries, isn't it?

Two weeks later, after putting in 15 hours of work per day, I returned to the EC with a detailed staffing plan. 'Well done! Approved,' they said. Then, finally, the President stood up, shook my hand and told me, 'Congratulations, Paolo, now make it happen. What are you waiting for?'

My team and I started working around the clock. We even had a joke: *If you don't come on Saturday, please don't bother to come back to the office on Sunday.* Taking an entire weekend off was not an option. I became a ghost father and husband, showing up at home at 10 p.m. only to sleep before heading back to the office at 7 a.m.

I was living in London at the time and one of my favourite parts of the day was walking from home to the tube, as I needed to cross Holland Park. I was always the first person to enter the park at 7.30 a.m. I loved the few minutes when, all alone, I met the squirrels, the peacock, even foxes. At first, we avoided each other and then we learned to respect one another. Finally, I felt they knew me and I knew them. I breathed the fresh air of the early morning, stopping and meditating a few minutes by the little pond – icy in winter – before taking the tube on the overcrowded Central Line. It was my mental medicine. I still miss that walk, the magic of Holland Park.

A few days after the EC approved the proposed restructuring plan, I was in my park and started fantasizing: what if I were to ask for the severance package myself and leave the company? I toyed with this idea for a few days and then I thought: 'Be serious, Paolo, you can't ask that: you need to make this project happen and take a lovely holiday when it is over.' My inner voice was whispering something to me, but I brushed off these thoughts. How stupid of me even to conceive such an idea at age 44. A few months later, as I was enjoying my well-deserved vacation, this fantasy came back. I wished I had left the organization: I was not looking forward to returning. 'C'mon, Paolo,' I thought, 'isn't this what you always wanted? Are you crazy?'

The inner voice had returned, but I decided to ignore it. Again. But it was becoming louder and more insistent. As a result, one year later, I changed my job and returned to Washington, DC, at the World Bank. It felt right. I reconnected with old friends and I felt like I was going back home. My fantasies of leaving disappeared. I was *cured*. I only needed to take a break, change scenery and my job, and voilà, I solved the problem. My inner voice was no longer there; I had suppressed it.

But one year later, the fantasy unexpectedly returned as I was walking back home. I wasn't in Holland Park, but it wasn't difficult to recognize: it was the same voice. It did not gently knock at the door: it broke down my mental door and crashed back into my mind.

The inner voice was there to stay until I dealt with it. I needed someone to help and support me, so I asked to work with a coach and I met an outstanding one who asked me this question after a couple of sessions: 'Paolo, do you want me to help you to survive a little bit longer in your role or to support your quest to find what is next for you in your next 20 years?' Holy cow! THAT question truly destabilized me and I asked for some time to reflect.

But I have to confess: the question also made me upset. I had just joined the World Bank. I lead a team of outstanding professionals, 200 of them. I respected and admired my boss and the institution, yet someone was telling me something disturbing. 'Me, surviving, you are kidding me?' my ego was shouting in anger. Was my ego a friend or an enemy?[128] It took a while for me to think about and elaborate on my coach's powerful question. Finally, when I was ready, we met again for a coaching session that – honestly – changed the course of my professional life. I was 45 years old. To use a soccer analogy, it was half-time: I had 22 years of work behind me and probably a similar number in front of me. Did I want to play the second half the way I played the first half? Even better: *do I want to play the same game?*

My coach's question was simple: what do you want to do with the rest of your life? My coach observed that while I could do my job, it was unlikely I would have *survived* until retirement in the same position and organization for 20 years. No way! The path up was almost impossible. Then she told me something I've never forgotten: 'I've seen many people waiting for decades to retire and then die as soon as they get there.

---

[128] Ryan Holiday, *Ego is the Enemy*, Portfolio Publishers, 2016.

They are the lucky ones, as many live much longer and only survive and vegetate, after losing the only identity they have ever developed, their professional one. Only a few can find a new path, one of meaning and fulfilment. If you are ready to work hard, challenge assumptions, manage your ego and explore, I can help: so, what do you want to do?' I really wanted to find the answer. The inner voice, the fantasy I had been trying to ignore or suppress, was no longer a persistent noise. Instead, it was a professional and personal challenge squarely in front of me. I needed to look at it, bite the bullet, recognize it and, step by step, deal with it.

Denying the crisis was exhausting. It was a necessary midlife crisis but with long-term benefits.

Midlife crisis

'*Midway upon the journey of our mortal life, I found myself in a forest dark, for the straightforward pathway had been lost.*' If you are Italian, and maybe even if you are not, you will probably recognize these two lines. It is the beginning of the *Divina Commedia* by Dante Alighieri, an Italian poet and philosopher who wrote his masterpiece between 1308–21, considered one of the greatest works of literature of all time. It is divided into three sections: *Inferno* (Hell), *Purgatorio* (Purgatory) and *Paradiso* (Heaven). The beginning is crucial; we experience a moment of disorientation and crisis midway through our mortal life. During medieval times, middle age was around 35. Since then, life expectancy has increased, but the challenge still exists. We still need to handle our midlife crisis.

Elliott Jaques, a Canadian psychoanalyst, coined the term midlife crisis back in 1965.[129] 'This is a moment when we come

[129] https://www.nytimes.com/2003/03/17/us/elliott-jaques-86-scientist-who-coined-midlife-crisis.html

to terms with our limitations, restricted possibilities and our mortality.' We can relate to this principle. In our mid-forties, we have already worked for 20-something years. We probably have a mortgage to pay, elderly parents to care for, and growing and demanding kids.

Along with Dante Alighieri and Elliott Jaques, let me add to the list the brilliance of David Byrne. You may remember him as the frontman of Talking Heads, a progressive band active from 1975 until 1991. It's challenging to define the music they played as they roamed between new wave, post-punk, afro-electronic, funk and dance rock.

Do you remember their song, a true masterpiece, 'Once in a Lifetime'? '*And you may ask yourself, well: how did I get here? (...)*'

So, it has been a while since poets, psychologists, singers and everyone else shared the same point of view. We all have a crisis at a particular moment in our professional journey.

As an executive coach, I have noticed that when clients stumble – like myself in the past – it's a watershed moment. They stop believing in themselves and their power to persevere.[130] Roger Federer used exactly the same words in a remarkably honest interview he gave a few days after he retired as a professional tennis player. He said that his decision to retire came after he 'stopped believing' he could continue playing because of injuries:

> The last three years have been tough, to say the least. I knew I was on very thin ice for the last year ever since I played Wimbledon. I have tried to come back but there is a limit to what you can do. (...) I listened to my body and I stopped believing, to be honest.

Near the end of the interview, Roger shared the feeling of realization that that moment was coming.

---

[130] https://www.bbc.com/sport/tennis/62975292

I always pushed my retirement thoughts away. I said, the more I think about it, the more I'm already halfway retired and this is not the way to go to work, you know, for me as a tennis player, so we'll deal with it when it comes. And it did. And I dealt with it. I think writing those words was, for me, partially also like rehab, like going myself through all those words, feeling them.

So how do we understand, decode and manage the crisis? This crisis usually occurs in the mid to late forties. We are struggling to find a new path as the current one is no longer meaningful. And at the same time, we are terrified and preoccupied that, by leaving our comfort zone, we will get lost — like Dante — in a dark and scary place. But, better bored and safe than in danger, isn't it? So, the instinct is to stay where we are. Here are the critical criteria to understand if we are actually having a midlife crisis.

The motivational factors are different

Carlo Strenger and Arie Ruttenberg, in an impactful article from the *Harvard Business Review*,[131] explained that during a midlife crisis we are moving *from deficiency motivators* to *growth motivations*. Deficiency motivators are fed by a 'lack of', such as the wish to become a manager, make more money, get married and get a house: predictable goals that fill our life. The authors also made clear that the midlife crisis is an *existential necessity*. During this career phase, *our ego is in charge*: we care about external validation, visibility, money, success and status symbols. We seek security and importance. We ask ourselves: How can I progress on the corporate-social ladder? What can I get from

---

[131] Carlo Strenger and Arie Ruttenberg, 'The Existential Necessity of Midlife Change', *Harvard Business Review*, February 2008, pp. 84–88.

this world and other people? What is most convenient, lucrative and advantageous for me?

During this phase, we are highly motivated, focused, determined and looking to improve the Better Game and reap its benefit. Then one day, we sense a crisis; it's usually in a moment of interior peace and silence when we start to feel that something is not quite right. But, of course, we still don't know yet; we kind of feel like we're in a difficult spot, but **we are moving from success to significance** and our souls will slowly but surely conquer our minds and hearts.

Your meaning replaces success defined by others and by society.
Jung defines this process as individualization, a true work of art. It's about reconnecting with your true self. A good starting point is to remember what you used to love when you were a child. As we discussed in the Inner Game, what you left behind and reconnected with is what gives you energy, what gets you in the 'flow' – the magic moment when you lose track of time and you're absorbed by what you're doing because you love doing it.

Your brain works differently.
As we get older we feel and experience the pain of ageing. We tend to panic with disturbing and visceral thoughts when we walk through our apartment and by the time we get to the dining room we've already forgotten what we went there to do. Sound familiar? We notice that our body changes, but what about our brain? The ageing brain is networked differently, as our brain undergoes a great rewiring after age 40.[132]

A very interesting article from Steven Ross Pomeroy, editor at *RealClearScience*, shares fascinating findings. Researchers from Monash University in Australia evaluated 144 studies and scientific literature, seeking to summarize how the connectivity

---

[132] https://bigthink.com/neuropsych/great-brain-rewiring-after-age-40/?utm_source=pocket _discover_health

of the human brain changes over our lifetime. During our teenage and young adult years, the brain seems to have numerous, partitioned networks with high levels of inner connectivity, reflecting the ability for specialized processing to occur. But around our mid-forties, that starts to change. The brain starts becoming less connected within those separate networks and more connected globally across networks. By the time we reach our eighties, the brain tends to be less regionally specialized and instead broadly connected and integrated. Basically we become less specialized and more generalist. Proper diet, exercise and plenty of sleep can keep our brain in optimal condition, but it still changes: this rewiring has concrete, tangible effects on our cognitive skills. Daniel Levitin in his impressive book, *Successful Aging*,[133] debunks the myth that our memory and cognitive abilities are doomed to unstoppable decline.

You wonder: what am I doing here?
There's a moment when you realize that you don't recognize where you are, time is a limited resource and you no longer have decades ahead of you. The moment when you realize that the number of tomorrows is much lower than the number of yesterdays. As a result, you get increasingly irritated, frustrated and detached from specific debates, people and dynamics. You get this feeling by meeting former colleagues who are still worried and focused on the same issues. They are still stuck in the same place, but you have moved on, and you wonder how they can keep showing up to see the same old movie. You want to leave and stop investing in relationships with the people who belong to the place you want to escape from.

Sounds familiar? This moment is called 'restlessness' and can be experienced at different levels of intensity. It is a ***misalignment between what we do and who we are or what we are about to become.***

---

[133] Daniel Levitin, *Successful Aging: A Neuroscientist Explores the Power and Potential of our Lives*, Dutton, 2020.

A midlife crisis is a moment to reset and reconsider what makes sense to us, to search for our true calling. My clients have verbalized it many times with phrases such as, 'I want to get out, get off the train, I can't stand it anymore, I am tired-bored-frustrated, been there, done that, I know the movie, I can't stand it.' Have you ever felt the same?

The four typical responses to the crisis

How do people react to this tense, unpleasant moment of restlessness? In my experience, I have noticed four kinds of response behaviours, almost equally distributed.

- The Faithful Soldier
- The Red Ball
- Peter Pan
- The Brave Traveller

The Faithful Soldier
The main feature of faithful soldiers is that they keep their heads down by doing the same job forever, only faster and faster and with more complex tasks. It is equivalent to saying: I don't like what I'm doing, so let me numb myself by doing it even more. They remind me of jugglers. They start with three balls and they feel that they have to demonstrate their juggling skills by constantly adding new ones. How many balls can you juggle? These people are usually very reliable, dependent, hardworking and committed, and they work until – sadly – they burn out or worse.

Serena, an account manager, was recently promoted to senior vice president with a 10 per cent raise. They also doubled her customer portfolio, even adding clients from Asia. She has to travel there regularly, feels terrible leaving her daughter with her elderly mother and she's also chronically exhausted. She wants to give up and find her true self, a new life: in theory. In practice, she's interviewing with other companies offering an even bigger salary and even more work and travel. Serena is a top professional in her field, competent, sharp, reliable and no matter what, she always delivers. She is understandably proud of her track record.

Still, she has not grasped the difference between change and transition, as she thinks that by changing her job, her wish to take time for herself will come true. Serena feels guilty about going to the gym or not working on Sundays and she frequently calculates how many years she still needs to work before she retires. Right now, only 15: we're almost there, only 5,475 days to go. Serena's inner voice is telling her to stop or at least take some breaks, but the soldier's instinct prevails. One more bullet, one more battle, one more fight. Repeat.

The Red Ball

Have you ever tried to hide a ball under the water? If you have, you know it takes quite an effort to keep the ball under the surface, as it will suddenly re-emerge if you don't pay attention and keep pushing it down: if the ball is red, everyone will quickly notice when it pops to the surface again. Take Mike, for example. He's in the restlessness phase and wants to live, to do something else, but he keeps denying it. Mike makes a considerable effort to ignore what's going on (he's pushing the ball underwater) but sporadically, the ball (his wishes) comes out. Denying the crisis is exhausting.

The red ball in this analogy represents the evidence that everyone will notice, no matter how much effort you make to deny it. Typical behaviour is minimizing, blaming external circumstances and trying to convince us that it was just a bad day, it will pass. Tomorrow. Maybe. Or maybe not. The problem is that *one day* is not a specific day of the week. You are the main character in the legendary movie *Groundhog Day*. Like Mike, he put it off many times, denied the red ball's existence and minimized it. It shall pass. And in the meantime, he keeps hiding the ball. Maybe no one will notice and he can keep on smiling.

Peter Pan

This is a metaphor based on the idea of not growing up and the fantasy that you can even turn back the clock to your youth. For example, Silvio is not what he used to be anymore, physically, emotionally or mentally. He knows it and people notice it. He considers ageing a curse and will do anything to deny it. So he buys the new red sports car (ideally a Lamborghini or a Ferrari), he gets a new young lover, most of the time half (or better one-third) his age, invents a new image, conveys (feigns) youthful energy, enhanced at times by drug use.

These are the symptoms of Peter Pan syndrome. I'm sure you've met a few people who fully fit this profile. What are the main traits of this syndrome? Regression to a glorified past, socially immature behaviour, creating an alternative reality that does not exist. People affected by this syndrome frame the last part of their life as a descent to hell, not an opportunity to redefine what matters. The older they get, the more pronounced this behaviour is. It's sad to watch: the more they decay, the more they pretend.

The Brave Traveller

So, we must start our journey as brave travellers by dealing with this chronic restlessness and reinventing ourselves. But, of course, travellers and tourists have different mindsets: travellers seek new landscapes and experiences while tourists try to replicate what they left behind. The process is a transition; it takes time, but the journey is worth the price. It's an existential necessity, and while a coach can surely help, this task cannot be delegated to anyone else.

We should therefore embrace the moment of crisis, as masterfully described by the philosopher Alain de Botton.[134]

---

[134] Alain de Botton, *The School of Life: An Emotional Education*, 2019.

A (crisis) breakdown is not merely a random piece of madness or malfunction; it is a very real — albeit very inarticulate — bid for health and self-knowledge. It is an attempt by one part of our mind to force the other into a process of growth, self-understanding and self-development that it has hitherto refused to undertake. If we can put it paradoxically, it is an attempt to jump-start a process of getting well — properly well — through a stage of falling very ill. […]. We haven't become ill; we were ill already. Our crisis, if we can get through it, is an attempt to dislodge us from a toxic status quo and constitutes an insistent call to rebuild our lives on a more authentic and sincere basis. It belongs, in the most acute and panicked way, to the search for self-knowledge.

Indeed: the necessity of a crisis, an opportunity we cannot afford to miss. One more question for you: are you more similar to barnacles or lobsters? Yep, you heard me: they are two different kinds of crustacean.

Barnacles and Lobsters

Barnacles are crustaceans, hence related to crabs and lobsters. Early in life they are confronted with an existential decision about where they will live. Once they decide, they spend their life with their head cemented to it.[135] Barnacles don't move. Ever. Until they die. If you remove them from the rock with a knife, barnacles will try to return to the very same spot. They can resist storms, waves and temperature changes: they don't move from the rock they chose to live on, they don't even consider moving.

---

[135] John W. Gardner, *Personal Renewal*, speech as delivered at the Marriott Executive Development Program, September 1990, Maryland.

It's a different story if you're a lobster. Lobsters live inside a rigid red shell that does not expand. So as the lobster grows, the shell becomes very confining and the animal starts to feel uncomfortable. Eventually the lobster abandons the now-too-small shell, hides under a rock to protect itself from predators and returns to normal life when its body produces a new shell. Lobsters go through this process many times in their life. As Rabbi Dr Twerski[136] quite rightly said:

> 'The stimulus for the lobster to be able to grow is that it feels uncomfortable to live with a shell too small. If lobster had doctors, they would tell them to take this pill to avoid the pain! We must realize that times of stress [the restlessness we've been talking about] are the moments of growth.'

Unless we prefer to be a barnacle and we want to cement our head onto the same rock until death.

Lost in transition

In my coaching sessions, I ask permission from my clients to take a picture of their faces after one specific question I always ask them. A fraction of a second is enough time for the body and face to register the feeling, but not long enough to think and formulate an answer. They look a bit puzzled, but they agree. The question is, '*How do you feel imagining that you will be doing the same job until you retire?*' You may look at yourself right now: how does it feel? Your facial expression reveals more than words, as it is not yet filtered; it is spontaneous. I have seldom seen a happy face. Instead I have witnessed expressions of disgust, perplexity, doubt, thoughtfulness, nervous laughing and surprise.

---

[136] https://www.youtube.com/watch?v=dcUAIpZrwog

Playing the same game until retirement is not appealing to most people. However, we have learned that sometimes halfway through your professional life, you sense, almost smell, that something is not right and, little by little, your self-awareness increases. As I've shared with you, there are some typical and predictable answers and reactions to this crisis. Are you a soldier who keeps on fighting? Are you trying to hide the red ball? Are you a Peter Pan? I envy your Ferrari, I must admit, but nothing else.

Or are you — or do you intend to become — a brave traveller? Do you see yourself more as a barnacle or as a lobster? If you want to be an intrepid traveller, lobster style, bear with me. You don't need to be lost in transition because **shifts happen**.

Transitions by William Bridges[137] has been on my greatest hits list of books for a long time: I have read it five times. It's an excellent, practical manual that helps us understand the process of transitions that we go through when we decide to become travellers. But, first, we need to understand that transition differs from change, as we tend to confuse change and transition as if they were synonymous.

Change vs. Transition

Change is about adaptation. *Change occurs outside us, we are on the receiving end.* For example, we are moving to a new home or a different country, getting a new job, buying a new car, getting a new manager, or our company is going through a reorganization. Change management is challenging and requires adaptation and flexibility. We need to adapt to new circumstances but we are still the same person. Change is situational and can revert to the initial stage, e.g. we can still move back to (a) after moving to (b). Fundamentally, we are the same person; we're 'just'

[137] William Bridges, *Transitions: Making Sense of Life's Changes*, Capo Press, 2004, 25th Anniversary Edition.

managing change. Change is driven to reach a goal. Change is a set destination.

Transition is the process. The word comes from the Latin word *transpire,* which means 'to go across' and often refers to the process, not the result. Transition is psychological and irreversible. It requires self-awareness, self-reflection and the courage to embrace a transformation. A transition is 'into', never 'from'. It is not an escape but a journey into something very different.

Transformation is therefore the outcome, the final result at the end of a successful transition process. Transformation is inside us: we transform ourselves.

While many thinkers in different disciplines have proposed their models and frameworks, I always refer to the one brilliantly presented by William Bridges, with a little help from our friends, two other distinguished psychologists, Carl Rogers and Judith Viorst. The process of transition consists of three diverse and sequential phases – autumn, winter and spring.

Autumn: the ending

Yes, ending, because every beginning starts with an ending. I have found it remarkable that while the transformation process can be long, almost every person remembers perfectly the specific moment they realized – mainly by intuition – that something was coming to an end, like the first cold day after summer, anticipating the arrival of autumn. They understood that they were ready to transform and reinvent themselves. The pain of staying where they were was stronger than the fear of moving ahead. Like lobsters, they realized that wearing the same shell was no longer possible; it became too painful, too confining and limiting. Usually, it's a mix of ever-increasing frustration and a sense of wasting time.

Judith Viorst's book, *Necessary Losses*,[138] is challenging and intense, and it contains a real gem: *We grow by learning how*

---

[138] Judith Viorst, *Necessary Losses*, Simon & Schuster, New York, 1986.

to understand, manage and internalize losses. The first one we experience as soon as we are born, when we enter the world after living in our mother's comfortable womb and someone cuts the umbilical cord. When we think of losses, explains Viorst, we tend to associate this term with something terrible; something to avoid. Yes, losing is no fun but losses and endings are a vital part of our growing process, or else we become trapped in the *repetition compulsion syndrome, the same as it ever was.*

Yet the problem with this phase is that we find ourselves returning to where we were and social conditioning plays a big part. Society, friends and our families have developed a clear image of who we are and it is sometimes complicated not to fit into their frame.

Take Eric, for example, a partner in a reputable consulting company. Part of his perks is participating in a few selected events as a speaker or panellist. While highly frustrated by his job, he can't bear the thought of not being invited and feeling excluded from the circle he belonged to for many years. His whole identity is his professional one and he's almost jealous of it. The freedom to lose is both a gift and a burden, the price we pay for moving ahead and never looking back. Even when we tend to return to our former selves, the almost physical sensation of misalignment persists.

In *On Becoming a Person*, Carl Rogers[139] explains this with the concept of **congruence**: *an accurate matching between experiencing and awareness.* Happiness happens when what you think, do, feel and say are in the same place. By default, a misalignment creates incongruence, hence bitterness, frustration and anger.

How do you rate yourself on a scale from zero (no congruence) to 10 (total congruence)? Who are the most congruent creatures? Kids. Perhaps this is also an explanation for why most of us love

---

[139] Carl Rogers, *On Becoming a Person,* Houghton Mifflin Company, Boston, originally published in 1961.

kids so much. They are, by definition, totally congruent with themselves, even when they're annoying. According to William Bridges, endings have several steps: they all start with the prefix 'dis', meaning lack of, and the opposite. Everything starts with an end: then can we begin again.

The end phase is made up of *Dis-engagement, Dis-mantling, Dis-identification, Dis-enchantment and Dis-orientation*. It is essential to reflect on the difference between *disenchanted* and *disillusioned*. The disenchanted person moves on, while the disillusioned person plays the same game only with different people and contexts. For example, the disenchanted child learns that Santa Claus does not exist, but the disillusioned child believes Mickey Mouse or Cinderella can replace Santa Claus.

Some time ago, I coached two executives from the same organization, reporting to the same manager. One became disenchanted, lost faith in his toxic company and left. At the same time, the second was the disillusioned person who thought that things would be dramatically different because her manager just changed his title and office. She honestly believed that a cosmetic change could do the trick. It did not. The beginning starts with an ending and sometimes someone needs to internalize necessary losses to become a person.

Internalizing an ending is scary. It may look like we are dealing with grief and death. We're not. If we can use a seasonal analogy, the ending is like autumn: we're losing our leaves, but roots are still there, we're still grounded and ready to cope with the winter season. We're entering the neutral zone.

Some time ago, after giving a presentation, I was approached by a gentleman in his mid-fifties who wanted to explore 'next steps' in his career, so he needed a coach for his transition. He invited me for lunch and explained that after 25-plus years in senior roles in banking, he was almost ready for a move, a change. Almost. A few weeks later, he sent me a kind email informing me that with two daughters still at university it was premature to take a huge risk. Approximately three years later, he contacted me again: another invite.

'Both daughters left the nest, they graduated and got married, so I am really ready to start a new chapter.' We discussed how we would work together and set up the first appointment. He cancelled it and – guess what? – he cancelled again and again. And all went quiet. But recently he re-contacted me. He was ready to start, something that he had told me twice before. I politely declined but I wanted to listen to him. He told me, 'Paolo, I was scared to jump. I don't need money: simply I don't know what I would do when I wake up in the morning, because my whole identity is limited to my professional one. If I lose that, what's left of me?'

Winter: the neutral zone

Cuba, 1992: we rented a small sailing boat with a local skipper for a two-day trip. We left at sunset. Within a few minutes, the village's lights disappeared. The sky was magnificent. Suddenly I realized we were in complete silence and darkness. I did not know where I was, somewhere north of Isla de la Juventud, but where were we heading? A growing sense of anxiety replaced my inner peace as I could no longer see the lights on the shore and could not yet see where we were going. I had a moment of fear and thought, 'Maybe I could offer a large tip and return to a safe harbour.' Entering the neutral zone is scary because you know what you left behind but don't know where you are going. Yet.

I have found the courage to continue on every journey in my life by reading a poem a hundred times: 'George Gray' from the legendary *Spoon River Anthology* by Edgar Lee Masters.[140]

I have studied many times
The marble which was chiselled for me–

---

[140] Edgar Lee Masters, *Spoon River Anthology*, 1915, now in public domain.

A boat with a furled sail at rest in a harbor.
In truth, it pictures not my destination
But my life.
For love was offered me, and I shrank from its disillusionment;
Sorrow knocked at my door, but I was afraid;
Ambition called to me, but I dreaded the chances.
Yet all the while I hungered for meaning in my life.
And now I know that we must lift the sail
And catch the winds of destiny
Wherever they drive the boat.
To put meaning in one's life may end in madness,
But life without meaning is the torture
Of restlessness and vague desire–
It is a boat longing for the sea and yet afraid.

This poem has had an everlasting impact on my life: every time I venture into something new that may appear dark from a distance, I think of George Gray. Of course, I don't want to live with the regret of not living fully and I am sure you don't want that either. But entering the neutral zone does elicit some anxiety. At times I have the distinct feeling that we have to choose between anxiety and depression, like the George Grays of this world, who will take to their graves the bitter disappointment of a wasted life filled with regrets. Bob Dylan explained it in just two lines in one of my most revered songs, 'The Man in the Long Black Coat': 'People don't live or die, people just float.' Dylan won the Nobel Prize in Literature in 2016[141] 'for creating a new poetic expression within the great American song tradition'.

I have always wondered if a caterpillar knows that, eventually, it will become a butterfly. If so, good for them as they can sleep well, knowing that they will become colourful, gentle creatures. They trust the process, but perhaps they don't know there is one.

[141] https://www.nobelprize.org/prizes/literature/2016/summary/

When they are no longer caterpillars and not yet butterflies, do they have doubts and suffer from anxiety or even panic attacks? Maybe they wake up in the middle of the night wondering: and now what happens?

The neutral zone starts precisely this way, with the sensation of venturing into the dark, with the anxiety that you don't know who you will be after your transformation. It's normal to feel this way. I bet you will feel two reactions, mainly governed by your amygdala, your reptilian decision-making system. Your inner voice will push you to 1) return to the safe harbour you left behind, or like George Gray, not even leave the harbour at all, or 2) abandon the journey or postpone it until *the time is right*, knowing that this time will never come. *Mañana*, as they say in Spanish.

My learning is not to settle for nice, pleasant, or familiar. We need to find what really moves us, what resonates with your heart and mind.

While the midlife crisis is comparable to autumn, the neutral zone is equivalent to winter. Everything seems frozen and dead; you will experience a sense of existential emptiness. Winter always comes before the spring. It is the quality time you need for yourself to complete the reinvention of your true self. But there is one more trap you need to avoid. Ironically, it is a trap you have created yourself.

What's the trap? 'Do whatever you can just to fill the emptiness.' So what do we do when we feel anxious? We tend to replace emptiness with activities. Let's start with the wrong ones: we do random things like over-eating, drinking, feeding our addictions and wasting hours on social media, which is medically proven to be the fastest road to chronic depression and Attention Deficit Disorder. Addictions make us their prisoners. We are stuck again, only in worse condition than before.

Doreen is a senior executive with 30-plus years of experience in Sales and Marketing. She was fired from her job following burnout. She has not yet figured out what she wants to do while recovering from a crazy life spent on intercontinental flights and in meetings with corporate clients. She's driven, probably obsessed, to demonstrate to her former company that 'I am still a hot commodity, not damaged goods.' I asked her if her former company manager and colleagues really cared about her next job. She started crying and told me almost no one had come to her farewell party: 'They didn't give a toss about me.' One second later, she realized that her efforts to take revenge on her former colleagues with a senior vice president role were a total waste of her already-depleted energy. She has lost her sense of direction. We smiled together when I shared a quote from *Alice in Wonderland*: 'If you don't know where you are going, every street will get you there.' 'I need to stop,' Doreen told me. Luckily, she did. She needed to reframe rest not as the *opposite* of work but as a precondition to re-start.

Yes, we must stop, put on the brakes before using the accelerator again and driving off in a completely new direction. We need to let go of our innate propensity towards action: we are human beings, not human doings. *Surrender is not an act of bitter defeat; it is an act of gracious acceptance.* The past is behind us and cannot be changed, but we can start to visualize a new future. We realize that we don't want to be soldiers fighting in the same trenches; there is no point in hiding the red ball or regressing by wearing Peter Pan's clothes: we are now brave travellers with a compass and a radar. We know where we are heading: towards a new self with an authentic transformation. If we want to fly like a butterfly, we need to give up everything that weighs us down. The more we let go, the higher we rise. A new optimism and fresh energy are now a part of our being and a sense of inner calm will start to replace chronic anxiety. Winter takes time; sometimes you even get snow in April. Give yourself time, don't rush the process. It may take a while, but rest assured, spring will come. Trust the process. The quality time invested during winter will pay off in a glorious spring. But first we need to ask ourselves some powerful questions and become independent thinkers.

Questions are the answer[142]

Who is the most relevant influencer of all time? Please think about it. Are you coming up with some famous singer, actor, politician or sports star? Let me help you: the most critical influencer of all times 1) is not and never has been on any social media; 2) has not written one single line in his life; 3) he does not sing or dance or act; 4) we don't have any picture or image of him, but we know he was not attractive, and even frequently ridiculed for his ugliness, and – ready? – 5) his fellow citizens voted to execute him. Then, he peacefully drank a glass of hemlock (please don't try this at home) and was gone.

So let me introduce him to you: Socrates. He's perhaps the most recognized philosopher of all time and yet we know so little about him. What we do know comes from his fellow philosophers Aristotle, Plato, the playwright Aristophanes and the historian Xenophon. But, interestingly, he didn't leave us with any philosophical theory or any formula such as $E=mc^2$ that made Einstein famous.

So, why is Socrates still so influential in our lives?

We have learned from him an approach to life, not a theory or a formula. I guess that teaching people to use their minds is still dangerous, even if people who do so are not forced to drink poison anymore. Socrates was interested in seeking the right question rather than providing a plausible answer. His method is called *maieutic*, the art of midwives. The difference is that he devoted his life to supporting people to give birth to ideas and solutions rather than babies. Wait: isn't this the beginning of becoming an independent thinker? Socrates is, therefore, the person who created coaching.

[142] Hal Gregersen, *Questions are the Answer*, HarperCollins, USA, 2018.

Spring is coming: preparing to reinvent

We are starting to get ready to visualize and to prepare the next game, **reinvent**. In the following two pages, I will provide you with some of the questions you need to ask yourself. Take your time to let them sink in; take your time to reflect on them and then act on them. So, please take a pen, switch off your phone, sit comfortably, get a glass of water, focus on yourself and breathe deeply 10 times. Ready?[143]

Phase one: visualize, reflect, imagine, create

What do you stand for? What matters to you?

Begin with the end in mind. What is **your** definition of success?

What are you doing for others?

What value do you create for others?

What are you good at now?

What do you want to be good at in the future?

What are you doing now to help yourself to get there?

What are you doing that is derailing your journey?

What are you NOT doing that you should start immediately?

What are you doing that you should stop immediately?

What do you do when you don't know what you are doing? (How, where and with whom you spend your free time will give you a hint.)

---

[143] Tom Rath, *Life's Great Questions: Discover How You Contribute to the World*, Silicon Guild Books, 2020.

Phase two: relationships, allies and bridges

We have discussed the importance of relationships and building trust. Here are the relevant questions for you to reflect on:

Who do you need to talk to — listen to?

Who is your ally?

Who can you help? How?

How can you establish win-win relationships with others?

Which mistakes did others make that you don't need to repeat?

This phase is comparable to late winter: the snow is starting to melt, but you haven't seen any flowers blossoming. Yet. Let me provide practical tips and approaches.

Dating ideas

I assume most people don't decide to marry their partner 10 minutes after meeting them, unless they are both in Vegas and have had too many tequila shots. *Dating ideas* is a process where you must understand various alternatives better and explore them before deciding. You apply the same technique when purchasing a house, the most crucial financial commitment ever. The point is simple: before taking a critical decision, we must investigate, do our homework, understand our emotions and visualize a different future. We must take our time and *date ideas* when considering a different professional future.

When I wanted to become a coach, I started by taking five clients pro-bono, 10 sessions each. I thought it was a sizeable investment of my time. But, on the other hand, it allowed me to experience fully life as a coach. I never thought of it as working for free; on the contrary, I enjoyed the experience. My pro-bono clients were happy, too, and they started recommending me to their colleagues, and two even introduced me to their companies. I started to get paid.

Dating ideas means you can have several 'dates' simultaneously, starting small before committing to larger projects. If you want to write a book, start by writing an article, get peer feedback, improve the idea and ask for advice. It will be a better book if you listen to others: what sticks, what doesn't, what is relevant and what is maybe nice but superfluous. A significant indicator is the financial one: it seems counterintuitive, but at the initial stage, economic considerations are not part of your thinking process. Again, as a coach, my initial question to myself was, 'How can I add value to my clients?' It was not, 'How much can I charge?' Interestingly, if you can answer the first question, you don't have to worry about the second. Ever. Still, if you start with the second question, you will compete on the price and eventually lose your battle in the marketplace or become just one of the many competitors who have to offer discounts because they don't provide value.

I still remember my eye doctor in Washington, DC. He was very successful in his practice. The waiting list for new patients was several months long. From every angle, he was at the top of his game. One day he wanted to talk with me. He told me, 'Paolo, I always wanted to be a baker and I want you to describe the kind of bread and bakery specialties you eat in Italy.' I still recall that conversation, which lasted two hours. While discussing the wonders of Italian bread, the focaccia from Liguria, the grissini from Piedmont, and *taralli* from Puglia, I noticed a spark in his eyes. He was dating his idea: in less than one year, he sold his practice and opened a bakery. I frequently stopped by, mainly to buy *taralli*.

Don't jump too fast

The first date was great, but hold your horses; there is more homework to do. For example, Rick is a food enthusiast, an excellent cook and in love with Thailand. He worked in an investment bank and – spoiled by a generous compensation – he treated clients and colleagues to the best restaurants. After watching a few series on TV about world-famous chefs, and loaded with sincere enthusiasm, he resigned, decided to open his own Thai restaurant and offered a job to a reputable Thai chef. He had money, energy and enthusiasm: what could go wrong? Well, you know the rest of the story: his passion for food was necessary but insufficient when he had to compete – according to TripAdvisor – with 20,847 restaurants in London, 507 of which are Thai. 'I wished I had done more homework before starting,' he said over a delicious Pad Thai, served in someone else's restaurant; he closed his after one year with no money left and less energy than before.

Less is more

When I started my management and executive coaching practice, I felt like I had opened an ice cream shop with a hundred different flavours, meaning potential services to my clients. I helped a client redesign their corporate structure; another organization asked me to conceptualize and write their leadership development strategy, another asked me to provide options for a new incentive system and another wanted to revamp the leadership team with executive coaching. Other clients asked me to interview several candidates and become the CEO's advisor, evaluate the effectiveness of their training courses and develop a staff survey; two clients asked me to sit on their board. I started collaborating with several universities by lecturing in many countries on several subjects in Italian, English and French. I also agreed to give keynotes at events mainly in Europe and Asia while supervising the publication of my book in seven different languages and preparing two TEDx Talks. And since that wasn't enough, I decided to collaborate with six magazines and engaged with four speaking agents in the

UK, USA, Italy and Latin America. I had to deal simultaneously with 80 or 90 people in four languages in many countries.

It was fun initially, but I soon realized it was too much. Sure, my fees were coming in nicely, perhaps better than expected, but at what price? I became a jack-of-all-trades, but some projects I didn't even enjoy. I started to feel overwhelmed; my working week was close to 80 hours and the weekend was gone. I missed two deadlines and felt terrible about it. My wife told me I worked for 107 consecutive days. I needed to learn to say no, to have my criteria to accept engagements and decide – in my ice cream shop analogy – which flavours I would drop and which ones I would keep improving. My new mantra became selectivity, value for me and impact for my clients.

I decided to use the following framework:

1. Do I add real value to my client? Can I demonstrate it with granular evidence? Anecdotes do not count.
2. Do I learn something new by doing what I am doing?
3. Which ice cream flavour do I want to master and which one can I drop? Which areas do I want to improve and which am I not interested in pursuing?
4. Do I want to be associated with this client or organization?
5. Are we able to develop mutual trust and respect?
6. Do they agree to pay me for the value, experience and integrity I can provide?
7. Can I learn to say no and avoid FOMO, the fear of missing out?

I produced a list of my clients and engagements and made some decisions: I closed the relationship with one organization because I felt disrespected. They were my top-paying client but were dismissive, arrogant and condescending. I was not happy: *out*. One client was genuinely nice, but I realized I would be trapped in more of the same, a tired repetition of the same debate. Boring: *out*. One client had a limited budget, but I accepted working with them as I cared about the affiliation with that company and also respected the CEO. *In.* I also closed my collaboration with three speaking agents: it was a waste of time, or they were overcharging me for their limited shallow services. *Out.* Collaborating with several universities was impossible, so I just kept Bocconi, my alma mater, and said goodbye to others, realizing that an academic career was not what I wanted. I reduced my collaboration from six to three magazines and most importantly, I learned to say no, graciously but firmly.

I decided NOT to take on tasks in areas where, honestly, others were more qualified than me, such as designing compensation systems that imply a deep understanding of taxes. I was not interested in developing my skills in this area. I declined a few projects and recommended some colleagues, trying to establish a relationship of trust with them. With some sporadic bumps in the road along the way, I began collaborating with other excellent professionals by building new bridges based on trust. The result? I reduced the number of clients by 60 per cent and – guess what? – my revenues, life and impact improved. 'What a lesson to learn,' I thought.

Rite of passage

I've found it helpful and uplifting to have my little celebration for the transition, my rite of passage. I take my old business card and a small object from the former company, such as a notebook or a pen. I give a gentle kiss to both, thanking the universe for the opportunity to work there, to meet great people and – hopefully – for the contribution I have provided. By pronouncing their names, I thank some of the best people I had the pleasure of collaborating with. The most intense moment is when I say – loud and clear – that I also forgive the malicious villains I invariably met on my journey who have hurt me. I calmly say their names and surnames. I then burn the objects and never pronounce their names again. They are gone, forever. Vanished. I never take revenge; I just 'delete' people from my life.

I forgive them and they don't exist anymore, as I am processing a healthy emotional detox. I can move on because I can feel that spring is coming.

The midlife crisis is not a moment to fear but an existential necessity, a fantastic and challenging opportunity to take stock. After the season of loss – autumn – and the season of anxiety – winter – you enter into spring, all its energy, the land of hopes and dreams. The transition is complete and you are now a butterfly. Yet, there is much meaningful work to do: this time, the work you choose to do, the work you want to do, on your terms, not the job imposed on you. Rebirth means reinventing yourself. It's fun and a lot of hard work but is worth it. So let's dive in.

6

GAME #5 – Reinvent, GAME #6 – Revolution and GAME #7 – Letting Go

'Life isn't about finding yourself – life is about creating yourself.'

GEORGE BERNARD SHAW[144]

Reinvent yourself

What happens after Game Four: Crisis? The joyfully intense, intensely joyful Game Five: Reinvent.

> Invent yourself and then reinvent yourself, don't swim in the same slough.
> Invent yourself and then reinvent yourself and
> stay out of the clutches of mediocrity.
> 'No Leaders Please'[145] by Charles Bukowski

Let's take a short trip to Japan and then to the United Arab Emirates, Dubai, one of the most popular destinations on the planet. First, we visit the Ise Grand Shrine, Japan's holiest and most culturally significant temple, and the spiritual home of the Japanese people. Ise Grand Shrine (or *Ise Jingu*), which

---

[144] https://www.pcs.org/features/7-brilliant-quotes-by-george-bernard-shaw
[145] Charles Bukowski, *The Pleasures of the Damned: Selected Poems 1951–1993*, Canongate Books, 2018.

dates back almost 2,000 years, is the home of the sun goddess Amaterasu, Japan's supreme deity, and the location of the Sacred Mirror of the Emperor. One of the most surprising and unique features of Ise Grand Shrine is that both the inner and outer shrines and Uji Bridge over the Isuzu River are completely rebuilt every 20 years.[146] The shrines are designed according to the *Yuitsu-shinmei-zukuri* architectural style, known for its simplicity and antiquity: it cannot be used in any other shrine. The buildings also use wooden dowels and interlocking joints rather than nails. The wood from the previously dismantled temple buildings is recycled to make a new *Torii* gate at the shrine's entrance and is also used in shrines across Japan. The current Ise Grand Shrine buildings were constructed in 2013 and will be rebuilt again in 2033.

What is the symbolic meaning that the Ise Grand Shrine is wholly rebuilt every 20 years? To represent the Shinto understanding of death and renewal, the inner belief of constant rebirth and renewal, the impermanence of all things. Eternity is not 'fixed' but constantly reinvented. This custom also ensures that building techniques and knowledge are passed from one generation to the next. What's more, reusing and recycling the old material is a way to acknowledge that 'the old' cannot be thrown away because it contains our experience and learning.

One of the most fascinating recruitment searches I have ever done was finding the World Bank's art curator. When I joined the organization, I was unaware that the World Bank had an impressive art collection, primarily gifts from various governments. I met several candidates who were curators of the most prestigious museums in the world and learned the difference between curating a museum (or part of it) and putting together an exhibition. The job of a curator is to help people to remember and glorify the past: an artist, a city, a country, an event, or a well-defined period.

[146] https://en.wikipedia.org/wiki/Ise_Grand_Shrine

Then, a few years ago, an announcement in the *Economist* caught my eye: Dubai was looking for the art curator for the *Museum of the Future.* I thought, this is a different story. It's not about remembering or glorifying the past but about imagining the future. How can you find objects and ideas in a museum for a period in time that doesn't yet exist? The Museum of the Future[147] is outstanding, starting from the impressive and (easy guess) futuristic building. One section, or I should say one distinct experience, is Future Heroes: a fantasy world for children focused on future skills.

Reinventing yourself is demolishing – not destroying – and reassembling, like the temple of Ise Grand Shine in Japan. Reinventing yourself is reimagining your future self, like the Museum of the Future in Dubai. *Reinventing is a transition*, a Janus moment, the god of transition according to the Romans, as we have learned at the beginning of this book. Why should we reinvent ourselves? Wouldn't it be much easier to stay put, to enjoy the status quo, our comfort zone? Maybe we should ask a different question: do we have a choice?

How to create a mindset of permanent reinvention – by Aidan McCullen

Aidan McCullen[148] is a gifted and creative author. How can we co-create a mindset of permanent reinvention? I asked him to share a story of reinventing a career: he talks about ants, stem cells, vacuum tubes and rust, inspired by his book, *Undisruptable.*[149]

[147] https://museumofthefuture.ae/en
[148] https://www.linkedin.com/in/aidanmccullen/
[149] Aidan McCullen, *Undisruptable: A Mindset of Permanent Reinvention for Individuals, Organizations and Life*, Wiley, 2021.

A team of Swiss researchers[150] led by Danielle Mersch painstakingly monitored individually tagged carpenter ants in six colonies over 41 days and discovered something remarkable. They already knew that ants specialized in specific tasks like cleaning, nursing and foraging, but they discovered that 40 per cent of the ants follow a predictable career path as they age. Younger ants start out as carers before levelling up to cleaners and then graduating as foragers. Foragers remain in their role until death, which makes sense because they are older, wiser and more street-smart when facing the dangers of foraging. This research teaches us new lessons about these ancient creatures, which have survived on the planet for much longer than us, so perhaps we can learn from them.

This research about role specialization made me think of stem cells. Stem cells start out as unspecialized embryonic cells and develop into different cells as needed by the organism. During the development of a foetus, embryonic stem cells differentiate into increasingly specialized cell types. The environment signals what stem cells should become and what they should specialize in. (I am simplifying here.) Our bodies are composed of 100 trillion (1 trillion = 1,000 times 1 billion) cells working in unison. Our bodily cells regenerate and renew at varying rates. For example, we shed almost 40,000 skin cells every hour, so it only takes a mere month for us to have a whole brand-new layer of skin. Cells continually die and renew simultaneously and stem cells play an important regenerative role in our permanent renewal.

To be considered a stem cell, a cell must have two characteristics:

1. The ability to self-renew.
2. The capacity to differentiate into more specialized cells as required (known as potency).

---

[150] https://www.science.org/doi/10.1126/science.1234316

Now that sounds like preferential characteristics that I would like my friends, family and workforce to develop in a world of flux. Adapting as the environment changes is natural for us. Our bodies change regularly and so do our careers; sometimes it happens but we don't even notice. Take engineering, for example. If you are an engineer born in the 1940s or 1950s, you studied vacuum tubes. Shortly after college, you needed to learn about transistors, a technology with nothing in common with vacuum tubes. Then you levelled up to integrated circuits and later moved to the world of computer programming. Then all of this moved to the cloud. You evolved with the times and a changing digital environment. That's a lot of change in one career, a lot of new learning that demands a stem cell mindset, a learnability outlook and a willingness to change.

Our bodies regenerate every seven years; so do our careers, so do our relationships and so does our planet. Yet, many of us still resist change. When we resist, we linger in stasis and we start to rot. When we cling to the past, we straitjacket our potential. Movement, reinvention and evolution are the only way forward. Our cells live in the present; they are constantly adapting and renewing as needed. We must adopt the same approach and embrace change or it will consume us like rust consumes metal.

Life quakes vs. life decisions

The need to adapt is nothing new: we learned it from Charles Darwin and Benjamin Franklin too, who said: *when you are finished changing, you are finished.*

We need to reinvent ourselves, constantly. Reinvention is not a destination but a process created by a mindset. The problem is most people start this process only after a life quake hits them hard. A life quake is an event that leaves us traumatized and affects our families and us for the rest of our lives. Managing a transition following a life quake is often an impulsive and not well-thought reaction driven by desperation, done when we are not at our best in terms of our abilities. It is different from a WTF moment when we only shake our heads in disbelief. A life quake leaves us lost in the flood, a tsunami of pain we need to deal with.

The sad list is long, and we all know it. What unites us all is that we are all survivors: some people have lost a dear friend or a beloved family member, some their job and their identity, or their health; some are prisoners of their addictions; some have severed their roots because they had to leave their homes and country; some have lost their loves (at times with a nasty divorce). No one is immune, even if some believe they are until it is their turn.

Reinventing yourself as an immediate reaction to a life quake is like running a marathon with a broken leg. It takes a long time to heal. Typical is when someone, after being fired, accepts any job just to prove that they're still valuable without considering if the new role makes sense. It's the professional equivalent of rebounding, getting a new partner shortly after a failed relationship. It may fill a void but it does not solve the problem. How can you reinvent yourself, following a conscious and deliberate decision? We initially focus on why, when and how to play Game Five: Reinvent.

Why

'The dangers of life are infinite, among them safety,'[151] Johann Wolfgang von Goethe reminds us. The point is: *linear life is*

---

[151]   https://www.goodreads.com/quotes/8875990-the-dangers-of-life-are-infinite-and-among-them-is

dead, gone forever.[152] If we have learned something in the last few years, it's that planning can serve us up to a certain point. Perhaps we should call these events not megatrends but Mega Threats,[153] based on the clever definition coined by Nobel laureate Nouriel Roubini. We must embrace flexibility and internalize our capacity to adapt and reinvent ourselves: we are works-in-progress. Our journey is not linear, as life involves several life transitions.

Harvard researcher Todd Rose and neuroscientist Ogi Ogas[154] tried to understand how many people had a tortuous career trajectory. They anticipated that most people had a relatively linear career, but they were wrong. The choices we make over the years are constantly changing. For example, a job that appears appealing in our thirties is not suitable when we are in our fifties.

Harvard psychologist Dan Dilbert[155] measured the preferences, values and personalities of 1,900 adults between the ages of 18 and 68. He divided them into two groups and asked group one how much they thought they would change in the next 10 years and the second group how much they had changed in the last 10 years. The first group answered that they expected few changes, while the second group responded by listing many significant changes in their lives. We constantly tend to underestimate the challenges ahead of us: often, this attitude results in our lack of preparation and foresight. Managing life transitions and driving meaningful reinvention are necessary skills we can all learn.

[152] Bruce Feiler, *Life in Transitions: Mastering Change at Any Age*, Penguin Press, 2020, p. 24.
[153] Nouriel Roubini, *MegaThreats: Ten Dangerous Trends that Imperil Our Future, and How to Survive Them*, Little, Brown and Company, 2022.
[154] Todd Rose and Ogi Ogas, *Dark Horse: Achieving Success Through the Pursuit of Fulfillment*, HarperOne, 2018.
[155] Quoidbach, J., Gilbert, D. T. and Wilson, T. D. 'Your life satisfaction will change more than you think: A comment on Harris and Busseri', *Journal of Research in Personality*, 2019, p. 86.

When

When is the right moment to reinvent yourself? Short answer: Now. One day or day one: you decide. Reinventing is a long-term process, not a final destination.

You need to reinvent yourself when: you start thinking about the weekend on Tuesday afternoon. You'd rather be sick than go to the office. You wake up in the middle of the night worrying about the work waiting for you tomorrow morning. You are expected to be at the office even when your kids will be performing in the school play. You can't respect your boss and you have good reasons to feel that way. You are not learning anything new: you use 100 per cent of your time and energy but 40 per cent of your brain. You are over-used but under-challenged, a lethal combination. You get a promotion with a 5 per cent raise but your workload magically doubles. When the rate of change outside your organization is higher than inside; when your company is over-managed but under-led; when you would like to be the guest of honour at the farewell party.

But also: when you are excited to start something new or when you want to prove what you can do, not only what you have done. When you feel that you will learn and become a better person. When you are scared to leave your comfort zone while the best part of you is prodding you to jump, to try: and you do. When your eyes are sparkling, just by thinking of the idea of a new project or a new role. When you would work for free if only you could afford it. When the people who love you fully support you. When you can't wait to start, you feel the positive energy flowing through your veins. When you want to help others and you learn and love what you do. When you know that you will be great at doing what you have in mind and working feels like fun. When what you do, say, feel and think are in the same place: in your heart. In a nutshell: how do you feel on Sunday afternoon? Excited as you are working on a challenging project, or depressed as you would rather be anywhere rather than at the office?

How

Take quality time before committing

Managing a change is easy, for example, moving from Company A to Company B to take on a similar role. You need to understand and adapt, of course, but you are in the same game, the Better Game. Reinventing is a transition because *you* have changed. As I am specialized in transition coaching, my experience is that completing a successful transition to reinvent yourself takes at least nine months and up to two years. While looking for a job is a job, reinventing yourself is a vocation and a life mission.

Examples: do you want to write a book? Start by writing an article. Do you want to be a coach? Do it pro-bono for four or five clients for a limited period. Do you want to become a professional speaker? Start giving a few speeches for small audiences and ask for feedback. You may volunteer to help on a project, take on some additional tasks, or try job shadowing as an extra assignment or a development opportunity.

Who are you? What is your reputation?

Dick Bolles is the author of *What Color is your Parachute?*, a reference manual for job searches and a top seller for 40 years. He says, '*Most job hunters fail to find their dream job, not because they lack information about the job market but because they lack information about themselves.*'[156] So while playing Game Six, we need to return to the Inner Game to reassess our self-knowledge. We all change over the years; we must re-evaluate who we are and what motivates us. You may find it helpful to reread every performance evaluation you have received from supervisors and reconsider client and colleague feedback. What traits and behaviours constantly emerge? What do you need to improve? What have you learned from your mistakes?

---

[156] Richard Bolles with Katharine Brooks, *What Color is Your Parachute?*, Berkeley, Ten Speed Press, 2022.

What is your online presence? Google your name and read the results. Do you like what you see? Please be aware that several companies, such as Active Screening[157] or DataCheck Inc,[158] will probably check your references and your online presence. Most importantly, ask yourself if your online presence is *congruent* with your future self.

Can you see what is not visible?
Abraham Wald, the son of a rabbi, was born in 1902 in Romania, which was part of the Austro-Hungarian Empire. Wald excelled academically, earning a bachelor's degree and a PhD in mathematics, but he couldn't find employment in academia due to anti-Semitic discriminatory laws, so he moved to Austria.

On 11 March 1938 came the *Anschluss,* Hitler's annexation of Austria. The Jews' situation went from difficult to dramatic. Luckily, Wald managed to emigrate to the USA. In July 1942, the United States created the Statistical Research Group (SRG) at Columbia University. Eighteen scientists, a fantastic team with the most brilliant minds in mathematics and statistics on the planet: many were fugitives from the Nazi regime like Wald. Their job: to help the US win the war. They did not have weapons or bombs, but *only* their brains, science and probabilities.

One of the most vital tasks of the SRG was to help the Allies figure out how to better protect aircraft from enemy artillery. The dilemma was that adding armour to the planes also slowed them down, making them an easier target. The researchers needed to find out where to position the armour so it would be most effective. By observing planes returning from bombing campaigns that were often riddled with bullet holes, Wald realized something counterintuitive. When Allied aircraft were shot in the wings, tail or fuselage, they returned to the base, damaged but safe. But when the planes were hit near the

[157] https://www.activescreening.com/solutions/social-intelligence/
[158] https://datacheckinc.com

engine or the nose, they did not make it back. Wald's team were studying only the aircraft that had survived. They did not 'see' – and could not see – the planes that the Nazis had shot down, the ones that mattered.

Wald was exposing *survivor bias*, or the tendency to focus on a subset of visible information, people or things that have made it through a particular process: in this case, planes that returned safely to the base. The idea is simple – as explained by Brian Klaas in his fascinating book, *Corruptible:*[159] you need to study all the cases, not only the ones that survive. Equally, reinventing means: which options *don't* we see? For example, most jobs are not advertised; most opportunities are imagined and created.

Creating the job of your dreams is easier than finding one.

You may have seen the 2010 movie *The Social Network,* the story of Facebook. There is a scene when Harvard's dean Larry Summers tells Mark Zuckerberg, '*The most important thing you learn at Harvard is that it is easier to create a job than to find one.*' I agree. When you are in the business of reinvention, it starts with you. I am convinced that you can design your dream job, through a process of actively seeking and co-creating it, as explained by Bill Burnett and Dave Evans in *Designing Your Life.*[160]

Let me share one example. I was HR director for 16 years, from 2002 to 2018. I have always loved the people-leadership and development aspects of my role and sharing my ideas by writing, posting and giving speeches: in a nutshell, sharing my experience for the sake of helping others. My instinct is to go deeper into topics that interest me so I keep on studying, reading and learning. But on the other hand, I have never found

[159] Brian Klaas, *Corruptible: Who Gets Power and How it Changes Us*, London, John Murray Publishers, 2021.
[160] Bill Burnett and Dave Evans, *Designing Your Life: How to Build a Well-lived, Joyful Life*, Borzoi Books, 2016.

the compliance-regulation part of my job interesting. In fact, in the last few years in that position, I even started to deeply resent managing misconduct: basically resolving conflicts created by others, mostly toxic and incompetent managers, and finding myself in emotionally charged situations to the point that I started losing sleep.

So I decided to create my dream job where I would focus only on the part I always loved, knowing that I was reasonably good at it. I am now the executive coach of many senior leaders, primarily CEOs. I teach at a university and give on average 40 to 50 keynotes annually. I am happy to write for and collaborate with several reputable magazines and I am a mentor and advisor to several organizations and senior executives. I learn from them every day.

I give my best when I work with complete autonomy, so you may find me working on a Saturday evening or riding my bicycle by the lake on a Tuesday morning. I start the day by reading for at least one hour: I do what I love, what I was born to do; I can choose when I work and who I work with. If it works for me, rest assured it will work for you too. Creating a job does not mean securing an open-ended contract working full-time for a company: it can be achieved by developing a portfolio career by engaging with different clients and projects.

Focus first on the value you add.
Yesterday a reputable company contacted me to ask for my support as executive coach. I can reply to them in two different ways.

1. Please note that my fees are (...), with 50 per cent payment upfront.
2. I have worked for and helped X number of people to become CEOs and Y people to manage successful transitions. Here's the list of people. Feel free to contact ANY of them for references.

Which one is more convincing? What are you good at? Where and how can you demonstrate the value you bring to the table? To demonstrate your value, you need to become a Thought Leader, a reference point in your domain. This happens only when you develop your own content and you can prove the value you create for others, not just the fees you charge for yourself.

Who can help you?
It would help if you had a mentor to give you feedback candidly and/or an experienced coach. Ask yourself: who are your allies? Who can help you? Who can introduce you? When someone gives you some of their time, be grateful, tactful and respectful. Leave the meeting with other possible contacts and don't forget to send a thank you note. Do serious homework before meeting anyone.

Develop a narrative with an authentic story.
People want real, credible, authentic stories, not perfection or an impressive (at times inflated) list of accomplishments. What is your story? Branding is the packaging, but – apologies to vegetarians – where is the meat? You may remember Chapter two when we discussed the importance of credibility vs. visibility (*see* pp. 71–2), as your reputation matters. Put your heart into it: two careers – and two hearts – are better than one.[161]

Game Six, **Revolution**, is an intense and wonderful moment of reconnecting with your true self; it is a liberating feeling to be who you really are and offer your best to others. It is not about destroying: it is about reassembling and reimagining. 'Golden Feather'[162] is a magic song written by Robbie Robertson in honour of the Native Americans: '*When you find what is worth keeping, with a breath of kindness, blow the rest away.*' Listen to this

---

[161] https://hbr.org/2017/04/why-you-should-have-at-least-two-careers
[162] https://www.youtube.com/watch?v=CSM78BH-M18

song when you are playing Game Five. Ironically, Game Five never ever stops: reinventing you, as noted by Dorie Clark,[163] it is a continuous process of self-improvement and self-discovery: it is not the final destination.

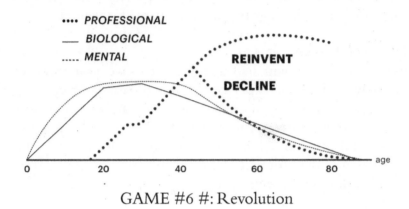

GAME #6 #: Revolution

'It's not rebels that make trouble, but trouble that makes rebels.'

Ruth Messinger

The difference between heroes and revolutionaries

Who is your hero? I asked this question of 200 people. Who is at the top of the list? Charismatic politicians? Sports legends? Hollywood celebrities? Rock stars? You can bet the answer is none of the above. Many mentioned a parent and even more frequently, a grandparent, at times a teacher from the past, an old friend or a colleague, or a mentor. Our true heroes are in our hearts, not on Instagram or Twitter. We tend to disregard narcissism and visibility, as we prefer the consistency of behaviour and authentic courage.

[163] Dorie Clark, 'Reinventing You: Define your Brand, Imagine your Future', *Harvard Business Review*, HBR Press, 2013.

I listened to the narrative explaining their choices and realized something else. Becoming a hero, a role model in someone's life, is not the result of one solo brave act. No one has ever said to me, 'I wish I could save a granny trapped in a burning building', or 'I hope to convince a suicidal person not to jump off a bridge', even if some remarkable people have done both these good deeds. God bless them, as they have our respect and admiration, of course.

Becoming a role model means the discipline of following up daily on our life choices and *having the courage of our convictions.* Our grandparents and parents did it for us: a life of sacrifice, dedication and devotion focused on what matters. Many have used the term 'revolutionaries' to describe their contribution and legacy. Heroism is limited to a commendable but solo act. But, at the same time, true revolution means something that will have a lasting effect on someone's life, in a family, in a community, country, or on our planet long after we are gone.

The common traits of the stories people told me were compassion, caring, love, faith and some healthy craziness to offer others something unique, an actual Revolution. For them, it's about giving to others, not accumulating for themselves. For these revolutionaries, improving somebody else's life was a life mission, not a career; they kept a low profile and they just did it because it mattered to them.

Let me introduce three people: Dave, a plastic surgeon from California, Mattia, the Spider Man and Silvia, a restaurant manager from Milan. To be honest, I have introduced them to you by quoting their (semi) official occupations, but they are much more than what they do. I selected them because they are extraordinarily normal. Three true Revolutionaries – you don't need to go to Cuba to find a new Che Guevara.

Smiles in Guatemala
I struggle to find a word that can define Antigua, in Guatemala: maybe magical, magnificent or stunning? I've been to Guatemala several times and fell in love with Antigua.

The first time I went to improve my Spanish: many fellow students recommended visiting Obras Sociales del Santo Hermano Pedro.[164] So my wife Lalia and I went to see OSSHP, founded in 1981 by the Franciscan Order of Friars Minor. It is a non-political, non-governmental, non-profit association with operating licences in health and education. Its mission is to provide medical, educational, spiritual, moral and social assistance to all poor, orphaned or abandoned people. The centre attends to patients through medical consultations and organizes specialized surgeries with the help of volunteers, doctors and professionals. There I met Dave. He came from California with a team of six specialized dentists and surgeons to operate on kids with cleft lips. Sadly, the Guatemalan Ministry of Health estimates that cleft lips and palates account for 15 per cent of all reported congenital anomalies in the country.[165] Rural Guatemala is extremely impoverished and poverty presents numerous additional challenges for families with cleft-affected babies and children.

Dave told me about his career as a plastic surgeon. He has been very successful and says, 'I made tons of money by enhancing people's attractiveness: they are mainly extremely rich, old and bored.' Yet something did not click in his mind. He accumulated money for 30 years, but 'I found purpose only here in Antigua.' Dave goes (with his colleagues, now friends) twice a year.

'I have the best time of my life: I can help these kids who are not only handicapped but also stigmatized by having cleft lips. I know it's a cliché, but coming here made me realize what gives me joy. Putting a smile on a child's face is more meaningful than implanting silicone breasts. It's strange: when I work in California, I am exhausted at the end of the day. When I work here, I can't wait to start again and I don't feel tired at all.'

[164] https://hermanopedrogt.org
[165] https://www.lovewithoutboundaries.com/blog/preparing-for-our-cleft-trip-to-guatemala/

Maybe Revolutionaries are the least tired and happiest people on the planet?

Spider-Man

Wait a second: did I just see a picture of Pope Francis shaking hands with a guy in a Spider-Man costume?[166] Oh yes. This story begins with a seven-year-old Mattia looking out the window, hoping that Spider-Man will appear at any moment. Mattia is at the hospital where he spent many days of his childhood: his legs are not in good shape and will not allow him to play soccer or even walk properly. Fast-forward 20 years and many operations later. Mattia is an adult with a good job and a lovely family. What more can he dream of?

Yet Mattia feels that something is missing. So one day, he gets an idea: to wear the Spider-Man costume and go back to the hospital, this time to give the kids there a smile and the hope that Spider-Man might appear anytime: 'I want to give them a moment of fun and laughter.' He's done it a hundred times and eventually the Pope heard about his story and invited him to the Vatican. Mattia Villardita in his book, *Me and Spider-Man*,[167] tells us how to help others and describes the responsibility that wearing a mask entails. Spending one hour in a hospital courtyard with kids who have cancer changes your life. Mattia is not the superhero in his story: the kids are.

Welcome to jail

Silvia is now 74 years old. You may think she's 'just' a restaurant manager but she is far more than that. When Silvia began her professional life as an educator, she asked to be sent to teach where no one else wanted to go: the rough outskirts of the city of Milan. Then after 22 years of teaching, she decided to make

---

[166] https://roma .corriere .it /notizie /cronaca /21 _giugno _23 /papa -incontra -spiderman -mattia -che -visita -maschera -bambini -ospedali -85f2376c -d413 -11eb -8dcd -923bd7ac4a6d .shtml.
[167] Mattia Villardita, *Io e Spiderman: Storia Vera di un Super Normale*, Italian edition Salani Editore, 2022.

her dream come true. Since she was a child, Silvia loved cooking. So she decided to open a small catering company, which became quite popular, all the rage among Milan's upper crust.

But when Silvia turned 50, she discovered she had an irreversible rheumatic disease that would prevent her from keeping up with the frantic pace of her catering business. In the end, she decided to sell the company. No worries, though, her future was secure after 32 years of work. She could sit back and enjoy life, travel and relax.

One day, Silvia got a phone call from Lucia Castellano, director of the penitentiary in Bollate, just outside of Milan, suggesting she start a catering business run with a team of convicts, offering food outside the prison grounds. Silvia replied that it was an *indecent proposal*. At the same time, she realized that if she agreed, her life would change completely. So she accepted on the condition that she would be the one to choose the men/prisoners who would work with her. And she'd also open a catering school to provide prisoners with professional training. She made clear she wanted to run a business, not a charity. So, Silvia started up the catering business.

The prison administrators supported Silvia. As you can imagine, never before had anyone tried opening a catering service staffed by convicts. The bureaucratic complications seemed overwhelming, but Silvia fought like a lion and succeeded in setting up the catering company, working with inmates, thanks to an open-minded director who set up an agreement with the surveillance court, to reinforce the application of alternative measures, in compliance with a law that was passed in 1986 encouraging various options as forms of detention.

Silvia is well aware of the fact that these people were sent to prison because they committed crimes, so she uses military-like discipline to enforce the rules and run the company. She also makes the people who work for her wear formal uniforms with white gloves, in part to cover up tattoos and frightening scars. For two years the team did their catering service accompanied by undercover police officers, who guarded the prisoners and made sure they didn't escape.

Normally a prisoner who leaves the jail on work release must go solely where permitted, no detours allowed. The timing and mode of transport are dictated by the prison administrators, but he can leave alone. Obviously, to offer catering outside the prison, all these rules would be impossible to follow, which is why the prisoners were initially accompanied by guards and later by Silvia herself. The responsibility for the convicts always rests with the Surveillance Court and the prison director who proposed this arrangement. Instead, Silvia is responsible for immediately alerting authorities if any prisoners leave or commit an infraction during an event. Silvia knows very well that if just one of them ever tried anything, this project would be shut down, so she's taking enormous risks.

Silvia never asks any of the prisoners why they are in jail (what are you in for?), but only how long they have to stay (when do you get out?). She even decided to give prisoners serving life sentences a chance, people called 'lifers' – what a terrible concept!

One day she got a request to cater an event for a bank. Ironically, among the people on her team that day was a former bank robber, who told Silvia, 'I never would have imagined going back into a bank dressed in a white uniform and holding a silver platter full of pastries. Last time I went into a bank I was wearing a ski mask and holding a Kalashnikov.' Silvia laughed her head off when she told me that story.

After two years the prison director decided to stop sending along a team of undercover cops to control and monitor the catering team. We trust you, they told Silvia. In 2015, Silvia went to the new prison director, Massimo Parisi, and asked him, 'What would you say if we opened a restaurant?' 'Why not?' was his answer.

Initially, Silvia thought about locations in Milan for her new venture, obviously run by the prisoners too and managed by her. Then she had second thoughts: if anything happened, even a stolen wallet, everyone would blame her. So, Silvia decided to do exactly the opposite. She opened a restaurant in the Bollate prison and called it *In Galera* (In the Jailhouse).

Silvia worked shoulder-to-shoulder with the penitentiary police, the public administration and the Ministry of Justice. And on 26 October 2015, she opened her restaurant, The Jailhouse,[168] just like she said she would. *In Galera* was the first ever restaurant run by convicts, but it was followed by many more.[169] On 5 March 2016, the *New York Times* published an article titled, 'Italian Cuisine Worth Going to Prison For',[170] written by the renowned journalist Jim Yardley, winner of the 2006 Pulitzer Prize,[171] who had visited Bollate and spoken with Silvia. She realizes that The Jailhouse was the first restaurant in the world inside a prison, run by prisoners, and she gets requests from all over for interviews, but prefers to keep a low profile. She's more focused on rehabilitating convicts and encouraging them to follow the path to redemption while helping them to accept the damage they've done to the victims of their crimes. And what she's doing seems to be working: the reoffending rate in Italian prisons is 70 per cent but at Bollate, with its 1,350 inmates, it's only 17 per cent.

Silvia – whose nickname is 'Granny Galeotta' (*galeotta* means convict in Italian) – is truly a wonderful woman, a true Revolutionary who is moved to tears when she reads the thank you letters she gets from her 'boys', as she calls them.

Life is a mission, not a career.[172]

REVOLUTION

[168] https://www.ingalera.it/en/index.html
[169] https://www.standard.co.uk/reveller/restaurants/a-restaurant-run-by-prisoners-has-topped-famous-eateries-on-tripadvisor-a3703131.html
[170] https://www.nytimes.com/2016/03/06/world/europe/in-milan-diners-go-to-prison-to-get-a-good-meal.html\
[171] https://www.nytimes.com/by/jim-yardley
[172] Stephen Covey and Chynhia Covey Haller, *Live Life in Crescendo: Your Most Important Work is Always Ahead of You*, Simon & Schuster, 2022.

The stories of Dave, Mattia – Spider-Man – and Silvia prove you don't need to be a CEO, a president or a billionaire to start a revolution: it is the essence of Game Six, the Revolution Game.

Is being a rebel, then, caring about others? Giving a helping hand to the disenfranchised, the Ghosts? Is it leaving a legacy? How does this principle translate into our life? Has it anything to do with leadership? Let's find out.

What can you learn from 2,000 obituaries?

'What can you learn from 2,000 obituaries?'[173] This is a very interesting question and to me, one of the best TED Talks ever. Lux Narayan lives in New York City. He starts the day by having breakfast with his wife, wondering, 'Let's see who died today.' He reads the *New York Times* obituary section daily. Does he have a morbid curiosity? No. Actually, Narayan has a point: every newspaper's front page primarily reports terrible news. The last page, the one with the death notices, is about paying tribute and celebrating the life of remarkable individuals who have left a legacy in the world. Narayan is the CEO of Unmetrics, a social media benchmarking platform.

In 2016, he started wondering what he could learn by studying obituaries. So, his team took 2,000 obituaries from 20 months in 2015 and 2016 and divided them into two groups. In the first group, you will find famous people such as the musical genius Prince, the titan of boxing Muhammad Ali or the ground-breaking architect Zaha Hadid. The second group of people were not famous and yet achieved extraordinary results, such as Jocelyn Copper, who paved the way for the first

---

[173] https://www.ted.com/talks/lux_narayan_what_i_learned_from_2_000_obituaries?language=en

African-American congresswoman, or Reverend Rick Curry, who used stagecraft to help the wounded and disabled.

Then Narayan used natural language processing to distil the essence of these two groups. And finally, with delightful humour, he shared the outcome. What the two groups have in common is the fact that *everyone helped*. The legacy they left behind, whether famous or not, was that they contributed *by helping*. Their legacy was not to accumulate wealth or visibility but to donate, give, support and help. They are the real revolutionaries, not only heroes.

Lux Narayan closes his TED Talk with a thought and a question:

> The exercise was a fascinating testament to the kaleidoscope that is life. Even more fascinating was the fact that the overwhelming majority of obituaries featured famous and non-famous people who did seemingly extraordinary things. They made a positive dent in the fabric of life. They helped. So ask yourselves as you go back to your daily lives: How am I using my talents to help society? Because the most powerful lesson here is if more people lived their lives trying to be famous in death, the world would be a much better place.

Let it sink into your heart. Lux, you deserve a standing ovation.

GAME #7: Letting Go

'Knowledge is learning something new every day. Wisdom is letting go every day.'

Zen proverb

He wrote the following letter when he decided to let go of the love of his life, basketball.

His name is – not was – Kobe Bryant.

Dear Basketball,

From the moment
I started rolling my dad's tube socks
And shooting imaginary
Game-winning shots
In the Great Western Forum
I knew one thing was real:

I fell in love with you.
A love so deep I gave you my all —
From my mind & body
To my spirit & soul.

As a six-year-old boy
Deeply in love with you
I never saw the end of the tunnel.
I only saw myself
Running out of one.

And so I ran.
I ran up and down every court
After every loose ball for you.
You asked for my hustle
I gave you my heart
Because it came with so much more.

I played through the sweat and hurt
Not because challenge called me
But because YOU called me.
I did everything for YOU
Because that's what you do
When someone makes you feel as
Alive as you've made me feel.

You gave a six-year-old boy his Laker dream
And I'll always love you for it.

But I can't love you obsessively for much longer.
This season is all I have left to give.
My heart can take the pounding
My mind can handle the grind
But my body knows it's time to say goodbye.

And that's OK.
I'm ready to let you go.
I want you to know now
So we both can savor every moment we have left together.
The good and the bad.
We have given each other
All that we have.

And we both know, no matter what I do next
I'll always be that kid
With the rolled-up socks
Garbage can in the corner
:05 seconds on the clock
Ball in my hands.
5 ... 4 ... 3 ... 2 ... 1

Love you always,
Kobe

Letting Go: The Last Game

The last game, number seven, is called Letting Go. You can play it only when you attain wisdom, *gravitas* and a healthy detachment from what kept you busy, worried and awake during the long and tiring Game Two, the Better Game, the warrior phase of your life. It is not about developing indifference, cynicism or bitterness. It is about realizing what truly matters. It is a liberating moment not because you run away from something but because you finally reach out to your inner and most authentic self. It is about going back home. There are four preparatory steps before you reach and master the Letting Go Game. It's about 1) slowing down, 2) healing, 3) learning to lose and 4) quitting. Letting go will come flawlessly shortly after.

Stop by Sarah Sparks,[174] *Wait* by Frank Partnoy,[175] *In Praise of Slow* by Carl Honoré[176] and (one of my favourites), *The Things You Can See Only When You Slow Down* by Zen Buddhist monk and teacher Haemin Sunim…[177] You get the point: the dire need to slow down. Yet the problem seems that we all suffer from a cognitive bias: we know but we just don't do it. We're suffering from the disease of FOMO, Fear Of Missing Out, which increases our anxiety as if we are missing something important. We pay more attention to notifications (you may want to turn them off now) than our family members.

I understood the magical beauty of slowing down during a vacation on the splendid island of Favignana, off the west coast of Sicily. The first time I went with friends, we rented a car and sped around to get to the beach or rush to a restaurant. The second time I went to Favignana, no rental cars were available, so I rented a bicycle instead. Suddenly, I discovered the natural and wild beauty of the island, the scent of summer; I listened to the birds chirping; I saw the amazing butterflies; I noticed the unbelievable blue sky of Sicily; I bought delicious peaches, apricots and figs from the locals. Without the air conditioning of the car, I felt the dry heat and the breeze and wind from the sea on my skin. It was a different experience, almost another island.

---

[174] Sarah Sparks, Stop: *The Calmer Way to Future-proof Your Career and Wellbeing*, Known Publishing, 2021.
[175] Frank Partnoy, *Wait: The Art and Science of Delay*, Public Affairs, New York, 2012.
[176] Carl Honoré, *In Praise of Slow: How a Worldwide Movement is Challenging the Cult of Speed*, Orion Publishing, first edition, 2004.
[177] Haemin Sunim, *The Things You Can See Only When You Slow Down: How to Be Calm in a Busy World*, Penguin Life, first edition 2012.

To let go, we need to slow down, create the space, detox and walk away from social media and emails. We need to savour and feel how sweet slowing down can be, especially if you can get fresh fruit during the journey. In the slowing down phase, silence will become a friend and we realize that it is always better to avoid noise, distractions and interruptions or we become *The Shallows*,[178] a scary book about the mutation and decay of our brain when it is over-exposed to the internet.

Healing

Here is a short story, worth sharing. How heavy is a glass of water? Imagine holding one in your hand. The absolute weight does not matter: it depends on how long you hold it. A few seconds, no problem; 10 minutes, a bit annoying; two hours, your arm will start to ache; all day long, your arm will be in serious pain and you'll feel paralysed. The weight of the glass of water hasn't changed, but the longer you hold it, the stronger the pain. The same thing happens when we hold on to our problems. Put the water glass down. It's OK. We can't carry it with us all the time or we'll become paralysed.

I fell in love with Van Morrison's 1993 album, *Too Long in Exile*,[179] thanks to 'Till We Get the Healing Done', a nine-minute-long song with hypnotic, healing power. A *Melody Maker* music critic wrote, 'Never has one man's therapy sounded *this* exhilarating.' This song helped me realize – in a difficult moment – the importance of healing before moving to the next phase, or game, of your life. I am not referring to the medical-science element: I am not a doctor. Instead, I am referring to the power of forgiveness without which we carry 'the poison inside'. Forgiveness is the main ingredient in healing, not to be confused with forgetting. Silence becomes

---

[178] Nicholas Carr, *The Shallows: What the Internet is Doing to Our Brains*, W.W. Norton & Company, 2011.
[179] Van Morrison, *Too Long in Exile*, 1993. In fact, https://en.wikipedia.org/wiki/Too_Long_in_Exile

a friend. The beneficial effect of healing is to replace resentment with gratitude. When we forgive, we heal. When we let go, we grow. When you look at your scars, some on your skin, some on your soul, you will discover their significance and ambiguity. Here I got hurt *and* here I was able to heal.

Losing

Learning from mistakes seems easy compared to learning to lose. How can you learn from losses? I asked this question of one of my sports idols, Riccardo Pittis,[180] a former multi-championship-winning basketball player. I never would have imagined meeting Riccardo. I'm a huge basketball fan, and like all good Milanese, I cheered for Milan's team every Sunday. We had a legendary team with players who were the idols of the entire city. Dino Meneghin, the iconic pivot; Mike D'Antoni, the brilliant playmaker; Bob McAdoo, NBA superstar; and Riccardo Pittis a real fighter, a winner, a small forward guard.

A few years ago, I read on LinkedIn that Riccardo had written a book titled *'Lasciatemi Perdere'*,[181] an emblematic title that has a double meaning in Italian: Leave Me Alone and also Let Me Lose. I reached out to him and he was very kind, happy to talk to me. We had a wonderful conversation-interview.

Riccardo, during your 20 years as a professional player, you've won 24 titles, including seven Italian national championships. What have you learned from your victories?

Obviously winning is a great feeling: I'm really competitive. But I realize that winning doesn't happen by chance; it comes from focused determination, sweat, hard

---

[180] https://en.wikipedia.org/wiki/Riccardo_Pittis
[181] Riccardo Pittis, *Lasciatemi Perdere,* Roi Edizioni, 2022.

work and sacrifice. But victories are fleeting; they're gone before you know it. As soon as you win, you start thinking about the next game. I was lucky to play with amazing teammates – I consider Dino Meneghin, Mike D'Antoni and Bob McAdoo my 'basketball fathers'. Everything I learned, I learned from them, and I'm still grateful for the life lessons they taught me, beyond basketball.

What did you learn from your losses?
I would draw a distinction between losses in basketball and losses in life. Obviously, some losses on the court would burn, and others were crushing, but they also motivated me to improve, to train harder and better: I'm very competitive so I took it as a challenge. I rarely messed up two games in a row; I learned from losses and I didn't make the same mistake twice.

Losses in life leave a bigger mark. You don't have to manage the loss, but you feel like a failure and that impacts your identity as a man, not as a player. You learn more from losses than from wins, believe me.

I want to share a meaningful experience in my professional career. At a certain point, I couldn't shoot with my right hand anymore – and I'm right-handed – because I had a serious problem with my tendons. I had two choices, I could stop playing or learn to shoot with my left, but I never even used my left to dribble. I learned in just a few weeks and I'm not telling you this to brag. The truth is, I thought about it a hundred times: Why didn't I do this sooner? I was forced to make that choice, but actually we all have the power – and the ability – to choose.

When did you realize that it was time to quit?
For an athlete, it's a moment you hope will never come, but obviously, it comes for everyone. I knew it was time when I

realized that I couldn't be a player who made a difference on the court anymore. I didn't want to just be another number. I wasn't enjoying the away games or having fun during practice anymore. When I turned 35, I said enough. Time to move on.

How did you reinvent yourself?
It was a long, hard road, not a straight path at all! I made a lot of mistakes. I was used to learning fast, and I thought that was all I needed, but I was wrong. It's kind of like learning to play 'Für Elise' on the piano and then thinking you're ready to give a concert at the Met: I wasn't ready. I realized I had to take time out to train up, I had to take the time I needed to get good, like I did in basketball.

I also thought about why playing basketball made me happy. I think I gave my fans a lot of emotional moments and I wanted to keep doing that. With the help of a coach, I figured out that basketball was just a tool, but not the only one there is. The profession I'm doing now is my mission. I want to give people an emotional experience as I share what I've learned. Not only as a player, but more importantly as a man. I hope I can succeed.

Losing is a sobering moment of reflection: I have learned more from the experience of being fired — it happened twice — than from the experience to be promoted — it happened 10 times.

Quitting

It's 21 October 2000, in Wembley, London. We are at the British and Commonwealth boxing heavyweight title match. Danny Williams (nickname: *The Brixton Bomber*) versus Mark Potter (*The Great White Shark*). The fight is absolutely brutal and dramatic: during the sixth round, Williams gets violently hammered to the point that he dislocates his shoulder. The pain is unbearable and the TV commentator shouts, 'He can't fight; the shoulder is completely gone, he needs to stop now!'[182] Williams looks at the corner and the referee, hoping that the match will be called. But after a few long seconds, Danny continues his fight with one arm. He's fighting for pride and doesn't want to give up. Everyone's thinking: it's only a matter of time, he can't fight with a dislocated shoulder. Then, less than 15 seconds later, Danny throws a devastating punch and knocks Potter out.

It is a stunning, unbelievable ending: to this day, one of the most legendary fights in the history of boxing. The Brixton Bomber is famous for his ferocious grit and determination. Then, four years later, Williams has another crucial fight against Mike Tyson, who enters the ring as a nine-to-one favourite. But, Williams wins again. He's 31. He's at the peak of his career.

The next challenge is against Vitali Klitschko (now the Mayor of Kyiv) for the world heavyweight title, but the Bomber is beaten this time, so he returns to fight back at home. Williams takes part in a boxing tournament in October 2009. In the run-up to the match, Williams says he would prove that he's the best British heavyweight. In his first bout of the night, Carl Baker beats Williams on points after knocking him down twice in the opening round. William is now 36 years old.

In May 2010, Williams promises that win or lose, this next match will be his last. He loses again. The British Boxing Board of Control states they have concerns about Williams' severe decline and inability to box. But Williams continues to box in events sanctioned overseas. He racks up loss after loss and finally retires 11 years later, in 2021, aged almost 49. His boxing record in 2008 (when he was 35) was 40 wins vs. six losses. When he retired in 2021, it was 54 wins and 30 losses. The grit and determination that allowed him to win with a dislocated shoulder in 2000 and

---

[182] https://www.youtube.com/watch?v=-hE965aKKVU

to beat Mike Tyson did not serve him well, as he continued boxing far too long. His decline was obvious to everyone and there were so many embarrassing defeats on his way down. The lesson here is that persistence is not always the best decision. Annie Duke, the author of *Quit*,[183] explains:

> That's the funny thing about grit. While grit can get you to stick to hard things that are worthwhile, grit can get you to stick to hard things that are no longer worthwhile. The trick is figuring out the difference. Some do, some don't, no matter the evidence of their decline: sad to watch.

When you climb a mountain, it is paramount to strictly observe your *turnaround time*, when you must return to base camp, no matter where you are. The turnaround time is decided well before the climbing starts to protect climbers from danger, as the descent is far more dangerous than the ascent. In fact, eight times more people die on Everest on the way down than on the way up. Annie Duke, who has also been a professional poker player, suggests using two practical tools to avoid relying on grit when it is no longer helpful, beneficial or feasible:

> a) Decide the turnaround time before ascending. The biggest mistake most people make is to 'renegotiate' the turnaround time while you are 'in'. You may be only a few hundred metres from the summit; you know you have put in so much effort you want to give one more push, just one more try. Unfortunately, many have died in climbing for this last push, obliterated by fatigue, darkness and weather conditions. Many have failed and wasted so much time, resources and love; for example, surviving in relationships that don't work or staying in dead-end jobs and occupations. What I find relevant is the

---

[183] Annie Duke, *Quit: The Power of Knowing When to Walk Away*, Portfolio Penguin, 2022.

fact that Morgan Housel, in *The Psychology of Money*,[184] shared the very same idea. When investing, choose the turnaround time, the time to walk away. But remember, quitting on time usually feels like quitting too early.

b) Every goal needs at least one 'unless': a straightforward way to frame our goals. Yes, we want to achieve 'that' unless, for example, our health deteriorates or we stop talking and listening to our kids. We need to consider the price we pay for the money we get.

Annie Duke suggests that 'the opposite of a great virtue – such as Grit – can also be a great virtue, such as Quit'.

Letting go

You maybe know the legend, attributed to the Native Americans, of the two wolves that battle within us. In the story, a wise elder explains to his grandson, one wolf is filled with bitterness, anger, resentment, jealousy, arrogance and vindictiveness. The other wolf is just the opposite: he's loving, generous, humble, hopeful, compassionate and caring. The boy asks his grandfather, 'Grandpa, which wolf wins?' The elder replies, 'The one you feed.'

According to David R. Hawkins, author of *Letting Go: The Pathway of Surrender*,[185] 'Letting go is like the sudden cessation of an inner pressure or the dropping of a weight. It is accompanied by a sudden feeling of relief and lightness, with increased happiness and freedom.' Letting go is not about repression, suppression, denial or escape from our feelings. On the contrary, it's about being aware of our feelings, because it's the accumulated pressure of feelings that causes our thoughts. But we are not our thoughts:

[184] Morgan Housel, *The Psychology of Money: Timeless Lessons on Wealth, Greed and Happiness*, Harriman House, 2020.
[185] David R. Hawkins, *Letting Go, the Pathway of Surrender*, Veritas Publishing, first edition 2012.

thoughts are just thoughts. We have negative thoughts, the bad wolf, and positive ones, like the caring and compassionate wolf. By feeding the good one, we experience positive energy and we ignite the process of letting go. The more you let go, the higher you rise.

The writers Henry Miller and his lover, Anaïs Nin,[186] exchanged intimate and profound letters for over 20 years. In one letter, Henry Miller shares his reflection about Letting Go and Surrender.[187]

> 'When you surrender, the problem ceases to exist. Try to solve it, or conquer it, and you only set up more resistance. I am very certain now that if I truly become what I wish to be, the burden will fall away. The most difficult thing to admit, and to realize with one's whole being, is that you alone control nothing. To be able to put yourself in tune or rhythm with the forces beyond, which are the truly operative ones, that is the task – and the solution, if we can speak of "solutions."'

Letting go will take us to the surrender state: we understand and internalize that happiness is the result not of external circumstances but the natural and unforced outcome of our decisions, our mindset. Optimism is not about 'things will go my way, no matter what', but knowing that, regardless of the outcome, you will be able to manage. The ultimate form of preparation is not rigid planning for a predetermined scenario but a mindset that can handle ambiguity, uncertainty and surprises, bad or good. The source of happiness is within us – so we can control it, not outside us. The elusive search for the Holy

---

[186] *A Literate Passion: Letters of Anais Nin and Henry Miller 1932–1953* Edited and with an introduction by Gunther Stulhmann, Harcourt Brace Jovanovich, 1987.
[187] https://www.themarginalian.org/2022/07/31/henry-miller-control-surrender-despair/

Grail, but it does not exist. We do not find happiness by adding things into our life.[188]

Letting go is embracing a new identity, as you cannot define yourself by what you used to do and used to be but by what are you now. It's about honouring your past, going back home, like Ulysses when he returned to Ithaca. It's about asking a simple and powerful question: who will cry when you die?[189] What legacy do you want to leave behind?

What if you were to read your obituary when you were still alive?

Merchant of Death[190] by Aditya Agrawal

Alfred Bernhard Nobel was an engineer and inventor; he was interested in studying chemistry and fascinated with nitroglycerin due to its unpredictable and highly explosive nature. Despite the scientific community's aversion to nitroglycerin, the young man's mind was determined to tame the explosive substance and turn it into a commercially usable blasting agent.

In the 1860s, the chemist experimented with controlled explosions, looking for a stable combination. However, in 1864, a tragedy struck his company. A vat of nitroglycerin exploded, killing five people, including his younger brother, Emil. Rather than being put off working with nitroglycerin, Alfred threw himself into trying to find a safe way to detonate the chemical. To give up now would be, in his view, to allow his brother to have died in vain.

[188] Mo Gawdat, *That Little Voice in Your Head: Adjust the Code That Runs Your Brain*, Bluebird Publishing, 2022.
[189] Robin Sharma, *Who Will Cry When You Die?*, Jaico Publishing House, first edition 2003.
[190] Aditya Agrawal, blogger and writer for the *India Times*. https://www.linkedin.com/in/aditya-agrawal-87a3a1169/
This story can be found at: https://timesofindia.indiatimes.com/blogs/unheardshepherd/merchant-of-death-the-story-behind-the-nobel-prize/

He continued his work and ultimately produced dynamite, the first safe explosive. He was soon granted patents for his invention in Europe and the US and dynamite became Nobel's big business. It turned out to be an immediate success, with engineering companies from all over the world clamouring to get their hands on it. Business boomed and numerous factories and plants were set up across the US and Europe. Soon money started rolling in and virtually overnight, Alfred amassed a massive fortune.

The explosives created by Nobel spread rapidly around the world and brought great benefits to engineering and mining. But inevitably, they were also used intensively for war. He was often quoted as saying, 'As soon as nations will find that in one instant, whole armies can be utterly destroyed, they surely will abide in golden peace.'

Alfred considered himself a pacifist and strongly believed that his weapons would create deterrence, ultimately proving to be a boon to mankind. This, however, was a gross miscalculation. Wars continued and nations didn't recoil. His inventions failed to change the course of the world. His faith in mankind was sadly misplaced.

One particular incident, however, left him with a tortured conscience and changed his life forever: in 1888, Ludwig, one of Alfred's brothers, died while visiting Cannes. A French newspaper erroneously confused Ludwig with Alfred and published a scathing obituary entitled, 'The Merchant of Death is Dead'. It condemned Alfred Nobel for his inventions, criticizing him as the wealthiest vagabond in Europe who had become rich by finding ways to mutilate and kill innocents. Virtually every newspaper seemed to find glory in his supposed demise.

The error was later corrected, but life had granted Alfred the rare opportunity to read his obituary: the experience horrified him and left an indelible mark on his conscience. Fame and fortune now felt like a burden. He began questioning himself,

'Is this how posterity will remember me? Is this the legacy that I'll leave behind?'

He became concerned about his posthumous reputation and decided to make a positive mark in the world. In 1893, Alfred worked diligently on his will over the next two years: he selflessly bequeathed over 94 per cent of his fortune to set up the Nobel Foundation. By the time he wrote his will, Nobel was highly affluent and owned over 100 factories that made explosives and munitions. But this was not the way he wanted to be remembered. Now was the time for a much-needed change. His only intention was to work for humanity; to reward all those who have selflessly worked for society and have conferred the greatest benefit on mankind.

Then, on 27 November 1895, Alfred signed the testament unlike any other and officially donated 35 million Swedish kronor (almost his entire estate) to the Foundation, which presently amounts to nearly 265 million dollars. His will indicated a sense of apology with a strengthened resolution to work for the peace movement. This is how an erroneous obituary, a mistaken identity, altered the destiny of Swedish inventor and industrialist, Alfred Nobel, and made his legacy synonymous with peace. Sometimes even a small incident can bring about a profound change in a person's life.

Is Alfred Nobel the story of a successful man? He was extremely hard on himself. In a letter to his brother Ludwig in 1887, he wrote, 'Alfred Nobel: pathetic, half-alive, should have been strangled by a humanitarian doctor. Greatest merit: never a burden to anyone. Greatest fault: lacks family, cheerful spirit and a strong stomach. Greatest and only petition: not to be buried alive. Greatest sin: does not worship Mammon. Important events in his life: none.'[191] We disagree: his life was

---

[191] Kenne Fant, *Alfred Nobel: A Biography*, Arcade Publishing, 1993.

remarkable. He left a gift to humanity and a yearly celebration of human achievements. He wanted to leave a legacy different from the one he read in his obituary.

How can we increase our professional value? How can we remain relevant? How can we be employable rather than employed? Chapter Seven will answer these questions.

7

How to increase your professional value

'You have your brush, you have your colours, you
paint the paradise and then you go.'
                    NIKOS KAZANTZAKIS, Greek Poet

Knowledge, Relationships and Reputational Capital

If you were the portfolio manager of a private bank, your job
could be summed up in a few words: to increase the value of
the portfolio you are responsible for. If, for example, you have to
manage the wealth of a (rich) client, let's say 100 million, your
client expects that the value will be higher in the future. 110?
120? Whatever the figure, the key is growth.

What if you were the portfolio manager of yourself? The
real question is: *how do you increase your value?* What is your real
wealth? What are the assets you will need to grow? No, I'm
not referring to your bank account or whatever fortune you
may have accumulated. Instead, I'm talking about enhancing
your value as a professional, a crucial element in a fast-changing
economy squeezed between the speed of the Fourth Industrial
Revolution and the brand-new context we discussed earlier.

The question is relevant. What is the difference between
being one of the people who is shaping the new context and
will remain relevant and employable, and the ones who will

be considered a useless class or workforce, according to the definition of Yuval Noha Harari?[192]

As an executive coach, I have noticed that most people confuse value with salary. Sure, there must be a correlation between the two. Still, if you focus exclusively on boosting your salary without enhancing your actual value, you will find you've become too expensive for the job market and you'll be made redundant. Someone out there can do the job you're doing for much less. One typical example: people who have been over-promoted (not always based on merit) well beyond their abilities may find themselves in a difficult spot. And I guarantee they'll risk losing their jobs because the value they bring to the table is lower than the salary they receive. Sooner or later they will be asked to step down or just leave the organization. So, how can we increase our value? We have three assets to curate, grow and protect: Knowledge, Relationships and Reputation.

Learning to learn

Do you remember the day of your graduation, your wedding day, the birth of your child or your first kiss? Do you remember 9/11? Have you noticed that your kids can sing all the songs from their favourite singer yet do not remember two lines from their class yesterday? Or why do you cry when you listen to that certain song, but you forget you saw that movie only recently?

How does learning occur?
How We Learn by Stanislas Dehaene[193] is a magnificent book that opens the black box of learning. The author is a world-renowned neuroscientist and he provides science-based evidence about understanding how we learn. It starts with a question: what is a

---

[192] Yuval Noha Harari, *21 Lessons for the 21st Century*, Random House, 2018.
[193] Stanislas Dehaene, *How We Learn: The New Science of Education and the Brain*, Penguin Random House, UK, 2020.

memory? Each of our actions and thoughts relies on the activity of a specific subset of active neurons. When I meet, for example, a dear friend, some neurons respond to his face, others to his voice and others to where we are in that specific moment. Single neurons provide scattered information (e.g. his voice sounds like he's happy), but only several related groups of neurons encode overall memory. Memories are formed when neurons connect. If I haven't seen this friend in a long time, I may be excited, anticipating meeting him again. Therefore, my emotional system upgrades this experience as relevant enough to be stored in my memory. In Dehaene's words:

> To cement the event, the neurons that were recently activated undergo significant physical changes. They modify the strength of their interconnections, making it more likely that this set of neurons will fire in the future. Some synapses become larger, and some will even get duplicated. These changes are the physical basis of learning: collectively, they form a substrate for memory.

Even more interesting is what happens *after* forming a memory is completed: the neurons can rest, memory is dormant, but it is always available and retrievable. If we meet the same friend, let's say two years later, we will restart from this memory. Did it ever happen to you to meet someone after many years and feel that you saw him/her just the day before? Based on this theory, *each restored memory is a reconstruction;* to remember something is to play back what we have experienced before in our past life.

Memories are based on emotions and we tend to anchor our memories to emotions. Therefore, learning is also based on emotions; *without any emotional involvement, learning does not occur.* This is why our kids can remember their favourite songs and tend to forget yesterday's chemistry lesson unless it is compellingly taught. Let me demonstrate this to you.

Do you remember the song 'The Sound of Silence'? I am sure you know it, and you may well like it, but it probably doesn't mean much to you: it is a song you enjoy listening to and that's it. Well, it's the story of Sandy Greenberg, a boy from a modest Jewish family in Buffalo. He's a bright student and wins a scholarship to Columbia University, so he moves to New York and becomes another student's close friend and roommate. One day Sandy goes to a baseball match and suddenly, he becomes blind. Not a big deal – the doctor told him – it is only conjunctivitis; it will pass shortly. Sadly, the doctor was wrong, it never did. So Sandy, now blind for life, becomes depressed and decides to abandon his studies and return home. His friend goes to visit him and convinces him to return to New York to finish his studies. He pledges to support him; he does so daily by helping him in everything: 'I will be your light in your world of darkness.' Sandy recovers his energy and optimism. He graduates and then gets a master's from Harvard and – can you believe it? – a PhD from Oxford. His career is stellar and Sandy becomes a famous attorney, advising US presidents such as Gerald Ford and Jimmy Carter.

Now let's go back to March 1964: Sandy's roommate asks to borrow $400 from Sandy. He needs the money to rent a recording studio at Columbia Studios in New York City. Sandy lends him the money so he can produce his record along with another friend, also a passionate and talented musician. Sandy's friend is Arthur Ira Garfunkel, whose friend is Paul Simon. The song is entitled 'The Sound of Silence' and it was written and dedicated to Sandy Greenberg.

If you want to fire your neurons, listen to the song while reading the lyrics.[194] The experience will be even more emotional, as you will be using the auditory sense, reinforcing synapses, and you'll never forget the story of the blind boy, Sandy, and his friend, Arthur. It will no longer be a song, but an experience in your mind and heart. Forever.

[194] https://www.youtube.com/watch?v=DCtouot15cA

How do we make sure that learning does not disappear?

First, we need to challenge an assumption, the myth of learning styles: there is no scientific evidence that supports that we differ radically in our modality of learning. If this is the case, what are the critical elements of our knowledge? According to *How We Learn,* there are four pillars of learning.

1. **Attention.** Are we paying attention? Or are we misdirecting our attention? Learning how to pay attention is critical, especially when we live in a society where distractions are social media's business model. We have three attention systems. Alerting: when to pay attention. Orienting: what we need to pay attention to. Selecting: how to process and choose our information. *The quality of our experience is based on the quality of our attention.*

2. **Active engagement.** Curiosity did not kill the cat: far from it, curiosity is the secret sauce permeating effective learning. Curiosity is embedded in our genes. Kids' most frequent question is, why? They want to know why all the time. How we respond to them will pique their curiosity, stifle or suffocate it. Memory and curiosity are linked and the more intense the curiosity, the better the retention. Please note that curiosity is not the nosy kind, wanting to know if your neighbour is having an affair with the lady on the second floor. It is the insatiable desire to learn, which creates pleasure via dopamine. Yes: once your brain is driven by genuine curiosity to learn and gets hooked on the joy of learning, it produces dopamine and we are in some sense forced to continue learning. It's the best kind of addiction you can have.

3. **Error feedback.** Our brain learns when there is a gap between what we expect and what has happened. If you play tennis, you will probably discover that if your forehand is too weak, the ball goes into the net;

too strong, it goes way too long. So you will learn how to calibrate the power and direction of your forehand. Feedback is supposed to be a form of encouragement, not a punishment: many kids lose their motivation, as the school system tends to punish failure. We have explored the importance of failures in learning in Chapter Four: it is essential to repeat here that failures are the avenue to success. Equally, performance systems where most employees are rated average or below average are suicidal machines able to produce massive quantities of demotivation, resentment and bitterness.

4. **Consolidation.** I had a weird experience recently. Several people told me that I had agreed with their proposals only a few days earlier. I assure you, I did not recall my agreement, which is quite an uncomfortable place to be. I was curious, so I asked them: 'When did I agree to your proposal?' I gave all my approvals on the same day when I returned from a long trip to Asia and I did not sleep for almost two days. My lack of sleep obliterated any recollection of these meetings. I was physically present but my brain was switched off. Consolidation of learning occurs by sleeping, constant repetition and regular intervals between theory and practice. You don't learn to play tennis only by watching Federer, or by playing alone against a wall, or by practising with a tennis partner. It would be best if you used a combination of all methodologies.

Only after learning to learn can we then decide why, what and when to learn.

Knowledge

I have said this before: to cope with machine learning, we need to become learning machines. How? Learning never stops and we need to keep on 'sharpening the saw', as brilliantly explained by Steve Convey in his legendary *Seven Habits of Highly Effective People*. But learning has to find some concrete application. If I were to say that I know all the recipes of Italian cuisine by heart, but I've never cooked a dish in my life, I won't have any credibility. Learning for the sake of creating value is what counts. So I guess we can all agree that learning is essential. Aristotle wrote that *the purpose of knowledge is action*. Passive learning creates understanding, but only active learning develops skills. I had a manager who once told me that he took people seriously only when they were sweaty. I understood what he meant years later.

Can I share with you three rules for learning?

'The beginning is always today,' wrote Mary Shelley. Every day is a good day to learn. Whenever I look at my university diploma hanging on the wall, I smile because everything I learned back then is no longer relevant. But does that mean we should stop wasting all this energy, time and money on university? Not really. Instead, as soon as we complete our formal studies, we need to become learning machines. I'll repeat it: we must become machines of continuous learning. We have no choice, or we will be out of the game and sitting on the sidelines.

Rule 1: Natural Curiosity
Every single moment, there is an opportunity to learn. But learning does not occur in classrooms: it happens in our minds; learning is a mindset, not a diploma. So the first rule is not to limit our learning to a single subject. And remember, one key element of learning is to be open to exploring new territories for curiosity's sake.

As Steve Jobs said in his moving 2005 commencement speech at Stanford University,[195] we will be able to make connections backwards. Jobs once explained why Apple products were so

---

[195] https://www.youtube.com/watch?v=UF8uR6Z6KLc&t=60s

stylish, clean and perfectly designed: he attended a calligraphy course when he was a student. He wanted to translate this aesthetic into his company's products. As a result, the design of Apple products is now iconic. Try to get out of your comfort zone and dismantle how you usually think. Learning will occur in mysterious and magical ways.

Rule 2: Failure is part of learning

Let's play a game. I'll tell you a word and you have to say the opposite word: simple, right? OK, let's start.

Cold. Yep, the opposite is hot. Tall, short. Rich, poor. Hard, soft. You get the picture. But what is the opposite of success? Please think carefully. Many in my seminars and workshops answer without hesitation, 'failure'. But let's hold on a second. Failure is NOT the opposite of success but the process – at times painful but always necessary – to arrive at success. We have learned it in our lives and we have explored it in the Better Game.

Rule 3: Learning never stops

I frequently ask in my workshops if anyone believes that whatever knowledge and experience they have gained up until today will be sufficient in five years. Almost everyone responds negatively, as we all understand that the best investment you can make is in yourself and your learning. So my second question is: what have you done or are you doing right now to sharpen your saw, to keep on learning and growing? Today, you buy a new car for $50,000. What would be the residual value of this car in five years? At best, it will be 20 to 30 per cent of today's value. The same concept applies to your skills. Today, your skills and experience are worth 100. So the residual value will be a fraction of today's value in five years; you need to invest in yourself, the best investment you can ever make.

According to a study done by Deloitte, learning is not limited to business activity but should be part of 'the flow of life'. They have a point, as now careers can last up to 50 years, and since the average tenure in one position is four and a half years, we will all do more than 10 different jobs. Learning agility is vital. The proof of your learning, if you think about it, is not a diploma but a growth mindset. For example, every person you'll meet in your life knows something more than you in at least three subjects. We are natural-born learners; even as kids, we are programmed to learn, and there is no limit to what we can learn.

But not all learning(s) are created equal. Learning something new and practising something new seem similar, but these two approaches produce two very different outcomes. Passive learning begins with knowledge; only active practice creates skills. It's the difference between memorizing a recipe and being able to cook it.

So, become a learning machine, enjoy successful failures and don't ever stop learning. Practice is more important than learning some formula or concept by heart. You can reinvent your future by investing in your learning. It will be a joyful journey to freedom (most of the time) and nobody will ever take away what you've learned and the choices you've made as a person. OK, now I can reveal the answer: the opposite of success is not failure but the absence of learning.

Relationships

I want to share a secret with you: how to be happy. A study done by Harvard Medical School pointed out something we know but haven't gotten a grip on. 'The surprising finding is that our relationships and how happy we are in our relationships have a powerful influence on our health,' says Robert Waldinger, director of the study and professor of psychiatry at Harvard Medical School.[196] 'Taking care of your body is important, but tending to your relationships is a form of self-care too. That, I think, is the revelation.'

[196] Robert Waldinger, MD and Marc Schultz, *The Good Life: lessons from the world's longest scientific study on happiness*, Simon & Schuster, USA 2023

The quality of our relationships with others – starting with our families – is an essential component of our wellbeing and happiness. But, wait. I'm not done yet; there's more here. Do you remember when we talked about complexity and the need to decode it and collaborate with others? In short, we all need a band.

If you have seen him live in concert, you'll remember him all your life. Yes, of course, I'm talking about The Boss, Bruce Springsteen. Towards the end of all his concerts, Bruce sings-recites a kind of gospel – usually standing on the piano: 'I wanted to be the rock 'n' roll apostle of this planet, then I had a vision... an Angel told me, "Son, you need a band, you can't do it alone."' The moments that follow are simply exhilarating. Bruce not only introduces his musicians to the audience, he does so with esteem, love and friendship.

I confess that I've realized the importance of the team thanks to the Springsteen concerts I've attended: 80 so far. Still, for years I didn't understand the tools and methodologies needed to manage a team and foster collaboration: not as a rock star (God knows how much I would have loved that!) but as a director of Human Resources. Relationship capital is essential not only to be healthy and happy but also to get things done. Bruce is right – we all need a band.

We need to foster and curate our social capital, the network we have built over the years. How do you develop your network? It's not having millions of followers on social media, it's about *being at the service* of other people. To a certain extent, your social capital is like your bank account. You can withdraw cash only if you have deposited and invested in building relationships based on trust. It doesn't work when people think of their relationships only when it's convenient for them and then disappear if they believe that others can't give them any value at that moment. This approach is purely transactional; it means that 'you exist just because I need you'. On the contrary, 'I exist because I can help you'. Building a solid relationship is the key to enhancing your value; if you do it ethically and with sound judgement by fostering collaboration with people and organizations you want to be affiliated with.

Gianfranco Minutolo[197] is an author and expert in networking. I have asked him for his insights and practical advice about the importance of building a solid network based on trust.[198]

Networking – by Gianfranco Minutolo

One of the most important assets that every person has is the network of their relationships in their personal and work life. But thinking of a network as a more or less extensive list of contacts is an overly simplistic, albeit common, mistake. Whenever people who know me say they envy my address book, I am convinced of their limited knowledge of the value of 'networking'. If I were to let these people import all the phone numbers in my smartphone, in terms of real value I would not have given away much. They're just numbers, essentially, that they could do very little with. And there is a difference between a number and a 'contact'.

The 'hidden' value is trust, that life force that keeps people bound together. Trust, which represents the quality of these bonds, is built over time, through a continual combination of knowledge and action.

My story can help you.

In 2010, I was called to develop the community of more than 100,000 Alumni of Bocconi University in Milan. I was very excited, but also anxious about the ambitious task I was hired to do: to revitalize and relaunch Bocconi's network with the goal of making it a pillar of the university.

Thanks to an invaluable, professional team of employees and volunteers, in the eight years of my stewardship we managed to revitalize the international network by taking on more

[197] https://www.linkedin.com/in/gianfrancominutolo/
[198] Gianfranco Minutolo, *Robots Can't do Networking (Yet)*, Guerini Edition, 2021.

than 200 volunteer leaders (up from the initial 40), organizing more than 300 events a year (up from the initial 50), reactivated more than 80,000 contacts and created many communities of interest and major initiatives on every continent.

The unit of measurement of the great results we have achieved is relationships. We have established tens of thousands of solid ties among people who previously did not even know one another by helping them build and maintain a network of relationships over time. How do we replicate this experience in our personal networks?

First, with knowledge. We built micro-communities by engaging people based on their skills and interests. We talked to them and listened to them, paying attention to each person's skills and needs.

Second, with action. Based on the evidence in the first relational phase, we created interconnections within the network. In this way, different, distant people can be each other's solutions, or combine their respective skills to their mutual benefit or to benefit a third person, who in due course could do the same for them.

This means nourishing the network by being willing to offer your services, creating a 'reciprocity loop' powered by the question: what can I do about this contact? Always in the spirit of 'gift' and not 'entitlement'. This is not about being a do-gooder; it's a successful, functional, collaborative strategy for professional as well as personal networking.

Our career path is a mix of our hard skills, soft skills and how we are perceived by others. When writing about hard skills, Paolo put it well in his earlier book, 'A person is hired for qualifications and experience, but he stays and gets ahead... only if he leaves his ego outside the door' (*The Compass and the Radar*, p. 202). So know-how is essential, but it is no longer enough. The mother of all skills is the relational skill.

We are the relationships we build over time. We need to be aware that we establish and strengthen our relationships in the daily exchanges with the people we engage with. We live immersed in the relational networks that we can create, consciously or unconsciously, every day. Think about your network by implementing three useful takeaways so that it stays active and generates value over time:

1. Value active listening. Get passionate about the person sitting in front of you; understand their strengths and needs.
2. Deepen your knowledge of people. Sharpen your curiosity by using social media as well.
3. Cultivate reciprocity by offering opportunities every chance you get. It is a quick and reliable way to ascertain a person's trustworthiness: their appreciation and availability over time will make them worthy of being part of your network. Reciprocity allows you to create two-way connections and to multiply the opportunities of each network member, who can then rely not only on their own skills and knowledge, but on those of all the other network members too.

My suggestion? Always follow through on your commitments. Be a farmer in your network. Continuity is nourishment: every day, water and work your 'crop' and gently remove the pests and become a role model of networking based on trust.

Reputational Capital

Pigs are clever animals, but they suffer from a terrible reputation: they are the subject of several proverbial expressions. My favourite is 'putting lipstick on a pig'. The etymology can be traced back to the sixteenth century: the phrase means to embellish something only on the surface while the actual substance remains unappealing and, in this case, smelly.

As an example, I always mention one of my 'favourite' companies: the unforgettable Enron: what are their corporate values in their mission statement? Integrity, Communication, Respect and Excellence. Sit down and enjoy the following line. Under the heading of respect, the Enron webpage read, 'We treat others as we would like to be treated ourselves.' I guess they spent a fortune on lipstick until the rest of the world and 29,000 employees found out the truth. Corporate reputation is vital, and rest assured, personal reputation is too. My experience is that sooner or later the skeletons in the closet will be visible to everyone.

Some time ago, I listened to one of the best, most hilarious presentations ever. The presenter took 10 profiles from 10 different people from four different platforms: LinkedIn, Facebook, TikTok and Tinder. He started with LinkedIn. First profiles: impeccable, perhaps too many buzzwords to describe their responsibilities and jobs, The presenter asked the audience of about 500 HR professionals, 'Would you recruit them?' The answer was overwhelmingly positive. Next, he showed the very same people on Facebook, TikTok. You can imagine. Here's the severe investment banker who won the bet to drink five pints of beer in three minutes. Here's the boring accountant performing Freddie Mercury in his underpants. Here's the schoolteacher with a military group with affiliations to Nazi propaganda. Oops! Now the fun became an embarrassment. The audience started to feel uncomfortable. The best part, the presenter claimed, was checking their profiles on Tinder; some pictures left very little to the imagination.

Then he posted their profile on LinkedIn again. He asked: would you still recruit them? You know the answer. He made the audience change their minds in five minutes. The presenter had a few legal problems: he obliterated some people's reputations. He was wrong to do it – no doubt – but this presentation raised an issue. Your social media presence is the first and easiest way to verify your reputation. What goes online will stay online no matter what you do.

I know several people who have had their careers ruined or derailed for a momentary lapse of reason. Avoiding a negative reputation is vital. We can do better by building a positive reputation. Do something for people without expecting anything in return; help people when they are having a hard time; call a colleague who has lost his job and introduce him to a friend or a new company. Help, be available, and offer a coffee to someone who needs to talk, do something unexpected, get in touch, or send an article or a book.

Reputation is what people say about you when you are not there. If you think about it, it's your ethical footprint. Ethics is defined by what you are NOT prepared to do to achieve your goals. We want to advance in our careers but not at all costs; we want to do it as decent people. Do you remember the difference between visibility and credibility?

Interestingly, the same applies to organizations. Back in the 1970s, the value of organizations was based on their physical assets. Today, 80 per cent is associated with intangible assets such as brand reputation; how they treat customers and employees, and the products and services they create and sell.

You can calculate your professional value by using this simple formula. Your professional value (PV) is equal to Knowledge Capital (KNC) plus Relationship Capital (RLC) multiplied by your Reputational Capital (RPC).

$$PV = (KNC + RLC) \times RPC$$

Why don't we just add the three capitals (C)? Because if you multiply any number by zero, the result is zero. So even if you invested in KNC and RLC but your reputation is zero, your professional value is also zero. So protect your reputation with the same energy and attention you protect your family. What is your Leadership Brand?[199]

We can be fantastic portfolio managers of ourselves, increasing our value by investing in our learning, relationships and reputation. It is the real value we offer to our society, our communities, and the people we love. I have seen too many people scared to lose their jobs: they have a point and a legitimate concern. But the game here is not to keep your job at all costs

[199] Dave Ulrich and Norm Smallwood, *Leadership Brand: Developing Customer Focus Leaders to Drive Performance and Build Lasting Value*, HBS Press, 2007.

but to keep investing in your professional value. It is the only insurance we can get: not a job for life but a role to play where our value is recognized and respected. So we will remain relevant and employable. It is our game, not theirs.

What is leadership? The Five Cs

The current leadership model has failed us; quite simply, it has forgotten 99 per cent of the people on the planet. The list of disappointments is so long that it would fill many volumes. Nobel Peace laureate Maria Ress provides a credible roadmap in *How to Stand up to a Dictator*.[200] So think twice if you believe that leadership is an empty word or just a topic to debate in academia.

If we focus on the corporate world, it's scary. Reading Jeffrey Pfeffer's book, *Dying for a Paycheck*,[201] you will find overwhelming evidence of how toxic organizations, psychopathic leaders and cruel working conditions are killing people. A fair illustration of a toxic culture is when:

> ...you survive long term if you're political, prepared to put in insane hours and not make enemies of certain people. It's a dog-eat-dog world. It breeds chest-beating, Spartan-like behaviour: 'I work longer hours than you.' You either fight and work harder or you're quickly out. It can be ferocious. Sadly, Toxic Leadership expects this behaviour: they provide an excellent example of it with frequent firings to make the point.

So, if we are indeed in the middle of a transformation, what kind of leadership does the world need? I don't want to bring up a few plausible points we all agree on, such as, 'we need good

[200] Maria Ressa, *How to Stand up to a Dictator*, WH Allen, 2022.
[201] Jeffrey Pfeffer, *Dying for a Paycheck: How Modern Management Harms Employees' Health and Company Performance – and What We Can Do About It*, Harper Business, 2018.

leaders with strong communication skills', or 'more diversity would be helpful'. The time to be politically correct without any accountability is over. Instead, I propose five key behaviours and character traits that will define future leaders: Five Cs to deal with the New Context created by the Five Cs.

Care starts with self-care

I always start my coaching session with a simple question: how are you? A few weeks after the pandemic began in the spring of 2020, I had 16 coaching sessions with people working for different companies. I was stunned to hear that everyone answered the very same way: 'Paolo, I am exhausted.' They did not say tired; they all – and I repeat, all – said exhausted. I asked them to elaborate. Their words were overwhelmed, stressed, anxious, scared, empty and restless. Some mentioned that they cried, asking me not to tell anyone. I felt I was not alone, as I have cried many times too.

With remarkable consistency, I am listening to people – not only executives – telling me that they are pushing themselves harder than ever before. By the end of the week, they felt exhausted. A good night's sleep was not enough to recharge batteries. I wrote an article titled *Why it could be time to hit the pause key*[202] that got 3 million views: it clearly struck a chord with many readers. Do you remember what Mike Tyson once said? 'Everyone has a plan until they get punched in the face.'

Well, COVID-19 is that punch. The war in Ukraine is that punch. The pressure – continual and constantly intensifying – is that punch. The potentially devastating consequences of climate change are that punch. I believe we got at least three punches. The first one as citizens, as every country has been severely affected by it. The second punch as professionals, as every business and

---

[202] Paolo Gallo https://irishtechnews.ie/why-it-could-be-time-to-hit-the-pause-key/

every sector is in a tough spot. The third punch is the hardest one for human beings as our lives have been disrupted on so many levels, also for the people we deeply love. Listening to the news, hearing what's happening, witnessing the dramatic stories: it's been a sobering experience.

Dr Seuss said: '*When something terrible happens, you have three choices. You can either let it destroy you, define you, or strengthen you.*' Let's explore the third option, shall we? How can we possibly manage this unprecedented crisis? How can we now start laying the groundwork for the solution to this crisis? In my view, we need to start by pressing pause.

Hold on a second here: is now the first time we are concerned about our wellbeing, or that stress is out of control, or that we feel exhausted? Not really. Let me share a story with you from a compelling paper by John Pencavel focused on the productivity of working hours. The setting: we are in the UK and the year is 1914. We are at the beginning of the brutal First World War. The Munitions of War Act of 1915 prohibited all restrictions on output and work rules in munitions plants. The war prompted the British government to suspend any limitation on working hours in plants producing war supplies. The working week went from 70 to 90 hours, more than 100 hours per week in some cases. Sunday work and night shifts were reintroduced. The military apparatus demanded 'men, more men and still more men'. All able-bodied men were sent to war, while women were obliged to work in ordnance factories because the war demanded 'munitions, more munitions and still more munitions'. By the end of the war, almost 80 per cent of factory workers were women.

The British government created the Health of Munitions Workers Committee (HMWC) in September 1915 'to consider and advise on industrial fatigue, hours of labour, and other matters affecting workers' health and efficiency in munitions factories and workshops'. It is essential to point out that HMWC's concern wasn't at all workers' health, it was the optimal efficiency of working hours. In 1916, the HMWC recommended reducing working hours because the total output would be unchanged. This study demonstrated back in 1915 that after a certain number of hours, productivity started to decrease. So the HMWC made some clear recommendations: 1) reduce working hours, 2) eating and resting come before work, not after; and 3) abolish both work on Sunday and nightshifts, as rest and sleeping are essential elements of productivity.

We may smile at this finding. First, however, we should know that it doesn't make sense to work 70 hours a week, at night too, or on Sunday; we also need to eat and sleep appropriately before working. The problem is, we don't do it: it's a typical example of cognitive dissonance, since 1915.

Yes, I am talking to you. I know you skipped lunch and just had a quick coffee and a snack on Monday in front of your computer. And on Tuesday, you needed to talk with a client in Asia at 7 a.m. and with your manager at 10 p.m., and since she works from the US, you only slept four hours on Wednesday. And on Thursday, you took a flight at 6.40 a.m. and by Friday, while eating junk food at the airport, you were exhausted. And you've been working the last three weekends. Am I right?

The question is: do you take care of yourself? No. According to an interesting study reported by Jordan B. Peterson,[203] people are better at filling and adequately administering medications to their pets than to themselves. Yep. We take care of our dogs, cats and parrots better than we care for ourselves.

Rule 2 of Peterson's book is my favourite. *Treat yourself like someone you are responsible for helping.* As an executive coach, I have learned that all my clients need to be emotionally supported. (I refer to them as partners because coaching is a true partnership based on mutual trust, respect and confidentiality.) But by the end of the week, I was feeling drained and I found myself in tears many times for no apparent reason. I needed to press pause, and I still do; I guess that you need it too. We cannot turn into high-functioning zombies.

[203] Jordan Peterson, *12 Rules for Life: An Antidote to Chaos*, Random House Canada, 2018.

Think about your favourite car. For me, it's the Ferrari Daytona, a true masterpiece of engineering and design. My question to you is, what feature allows this Ferrari to go up to 200 miles per hour? When I ask this question in my seminars, most people usually say the engine, the driver, aerodynamics, road and/or conditions, and so forth. These answers are technically correct, but that's not the whole story. The brakes. The brakes allow a Ferrari, or any car, to go fast. Without brakes, we couldn't drive even five miles per hour because we would have an accident at the first traffic light. The same is true for us: what allows us to go fast is our ability to slow down, to use our internal brakes.

Beyond that, we need to stop and check if we have enough gas in our tank. We have four different kinds of fuel: 1) physical energy, our general health and vitality; 2) mental energy, our clarity and focus; 3) emotional energy: our resilience and emotional self-control; and 4) spiritual energy, our inner motivations and values that drive our decisions.

Our four energy sources are like batteries: we need to constantly recharge with the same attention that we pay to recharging our smartphones. One hint: we can borrow from one battery if we lack the energy in another but only for a limited time. Here's a typical scenario: we are exhausted. We'd pay a million dollars to stay in bed, but we still manage to go to the office and deliver a first-class presentation to our colleagues. It worked! Yes, once, twice, maybe three times – but then we won't be able to do it anymore. So we need to stop to replenish our energy.

We need to manage our energy even better than we manage our time. Given the moment we are living through, we need to 'put on the brakes' by asking ourselves a simple question: which energy source has been the most depleted recently? Our emotional and spiritual reserves have been drained and, like a car, we are currently driving on fumes. Let's reflect for one moment on the duration of our careers and professional life. It's not a sprint, it's a marathon, and it's getting longer and longer as life expectancy rises, as we've learned at the beginning of this book. Jim Loehr and Tony Schwartz talk about 'The making of a corporate athlete'[204] in their eponymous HBR article. Their main point is that 'to bring mind, body and spirit to peak conditions, executives need to learn what athletes already know – recovering energy is as important as expending it.'

Many corporations have framed the problem the wrong way. We should start caring – for real – in the workplace.[205] It's not about creating never-ending resilience, a superhuman ability to work 24/7 with no rest. I once had a supervisor who expected us to always be available; he ridiculed people with burnout and would send emails such as, 'This is my agenda this week, 120 meetings: and you?' The real danger in running the extra mile, going over and above the call of duty, is to expect to run that extra mile every day. We have learned from the legendary Federer: he can win 20 Grand Slams, but he doesn't play in the Wimbledon final every day. Do you feel somewhat guilty when you are on holiday and not being productive?

Here's the point: we need to *reframe rest not as the opposite of productivity but rather as the prerequisite.* But rest isn't only about sleeping. According to Sandra Dalton-Smith,[206] there are seven kinds of rest: physical, mental, sensory, creative, emotional, social and spiritual rest. If you have a few minutes, you may want to do this test: www.restquiz.com. You will find out which rest you need the most right now. Want to learn the golden rule? 1+1+1. Every day, allocate one hour for yourself, one day per week with absolutely no work and – ideally – one month per year to unplug – holidays. If one month is not possible, at least two weeks.

We need to move, to exercise. The problem is that more and more often, organizations expect people to be willing to go the extra mile – in other words, to adopt habits at their discretion that

[204] Jim Loehr and Tony Schwartz, *The Making of a Corporate Athlete*, HBR magazine, January 2001.
[205] Dave Ulrich and Paolo Gallo, 'Why should you care in the workplace'? https://irishtechnews.ie/why-should-you-care-in-the-workplace/
[206] Sandra Dalton-Smith, *Sacred Rest: Recover Your Life, Renew Your Energy, Restore Your Sanity*, Faith Works, New York, 2017.

go beyond their formal roles. This expectation means anything from helping a colleague without being asked to taking on greater responsibilities, working longer hours or spending weekends or late evenings on call. These behaviours are generally associated with higher commitment, a sense of identity built around one's career and individual motivation. As a result, where extra-mile efforts are commonplace, organizations can gain collective advantages in developing social capital, boosting productivity and diminishing turnover. So there's no doubt that when people show they're motivated beyond the call of duty when they work hard and put in the extra effort, they generate positive outcomes for themselves, their careers and the organization.

But on the flip side, there is evidence of physical and cognitive limitations to this approach. These are particularly evident when 'the extra mile' isn't just one but turns into two, three, five, 10 miles – ultimately becoming an all-out marathon, a never-ending rat race.

The dark side of the extra mile emerged in a study run by SDA Bocconi, involving 650 participants. According to the findings, when people feel pressured by their company to do more than their jobs require, they experience a significant surge in fatigue. In fact, individuals under intense extra-mile pressure present a 50 per cent higher fatigue rate than others who are not subject to the same kind of stress. The study defined fatigue as 'an individual state in which feeling worn out, tired, or on edge is attributed to engaging in behaviours that go above and beyond individual duty'. But what are the reasons behind this outcome?

Briefly, people face a twin challenge: they're expected to go the extra mile as a matter of course; striving in a way that might once have earmarked someone for promotion or an excellent performance review is now seen as the status quo. But, at the same time, their core responsibilities haven't gone away, so people's limited stock of time and concentration is overstretched. As a result, expectations of excellence in the role are combined with pressure to go beyond the role. The cumulative effect of this is fatigue and – guess what? – exhaustion.

The most interesting aspect that emerged from the study is the spillover effect, which touches people's private lives. They need more time to recover the energy they've expended at work and they display more aggressive behaviour with family members at home. The study also involved employees' partners, asking them questions about the employees in the study, such as whether they get irritated quickly, are very critical, or ignore others when they get home.

To recharge our batteries, we need to use breaks and allocate serious and uninterrupted recovery time. Because we can give our best only when we are at our best, not when we try to survive with an extra dose of caffeine and inner conversations on self-motivation. So we need to pay attention to much-needed rest.

What will help us refill our tank? It depends on the person and the circumstances. We know, for example, that a walk immersed in nature, a deep conversation with the people we love, physical exercise, meditation, listening to music and regular sleep – all are positive sources of energy. At the same time, alcohol, over-eating, smoking, or too much screen time harms our power. Reading is a beautiful energy source, provided that it is done mainly with real books rather than with tablets.

Medical science can measure our physical fatigue and workload. We are now in the knowledge economy and we need to measure the 'cognitive workload' we are dealing with. Our cognitive workload (CWL) can be measured by three factors, according to Hinsta Performance. CWL results from Speed plus Switching and Interruptions plus Complexity of our task(s).[207]

$$CWL = Speed + Switching \& Interruption + Complexity$$

If you look at your job, do you think your cognitive workload has multiplied, remained the same or diminished? The bad news first: it has grown for almost everyone. The good news: we can

[207] James Hewitt & Aki Hinsta, 'Exponential: better life, better performance: from Formula 1 to Fortune 500', published in 2016.

control and minimize it, for example, by turning off notifications, so we can reduce interruptions, allocate quality time to one subject only, negotiate for more time, to set up clear boundaries in our life. 'Sorry, I don't take calls after 7pm or on the weekend,' for example. It works. Multitasking? Simply put, it's the biggest fraud ever. We need to focus and pay attention, not dilute our concentration in different activities. If multitasking is OK, why don't they allow us to text and drive at the same time?

So, we had a strategy and then we got punched. We are dealing with a disruptive crisis and several WTF moments; we need to use the brakes before restarting, check our energy level and refill our batteries with meaningful activities. To do so, we need to pause and reflect, to be ready to accelerate when we finally start again in a meaningful way.

Self-care is an essential component of wellbeing and the basis of healthy leadership. It's about maintaining the physical energy, mental focus and emotional and spiritual balance that allows you and me to be at our best to give our best. Self-care is essential to being a credible and focused leader, so it is necessary for your journey. But self-care alone is not enough. Now let's look at the rest.

Care

Somehow, conventional thinking has come to equate caring with weakness. Nothing could be further from the truth. Caring about people does not mean showing weakness but demonstrating empathy and compassion by taking concrete actions. Can you spell CARE? Sorry, it is not C-A-R-E, it's spelt T-I-M-E: it's time you invest in others and yourself. Have a look at your schedule for the next few weeks. How much time are you going to invest in care?

Cause

A cause – a sense of purpose – is the second essential trait of leadership. Why are we doing what we are doing? As people we are purpose seekers; we need to be connected with purpose. A true leader can motivate missionaries, people who have a notion deep inside, not mercenaries; people who have personal gain as their only goal. Losing the sense of purpose is like losing your compass: you may keep on going, but you've lost your sense of direction.

I learned this when working for the World Bank, for example, in the tragedy of the earthquake that struck Haiti in 2010. People found an immediate connection with their purpose and did their best to help by achieving results that were considered impossible just a few weeks earlier. And do you remember the sense of solidarity during COVID? We built hospitals in a few weeks rather than a few years. How is that possible? It's a sense of purpose, a cause that is entrenched in our minds and souls.

Connecting & collaborating

Co-ordination and collaboration: you don't need to go far to get the best possible example. It's our brain. We owe a great deal to two Spanish neuroscientists, Santiago Ramon y Cajal and Camillo Golgi, who won the Nobel Prize in 1906 in recognition of their work on the nervous system's structure. Our brain contains 86 billion neurons, which are different nerve cells. Neurons have complex shapes: each neuron has a vast tree composed of several thousand branches called dendrites (*dendron* means tree in – guess what? – Greek). Our brain, therefore, has a thousand trillion connections called synapses. These dendrites collect information from other neurons, while the axons are the cable transmissions of neurons; this is where electrical impulses from the neurons travel away to be received by other neurons.

As we learn, these elements continually change: this is neuroplasticity. For example, a child's brain can create or eliminate several million synapses – each second. Our brain weight, 1.2 to 1.4 kilos, is an exceptionally sophisticated organ hardwired for connectivity. Interestingly, while our brain is usually 2 per cent of our body weight it uses up to 20 per cent of our energy.

We have learned several lessons during the last few years. One is that the magnitude of the problem requires the capacity to co-ordinate and collaborate with many stakeholders. We can apply the same principle when thinking about climate change or other systemic problems such as unemployment.

What do we mean by connecting? The capacity to have a systemic approach to problem-solving, to understand how one problem is closely correlated to the solution, or the aggravation, of another one. If, for example, we raise the retirement age, we affect pensions and youth employment.

Let's consider another important point: problems are not only complicated but also complex. Machines are complicated but ecosystems are complex. A complicated situation demands technical expertise with a disciplinary focus. The traditional hierarchical structure can deal with this problem, as the chain of command is adequate to give an efficient response. But problems today are also complex, not only complicated. So we need to be gardeners, not mechanics, as per the fascinating book by Gary Lloyd.[208]

Solving complex problems requires three essential factors:

1. Platforms and networks rather than rigid structures;
2. Constant learning, flexibility and adaptation rather than rigid roles;
3. Full collaboration between people and institutions.

Collaboration is not just an excellent bullet point on a job description but one of the most critical behaviours that new leaders need to demonstrate. Every day. It applies to Nobel laureates and it applies to us.

Creativity
Listen to what Umberto Eco once said:[209]

> If by intellectual you mean somebody who works only with his head and not with his hands, then the bank clerk

---

[208] Gary Lloyd, *Gardeners Not Mechanics: How to Cultivate Change at Work*, Double Loop Limited, UK, 2021.
[209] 'Umberto Eco, The Art of Fiction No. 197', an Interview by Lila Azam Zanganeh.

is an intellectual and Michelangelo is not. And today, with a computer, everybody is an intellectual. So I don't think it has anything to do with someone's profession or with someone's social class. According to me, an intellectual is anyone who is creatively producing new knowledge. A peasant who understands that a new kind of graft can produce a new species of apples has at that moment produced an intellectual activity. Whereas the professor of philosophy whom all his life repeats the same lecture on Heidegger doesn't amount to an intellectual. Critical creativity – criticizing what we are doing or inventing better ways of doing it – is the only mark of intellectual function.

Given the new context generated by the Five Cs of Chaos, Crisis, Complexity, Confusion and Change, new leaders cannot rely only on updated operating systems, KPIs and procedures. They need creativity and the capacity to find innovative solutions to complex problems. It's not about inventing new products and services every day; it's about having a mindset and a creative process. One example of attitude is using knowledge and experience in one discipline and bringing it to a different one.

Steve Jobs did this when he fell in love with Andy Warhol's painting of the portrait of John Lennon. He used the same multicolour panel for the first Apple products. Apple was not the first company to use unconventional colours for its products. Olivetti started in the 1970s with a revolutionary typewriter called Valentina. This typing machine was available in several bright colours, such a revolutionary approach that one is now on display in the Design Museum in London.

Courage
Courage means remembering what we stand for.
Too many leaders choose what's convenient; they say or do what people expect by telling them what they want to hear. It's called populism. In corporate terms, it's a clear sign of mediocrity, as if leadership were a beauty contest. The problem with this

approach is confusing visibility and popularity with credibility and substance. We see this all the time: companies that measure their success based on the number of Facebook or Instagram followers as if they were teenagers with hormonal problems.

Courage is a different story. It is the capacity to do what is right even when it is not yet trending. For example, what's happening right now following the #metoo and #blacklivesmatter movements. How many companies have appointed qualified women or African-Americans in leadership roles?

Sure, it's easier to produce an elegant video and post it on Facebook: 2 million views are more important than substance, right? However, the courage of conviction is a different game: you will be looking at a leader when you see one. If not, you'll be looking at a clown.

Chaos, Crisis, Complexity, Confusion and Constant Change; the Five Cs generate a new context that opens up new possibilities as we deal with a historical transformation. This transformation will be possible only with a new leadership permeated with *Care, Cause, Collaboration, Creativity and Courage, the Five Cs.* Our journey as leaders and people will be successful only if we are equipped with a radar to understand the big picture unfolding at exponential speed and a compass that will give us a sense of direction in our journey.

Lessons from CEOs – by Peter Vanham

Peter Vanham[210] is the executive editor at *Fortune* and the author of several books including *Before I was a CEO*. I have asked Peter: what can we learn from people who made it to the top?

It's a question that most of us have asked ourselves at some point in our careers: how did those at the top make it there and

---

[210] https://www.linkedin.com/in/peter-vanham-9602ba6/

what can I do to get there as well? There is of course not one answer to this question, but over the years I spoke to dozens of CEOs about it, and some commonalities did emerge.

There's a depressing reality, first of all. Many of those who succeed share traits that were baked in at birth or latest in college. They came from affluent families with a successful business background, or went to Harvard, Oxford, or a handful of other elite universities. That's difficult for any one of us to replicate, post-factum.

But there are others too and they provide a more useful template to follow. From them, I learned almost philosophical lessons. Sure, there are some things you can aim for mechanically. 'I aimed to double my salary every four years,' one CEO told me. 'And if I didn't succeed, I knew it was time to change jobs.' I heard a few more of those very practical but mundane tips.

It was more useful, however, to take in some other reflections. 'I couldn't aim to become CEO of my company,' one other successful manager told me. Why? 'Because the company I now work for didn't exist yet when I was young and the term chief executive officer wasn't yet in use.' I looked it up and he was right: 'CEO' only became a thing in the 1970s in the US and later still elsewhere.

'Don't skip any steps on your way up,' another CEO advised me. He had gotten that advice from his mentor. The mentor told him that if he did try and go too fast, it would make people either resentful of him for skipping the line, or it could be too much, too fast, leading to a slowdown or failure down the line. It was better to master every role along the way. 'Go off the beaten path,' yet another CEO of a multinational said. 'If you do like everyone else does, 10 years into your career, you won't stand out. You'll have learned the same things your peers did and know the same people. It's better to go out of the spotlight early on, go abroad, get a wide range of experience and then when you come back, you'll have a unique résumé.'

That CEO also told me something very profound. When he ascended to the executive ranks, his then CEO told him: 'Remember to take your hat off to those who are coming down the stairs as you go up. One day, that person coming down will be you and you'll wish that whomever is coming up is as respectful to you as you have been to your predecessors.'

And he went on: 'I realized soon enough there was no point to wanting to become CEO. If this is your only goal throughout your career, only two things can happen: either you wait for 25 and you don't ultimately get the top spot. Then you'll have forever been unhappy. Or you do actually make it to the top and it will all be over in five or 10 years. Before that, you'll live in the future. After that, you'll live in the past.'

In the end, he said, it's better not to aspire to be CEO. It's better to find satisfaction in whatever you are doing in the moment. It will lead to a happier life and career, and it will probably make you more successful too. Will I ever become CEO? I don't know, and frankly, I don't care. Isn't that a beautiful life and career lesson to remember?

In the final chapter we will not draw conclusions but stimulate further reflections with – guess what? – storytelling and questions. We will go from…to something different. Personal development is a life-long journey: from…to.

8

From, to

'The meaning of life is to find your gift. The purpose of life is to give it away.'

PABLO PICASSO

Living the Seven Games

My daughter's question still resonates in my mind and heart: *what did I learn so far?* Can I ask you the same question about this book? Let's recap together.

Chapter One: by understanding the seven megatrends that are shaping the lives of our families, communities, company and countries, we have learned to celebrate Janus, the Roman god of transformation. We can connect the dots and 'see' the complexity of the new context. WTF moments will continue to pollute our lives, but we must focus on the big picture and what is relevant.

In Chapter Two, we learned to anchor our professional journey to our values and pay attention to the words we use. We remove assumptions and mindsets that are no longer relevant and understand what makes an effective team: our personal and professional development is not a solo act.

And finally, we played the Seven Games.

Game One is **The Inner Game**. We start by asking the following questions: what do we stand for? What are our strengths? What motivates us? How do we find our inner voice? What gives us joy and positive energy? This game is essential, like the foundations of a house. However, spending too much time on it may produce paralysis by (self) analysis. This game is **egocentric**; the keyword in the Inner Game is **self-discovery**.

Game Two is the **Better Game**. How can we improve what we do to gain expertise and master our skills? How can we learn from our mistakes? This is the Warrior Phase according to Carl Jung, one of self-definition, hard work and constant improvement. We shape our identity. The Better Game builds self-confidence and is an adrenaline-loaded phase. The drawback of this game can be exhaustion, being too focused with a narrow view; the risk is missing the big picture, the megatrends. At times playing the Better Game nudges us towards a pronounced narcissism, egoism or prima donna syndrome. This part of our professional development concerns external validation, competition, social adaptation, visibility and seeking security, a place in society. It is a long, tiring but exciting phase of building a career. Money is frequently used as the proxy for success. The keyword of the Better Game is **achievement. It is still an egocentric game**.

Game Three, the **Caring & Outer Games**: here we begin when we move from competing to collaborating; when we care for others and we learn to connect the dots. Becoming a leader happens when we help our team become successful: leadership is not about us, it's about helping and supporting the people we serve.

While the Better Game required strong muscles and resilience, Game Three demands empathy, social awareness, mental flexibility, curiosity, creativity and strong nerves. The perils of this game are twofold. First, from the emotional side, caring too much about too many issues or people can cause us to become emotionally bankrupt. The bad news: we cannot put people on 'mute'. The good news: we can build boundaries and teach people to respect them. Second, from the cognitive standpoint, being aware of what's happening does not translate into becoming an expert on everything. Instead, we need to know where to get the necessary insights and info; we need allies. Fear Of Missing Out is another drawback of this phase. The keywords of the Caring and Outer Game are **empathy and understanding. The game is sociocentric**.

Game Four is the **Crisis Game**: a painful, necessary and meaningful juncture of our personal and professional lives, usually occurring during our mid to late forties. The temptation is pretending that the crisis does not exist (loyal soldier), denying it (red ball), or giving in to regression (Peter Pan). But, on the contrary, we need to have the intellectually honest mindset and courage to tackle the crisis and become Brave Travellers, forging straight into the next phase of our lives. The keyword here is **questioning**. The game is mainly **introspective** – with feedback – as it requires reflection and self-awareness.

Game Five, **Reinvent**, is similar to remodelling and restructuring your house while you're living in it, an experience that (if you have lived it, as I did) you don't forget. It is messy, dusty, tiring, costly and frustrating. Still, it's a process worth going through by beginning with the end in mind. You will eventually end up in a new space with a new purpose, energy and enthusiasm. It is not rebranding with a new picture, logo, webpage, or business card. The old you is forever gone. The keyword is **awakening. The game is transformative, for you**.

Game Six, **The Revolution Game**, is also **transformative, but for other people**, as you have already completed your transformation. The critical word is **legacy**. The ego is gone: it has been replaced with the holiest part of yourself: your soul. It is not about your career anymore: it is about your **vocation**, your authenticity. The questions underpinning this phase are: does it make sense to me? How can I help? What does the world ask of me? The agenda is to grow as an individual rather than advance in your career.

Game Seven is **Letting Go**. When you let everything go, you see what stays. We have learned from Confucius, 'Happy is he who has overcome his Ego.'[211] It is **spiritual**, the final game when you seek meaning, reflection, solitude, reflection, depth and silence. The keywords are **giving away and fulfilment**.

Letting go is also about embracing *successful ageing*.[212] It is not only about living longer, it's about living smarter, thanks to cognitive enhancement and living better, because of meaning, significance and purpose. Scientist and immunologist Dr Anthony Fauci said it brilliantly: 'I am not retiring, I am rewiring.'[213] Letting go serves to regain your centrality; you are now in control. Time belongs to you. *You* are self-centred. You are what you were meant to be and to do. You will play again the same initial Inner Game, but with different maturity, gravitas and experience. You see life through different lenses.

The diagram below provides you with a framework of different elements in each of the Seven Games: coupled with the Spiral Development Framework and visualization of this book.

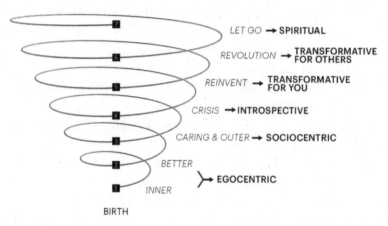

Spiral Development Framework – Paolo Gallo

[211] Siddhartha Gautama (c. 563–483 BC): the eightfold path is the means to eliminate desire and overcome the ego.
[212] Daniel J. Levitin, *Successful Again: A Neuroscientist Explores the Power and Potential of Our Lives*, Dutton Publishing, UK, 2020.
[213] Dr Anthony Fauci: https://www.ted.com/speakers/anthony_fauci

#	GAME	FOCUS	PURPOSE	KEY QUESTION	WHO CAN HELP YOU?	WHAT CAN HELP YOU?	BENEFIT	BLIND SPOT	POSSIBLE PROBLEMS
1	INNER	Egocentric	Finding your voice and path	What do you stand for?	You – intellectual honesty	Assessments	Clarity of direction	Confusing passion with talent	Paralysis by analysis
			Who are you?	What is meaningful to you?	Friends, colleagues, coach	Noticing, reflection	Realize what you are not good at	Not committed to anything, too vague	
			What motivates you?	What is your narrative, your story?	Assessments	Listening to others			
2	BETTER	Egocentric	Mastering your game	What am I good at?	Mentor-supervisors	Training	Mastering your domain	More is not better	Seeking perfection
			Improving credibility by achievements	How can I improve?	Mistakes/failures	Best practice	Measuring impact	Assumptions	burnout
				How can I measure my improvement?	Best – and worse – in the game	Asking questions	Focus on quality not quantity	Ego, arrogance	Too busy to think

(Continued)

#	GAME	FOCUS	PURPOSE	KEY QUESTION	WHO CAN HELP YOU?	WHAT CAN HELP YOU?	BENEFIT	BLIND SPOT	POSSIBLE PROBLEMS
3	OUTER	Sociocentric	Connecting the dots/contextual intelligence	How can I see the connections?	Diversity of network	Intellectual curiosity	Elevating your perspective	Stay in the comfort zone	FOMO
			Discovering opportunities – anticipating risks	What opportunities can I see?		Growth mindset	Gain insights	Too much to handle	Too much at once, overwhelmed
3	CARING	Sociocentric	Creating an impact for others	How can I help?	Clients. mentor, coach	Leaving EGO for IMPACT	Sense of purpose	Solving problems for people who don't think they have one	Exhaustion

		Move from independence to interdependence			Recharge your energy	Establishing long-term relationships		No time for self-care
								Neglecting who loves you
4 **CRISIS**	**Introspective**	Reassess to continue thriving	What is no longer relevant?	Coach, peers	Quality time to reflect	Energy of new scope in life	I can do it alone	Falling into the three syndromes (see Chapter 5)
		Discovering new motivations	What gives me joy?	Listening to others	Support system	Become a brave traveller		
5 **REINVENT**	**Transformative for you**	Reframe what is important	How can I find new meaning?	You	Noticing your energy level	Reframing your identity	Back to comfort zone	Going too fast or too slow
			How can I add value to others?	Coach	Evaluating business model	Reshaping a meaningful path		Cosmetic change
				Success stories and failures	Measuring real impact	Have fun		Unrealistic expectations

(Continued)

#	GAME	FOCUS	PURPOSE	KEY QUESTION	WHO CAN HELP YOU?	WHAT CAN HELP YOU?	BENEFIT	BLIND SPOT	POSSIBLE PROBLEMS
6	REVOLUTION	Transformative for others	Legacy	What really matters to me?	You	Reconnect with true self	Creating impact	Too generic	Misalignment with inner self
				How do I want to be remembered?	Coach		Being helpful to others		
							Replace ego with soul		
7	LETTING GO	Spiritual	Passing the torch to new generation	Did I contribute enough?	Role models	Wisdom and experience	Forging new identity	No one can replace me	Considering yourself essential and/or eternal
							Attaining wisdom	Define yourself by what you used to do	Pontificating rather than supporting

Becoming a Revolutionary Hero

How can we translate empathy, caring and collaboration into action? Let me share a practical tool that will help you, guaranteed. Look at the matrix below: on one axis, we have the severity of a problem from another person's perspective; on the other axis, the level that you are at fault – responsible.

RESPONSIBILITY

not mine   mine

	high	
	HERO ④	③ **RED CARPET**
SEVERITY OF THE PROBLEM	①	②
	SYMPATHIZE	**FIX IT**
	low	

Quadrant one: low severity coupled with not-your-responsibility or fault. What do you do? You sympathize, like when someone arrives late to a meeting due to a traffic jam. It is generally not a big deal; showing empathy will suffice.

Quadrant two: low severity, but it is your fault and responsibility. Again, you need to use and display empathy coupled with the capacity to 'fix it' or offer some remedial action. A few days ago, I forgot about a coaching session: after apologizing, I offered one free session.

Quadrant three: high severity and your responsibility. You need to apologize, acknowledge the problem you caused and immediately take corrective action. You will also need to go the extra mile. If the 'damage' is 10, offer 20. But I'm referring to something other than the financial side; I'm referring to the emotional side. A good idea is to send a written note to apologize.

Quadrant four: high severity level but not your fault or responsibility. Legally, we may say, 'Not my problem', right? But in reality, this is the space where we can become heroes to other people. *It occurs when we solve problems created by others; here's when we win the mind and hearts of individuals.* I am sure many examples come to minds right now. Maybe you have a colleague who has lost his job? Or a friend who lost a loved one? Or someone with challenges in their marriage? Or perhaps a family member struggling financially? We don't always need to solve their problems; we need to be there for them, maybe just listening, with our presence, without judging. Everything we think we know about addictions is wrong, Johann Hari told us in his moving TED Talk.[214] People in despair need our support, not our judgement or – worse – isolation.

We can become heroes by helping people struggling with significant problems and by expecting nothing in return. If we expect something back it's called opportunism, a behaviour not discussed in this book.

[214] https://www.ted.com/talks/johann_hari_everything_you_think_you_know_about_addiction_is_wrong?language=en

Lagom (by Gunnar George) and Ubuntu

I have been friends with Gunnar George[215] for many years since we shared a caipirinha (or two) in Rio de Janeiro, Brazil. Gunnar is a great guy from Sweden and, when he isn't listening to music, he's the founder and managing director at Compassion Communication. Here he explains the concept of 'Lagom', a word and belief integral to Swedish life:

> The best way to explain 'Lagom' is how the Vikings shared a meal when they had a ceremonial dinner to welcome guests. A big horn with mead circulated the table and you drank Lagom from the funnel. Not too much, not too little. If you took too much, someone at the end of the table would not get any. It was a sign of greed and not thinking of the common good. Trust was lost. If you drank Lagom, you shared equally and had everyone's best interest in mind. You gained trust. This Lagom can, in a larger sense, be a recipe for how we could handle many of the world's challenges today. It is a set of values, a philosophy, and a way of living and well worth exploring.
>
> The essence of Lagom is to include others and to share good and evil. This act of sharing is a sign of respect. Everyone is unique but also equal. This sharing is never taken for granted, as it is based on free will and on what individuals find reasonable. The underlying assumption and silent agreement are that no one should take advantage of others' openness, hospitality and goodwill.
>
> One example of Lagom is the 'Right of Public Access' in Sweden, which gives all people the right to walk freely in forests and mountains. In Sweden, you can pick berries, camp and make fires wherever you want, as long as you act responsibly and do not disturb the people and animals

---

[215] https://www.linkedin.com/in/gunnar-george-03a7741/

there. A shared belief is that no one will take personal advantage of it. And everyone knows that this trust is the source of great freedom.

Lagom means taking responsibility and ensuring everyone gets a fair share in the team, the community and the world. But, unfortunately, we are pretty far from there.

The opposite of Lagom is when the strongest take what they want and leave only leftovers to others: power instead of trust. It would be hard to face global challenges without trust and it needs to be built with some Lagom thinking. Climate crisis, war, pandemics, lack of food and water, AI and resource scarcity are challenges we must face together in collaboration. Lagom leadership takes responsibility for the whole and for inclusion to get away from all that 'them and us'. 'What's in it for me?' is the wrong question. It's about WE instead of me.

Doc Rivers has been one of the most respected and admired NBA coaches since 1999, after a brilliant 15-year career as a player. In 2004, he was appointed head coach of the Boston Celtics, possibly the most prestigious NBA team along with the Los Angeles Lakers. After three disappointing seasons, in 2007, the Celtics signed three superstars: Kevin Garnett, Paul Pierce and Ray Allen. Doc Rivers understood that expectations of winning were high, coupled with the challenge to transform three superstars into genuine team players, focusing more on winning for the team than scoring individual points.

One day, Doc Rivers[216] went to a business meeting and met a woman: 'Doc, your team is going to be amazing: but you have to be **Ubuntu**.' Doc had never heard the word Ubuntu before; the woman insisted, 'Ubuntu is NOT a word: *it is a way of living;* you need to know what it is.' Doc did not sleep that night: he stayed up reading everything to learn about Ubuntu, a

---

[216] *The Playbook: A Coach's Rules for Life*, Netflix documentary, first episode 2020.

philosophy of life. He read books and listened to speeches from Cape Town's Archbishop Desmond Tutu,[217] who popularized the term. In his short essay, 'Ubuntu: On the Nature of Human Community',[218] Tutu wrote:

> In our African Weltanschauung, our worldview, we have something called Ubuntu. This expression is complicated to render in English, but we could translate it by saying, 'A person is a person through other persons.' We need other human beings to learn how to be human, for none of us comes fully formed into the world. We would only know how to talk, walk, think and eat as human beings if we learned how to do these things from other human beings. For us, the solitary human being is a contradiction in terms. Ubuntu is the essence of being human. It speaks of how my humanity is caught up and bound up inextricably with yours. It says, not as Descartes did, 'I think therefore I am,' but rather, 'I am because I belong.' I need other human beings to be human. The completely self-sufficient human being is subhuman. I can be me only if you are entirely you. I am because we are, for we are made for togetherness, for family. We are made for complementarity. We are created for a delicate network of relationships, interdependence with our fellow human beings, and the rest of creation.

The Ubuntu's light reshaped South Africa under Nelson Mandela's leadership: it also reshapes Doc's thinking on how to coach his team. Doc Rivers believes that is the perfect incarnation of his basketball philosophy. He asks the team's rookies, the youngest players to be the ambassadors of Ubuntu. Ubuntu is initially met with irony and scepticism, but the group gradually embraces it. Kevin Garnett, before any game and

[217] https://en.wikipedia.org/wiki/Desmond_Tutu
[218] https://www.lookingforwisdom.com/ubuntu/

during time-outs, shouts '1, 2, 3...Ubuntu,' and the team follow him. The Boston Celtic's mentality changes: players start playing differently. The word Ubuntu becomes a way of life.

The team wins the NBA title against Los Angeles Lakers in 2008 after a 20-year wait. After the victory, one journalist told Kevin Garnett, 'You were superb.' Kevin replied, 'Me? It's Us, it is not me.' The most competitive players internalized that the better the team is, the better they are: all of them, not one of them. It is the very essence of the emotional speech by the veteran football coach played by Al Pacino in the 1999 Oliver Stone movie *Any Given Sunday*:[219] 'That's a team, gentlemen: either we heal as a team or we die as individuals.' I believe that the same principle applies to our families, communities, countries and planet.

Ghosts or Ancestors?

What do we remember from the people who left us, who are no longer with us?

Remembering is not a passive act; we need to play an active role. Remembering, in Italian, '*ricordare*', derives from the Latin *re-cordari* (from cor, cordis 'heart' with the prefix re-), to bring back to heart: the ancient Romans believed that the heart was the source of memory.

In his 2017–18 show, 'Springsteen on Broadway', the rock legend shared his life memories filled with many moving stories and moments, such as when he remembers his amazing and supporting mom and the sadness of losing his blood brother, Clarence Clemons. Then, near the show's end, he talks about legacy with disarming honesty and compassion. We have a choice to make, Bruce says, to become a ghost or an ancestor to our families, friends and – in his case – fans. Ghost, something

---

[219] https://www.youtube.com/watch?v=f1yWSePMqsk

we chase away, we avoid it the best we can; ancestor, a constant, a reassuring model and a reference point, maybe a guardian angel?

I frequently drive from Geneva, where I live, to Milan, my hometown, and back. The highway passes close to Ivrea, my father's hometown. I can't explain, but every time I used to drive by Ivrea, I could not stop crying. I was overwhelmed to the point that I had to stop the car. I never ever told this story to anyone, as I felt deeply ashamed. Then, a few years ago, a dear friend called me; 'Paolo, I need to talk to you, but please tell me that you won't think I'm crazy or that I perform black magic.' I laughed and said sure, I was happy to listen.

'*Listen: I have been dreaming about your father, whom I have never met.*' He described my father perfectly well and then continued: '*Your father told me to ask you to stop crying when you drive by Ivrea. He told me he's happy where he is, and you should be happy and grateful, too.*'

So, the next time I drove from Geneva to Milan, I exited the highway and went straight to Ivrea, nearly 45 years after being there with my dad. I booked a fancy restaurant, a table for two, and ordered a bottle of his favourite wine, Barolo, and his favourite dish, risotto. I asked for two glasses. I made a toast with my ancestor. Since that time, I stopped crying and started celebrating with him every single joyful occasion or event. I still have plenty of imaginary conversations. He's my coach, my secret weapon. I trust – actually, I know - that your ancestors are there with you too. They want us to be happy. They're still with us; they protect us.

I hope you can transform the acute pain of their physical absence into the deep peacefulness of their spiritual presence.

From, To

How do you know you are on the right track to complete your personal and professional development? When you move from something to something very different: in at least 50 different ways.

From autopilot to awareness
From ageing to growing
From distraction to focus
From dead-lines to life-lines
From busy-ness to clarity
From speed to depth
From qualifications to character
From success to significance
From pride to decency
From money to meaning
From visibility to credibility
From reaction to reflection
From legal to ethical
From anxiety to peacefulness
From chaos to harmony
From expedient to meaningful
From rules to values
From goals to purpose
From dreaming to awakening
From seeing to noticing
From mercenary to missionary
From obedience to critical thinking
From dependence to interdependence
From performance to impact
From branding to real
From languishing to thriving
From looking interesting to being interested
From external elegance to inner grace
From spotlight to candlelight
From judging to understanding
From reacting fast to anticipating first
From indifference to solidarity
From pretending to authenticity
From holding grudges to holding hands
From interrupting to probing
From answers to questions

From being distracted to being present
From knowing to understanding
From competing to collaborating
From using to caring
From money-making to sense-making
From anxiety to tranquillity
From blind spots to self-awareness
From wealth to health
From avoiding to exploring
From accumulating to simplicity
From emptiness to fulfilment
From ego to soul
From resentment to gratitude
From cleverness to wisdom

Which one do you relate to the most?

From FOMO to FOME

FOMO is the Fear of Missing Out, a feeling of anxiety or insecurity over the possibility of being left out of something, such as an event, an opportunity, or an update on your social media. It is also why we constantly check our phones (ready?) 2,617 times a day,[220] the main factor in creating Attention Deficit Disorder. This is a behavioural disorder, usually first diagnosed in childhood, characterized by inattention, impulsivity and, in some cases, hyperactivity. The constant acceleration at exponential speed has created an environment that is no longer suitable for our minds and our lives, no longer compatible and sustainable: it is simply exhausting living this way.

Furthermore, the oversupply of information has produced a breakdown in our capacity to pay attention, notice, reflect,

[220] J. MacKay, 'Screen time stats 2019: here's how much you use your phone during the work day', *RescueTime* (blog), 21 March 2019.

solve problems and engage with real people rather than digital followers. As a result, we have lost our connections and our focus, as brilliantly explained and convincingly researched in Johann Hari's books, *Lost Connections*[221] and *Stolen Focus*.[222] FOMO and continuous interruptions have created a fragmented, isolated life. The question is, how can we return to sanity? What is the antidote to insanity?

Nancy Kline[223] proposes building a thinking environment where we create focused attention, at ease but not in a hurry, an appreciation of others, equality and no interruptions. Hungarian psychologist Mihaly Csikszentmihalyi[224] coined the term, 'flow', the state and mindset of congruence, harmony and happiness. Flow occurs when 1) we choose a clearly defined goal, one that is meaningful to us; 2) we remove interferences and interruption from this goal; 3) the goal stretches our skills, just to the edge of our comfort zone; and 4) we focus on it for an extended period and when we delay gratification as the long-term goal is meaningful and essential to us. Sanity and happiness result when we replace FOMO with **Focus on Meaningful and Essential**: I call it **FOME**.

The spiral of the Seven Games is the visualization of our personal development. I am convinced that 'growing up', meaningful personal development, is the quintessential antidote to pain. In our lives, we have experienced, or will experience pure joy but also many difficult, if not traumatic, events that are part of us forever. Believing that time will heal, that we will forget these moments, that everything shall pass and that we will return to normal is delusional. Of course, it will not.

Counterintuitively, it's better to feel this way. Should we, for example, really aim to forget people who are no longer

[221] Johann Hari, *Lost Connections: Uncovering the Real Causes of Depression and the Unexpected Solutions*, Bloomsbury Publishing, 2018

[222] Johann Hari, *Stolen Focus: Why You Can't Pay Attention*, Bloomsbury Publishing, 2022.

[223] Nancy Kline, *Time to Think: Listening to Ignite the Human Mind*, Octopus Books, first edition 1999.

[224] Mihaly Csikszentmihalyi, *Flow: The Psychology of Optimal Experience*, Harper & Row, first edition 1990.

with us? Should we disregard the harsh but valuable lessons that life offers us? What will change is the relative 'space' that painful experiences will 'occupy' in our minds and hearts. Our continuous personal development will shrink the space of that event. Wounds will transform into openings. Initially, we will only grasp, then understand and finally internalize the true meaning and significance of pain and suffering. Events will become learning and growing opportunities: no more pain and suffering to suppress, avoid or deny. The size of the pain will not change nor will it be lessened by time. *The real antidote is not time, it is our personal growth.* The space taken by pain will progressively be reduced by our personal development. I am convinced that if we don't grow and develop as people, we will remain prisoners of pain. If we do grow, we will be able to give meaning to it.

We don't need drugs or addictions to numb our pain. Instead, we need to be wide awake, as we have a person, a family or a community to serve, or a promise to honour, a commitment to keep, with the help and support of our authentic human connections. **Personal development is the natural healing process.**

Understanding the big picture, rethinking your role as a vocation rather than a career, learning to master your personal and professional development with the Seven Games: all these efforts are lifetime endeavours of continuous evolution and growth in learning, contribution and influence. George Bernard Shaw reminds us that *Life isn't about finding yourself: life is about creating yourself.*[225]

Legacy. I always ask myself: if this project/task/job was the last one I did in my life, would I be content and satisfied? I was addicted to **FOMO**. It took some time: I am now an ambassador of **FOME – Focus On Meaningful and Essential**.[226] Two years ago, I decided to invest my time to write this book. If I can help even one person, I'd be happy. Could you please

[225] George Bernard Shaw quotes at https://www.pcs.org/features/7-brilliant-quotes-by-george-bernard-shaw

[226] Greg McKeown, *Essentialism: The Disciplined Pursuit of Less,* Crown Business Publishing, 2014.

let me know if you are this person by contacting me?[227] One of the most consistent impulses of my life is to help and to communicate with others, a burning desire and recurrent theme flowing in my veins.

Reflections, not conclusions

Two of the most critical questions of our existence are: *'How do we measure our life?'* The book and article[228] from a legend, Clayton M. Christensen, does not provide the answer but offers three subsequent questions. First, how can I be sure that I will be happy in my job? The author refers to a Life Purpose, not to climb the corporate ladder. Second, how can I be sure that my relationships with my spouse and family become a source of happiness? Third, how can I stay out of jail? Christensen refers to the determination to lead a life of integrity: 100 per cent of the time, not when it is convenient or someone is watching.

The second question, still about measuring, is, *'How do I want to spend the time I have left?'* I suggest you do the following exercise. First, take a paper ruler similar to the one you find at IKEA; it is 1 meter long, 100 cm. Life expectancy is (OECD countries) 82. So, please remove 18 cm, then remove the number of centimetres equivalent to your age. Then remove one-third of what is left, the time you spend sleeping. How much is left? When I do this exercise, I look intensively at 'my' 15 cm left. It is a sobering exercise that forces you to consider the importance of using wisely the time you (hope) you have left and how you want to use it.

---

[227] www.paologallo.net or https://www.linkedin.com/in/paolo-gallo-b996874/
[228] Clayton M. Christensen, 'How will you measure your life?' *HBR*, July-August 2010 https://hbr.org/2010/07/how-will-you-measure-your-life

Last: in life, we can negotiate everything. To sell is human,[229] Daniel Pink reminds us. Yes, but with one critical exception: we can negotiate everything except who we are, what we stand for, our values and principles.

This book starts with the definition of hell: on the last day of your life, you will meet the person you could have become. What is Heaven, then? It is about finding the ultimate response to every person's quest for meaning. It is becoming what you are meant to become. After understating the new context and learning to avoid too many WTF moments and challenge our assumptions, we start the Seven Games. First, discover the treasure inside you: your authentic voice in the **Inner Game**. Then learn the **Better Game** and master the **Caring and Outer Game**. Finally, after managing the **Crisis Game**, you can confidently **Reinvent** yourself, ready to leave a legacy with the **Revolution Game** before you attain wisdom with the **Letting Go Game**.

You may recall we have met Dante, the Italian poet, at the beginning of the Crisis game. Dante also wrote, '*Se segui la tua Stella, non puoi fallire a glorioso porto.*'[230] 'If you follow your Star, you cannot fail to land in a glorious destination.' So, I hope you have found your Star.

Indeed, '*the meaning of life is to find your gift, the purpose of life is to give it away.*'[231] It is our gift to the people we love, and to humankind. We can make it also because we are not alone, we will always have the support and the love of our families and ancestors. We can enjoy the never-ending journey of personal and professional self-development. By becoming your true self, who you are meant to become, you have mastered the Seven Games of Self-Leadership, the inner journey of Leaders, like you.

[229] Daniel H. Pink, 'To Sell is Human: The Surprising Truth About Moving Others', Riverhead, USA, 2021
[230] Dante Alighieri, *La Divina Commedia*, Inferno, Canto XV,
[231] Picasso quotes at https://spanishmama.com/picasso-quotes-about-the-meaning-of-life/

The true goal of the Seven Games of Leadership is to achieve your full potential. What did you learn by reading the Seven Games?

Let me close with ten questions and insights for you to consider in order to find out.

1. Can you see the big picture, the megatrends, and their connections? Then, *you have developed contextual intelligence.*
2. Can you avoid being derailed by WTF moments? Then, *you can keep your focus on what matters.*
3. Can you challenge outdated assumptions? Then, *you can foster a brand new mindset and open new possibilities.*
4. Can you play the Inner Game? Then, *you can create a genuine identity, self-awareness and internalize what you stand for.*
5. Can you play the Better Game? Then, *you can experience the joy of mastering a profession or a role by adding value.*
6. Can you play the Caring and Outer Game? Then, *you can help others also by understanding the new context.*
7. Can you play the Crisis Game? Then, *you demonstrate the courage to shape your new life.*
8. Can you play the Reinvent Game? Then, *you find a new purpose and refill your heart and soul with renewed energy and joy.*
9. Can you play the Revolution game? Then, *you are building a legacy for the people and communities you love and care for.*
10. Can you master the Letting Go game?

Then, you are Free.

With Gratitude (formerly known as Acknowledgements)

TV presenter Fred Rogers gave a short acceptance speech upon receiving the Lifetime Achievement Award at the 1997 Emmys.[232]

> So many people have helped me to come here to this night. Some of you are here, some far away, and some even in Heaven. All of us have special ones who loved us into being. Would you just take, along with me, 10 seconds to think of the people who have helped you become who you are, those who cared about you and wanted what was best for you in life? Ten seconds, I'll watch the time.
>
> Whomever you've been thinking about, how pleased they must be to know the difference you feel they have made.

Here are my 10 seconds.

My gratitude goes to Bloomsbury's amazing team for publishing – again – my book after *The Compass and the Radar: The Art of Building a Rewarding Career While Remaining True to Yourself* in 2018 and in paperback edition in 2020. The footnotes in my book are not *only* footnotes. They are my personal tribute to many artists and authors who have contributed to shaping the way I see life with their books, articles, songs, paintings, poems,

---

[232] Fred Rogers at Emmy Awards 97. https://www.youtube.com/watch?v=Upm9LnuCBUM

speeches, insights and questions. It is a tribute to each of them and a sign of respect for *you*, the intellectually curious reader, eager to learn and embark on the never-ending journey of self-development. Finally, sincere thanks to the (few) villains I have met in my journey: they push me to be better and to improve who I am, not only what I do.

My appreciation and gratitude to Alessandra Losito, for her generous support over the years, Jill Connelly for her help in editing The Seven Games and to the people who have contributed: in order of 'appearance': Marco Albani, Carlos Scartascini, Jennifer Blanke, Sandra-Stella Triebl, Fred Werner, Giuseppe Stigliano, Mirja Cartia D'Asero, Salvatore Pedulla, Riccardo Barberis, Bruno Bianchini, Francesca Corrado, Tobias Degsell, Alessandro Bogliari, Aidan McCullen, Silvia Polleri, Riccardo Pittis, Aditya Agrawal, Gianfranco Minutolo, Peter Vanham and Gunnar George – beautiful minds and friends. My sincere gratitude goes to Dave Ulrich, not only for writing the forewords but also for being a bright reference point in my personal and professional development.

Last, my deep, sincere gratitude to my family: Renzo, my ancestor, Anna, Francesca and Bianca. If you reflect on it, everything boils down to the last person you feel and think of when you go to sleep and the first person you feel and think of when you wake up. I have two special, caring, smart and loving persons in this category: I am blessed to have Lalia, my beloved wife, and Sadika, my joyful daughter, in my life. This book is dedicated, with gratitude and sincere love, to both: just hearing their voices makes me happy.

If you take 10 seconds for gratitude and thanksgiving, you will notice how many good and decent people have helped you become who you are, those who cared about you and wanted what was best for you. In writing this book, I hope you would consider me as one of them.

I trust you can see the magnificent beauty of a meaningful life waiting for you.

Go for it – it is here, now.

Index

active listening 227
Adams, John 70
Agassi, Andre 96
ageing, successful 248
aging and youthful populations/workforce 35–7
Agrawal, Aditya 210–13
AI (artificial intelligence) 39–43
Albani, Marco 30–2
ancestors *vs.* ghosts 258–9
anxiety and addiction 167
Apple 221–2, 241
Aristotle 169, 221
assumptions, challenging 84–8, 245
Athlete stage of development, Jung's 89–90
'atomic habits' 119–20
attention, paying 219

Barberis, Riccardo 53–5
barnacle *vs.* lobster characteristics 159–61
Behavioural Economics 136–7
Bianchini, Bruno 81–2
Binet, Alfred 73
Blanke, Jennifer 36–8
Bocconi, SDA 236–7
Bogliari, Alessandro 138–40
Bolles, Dick 185
bosses, relevance of 88
brain function, human 29, 123–4, 154–5, 167, 217, 239
Brave Traveller response to crisis 158
Bregman, Rutger 128–9
Bridges, William 161, 164
broker networkers 142
Bronson, Po 94
Bryant, Kobe 118–19, 198–200
Buffet, Warren 116
Bukowski, Charles 97, 177
burnout 167–8
Byrne, David 152

Cabral, Pedro Alvares 126
caring and responsibility - Caring Game 18, 126, 148, 238, 246, 253–4
   collaboration and its contribution to success 132–7
   creativity 132–3, 138–42
   Hobbes and Rousseau on human nature 127–9
   importance of empathy 130–2
   management roles 129–30
   networks and networking 141–3
   sabotage and backstabbing 137–8
   see also Outer Game
carpenter ants 180
Caribbean, inequality in the 33–4
Carrey, Jim 95
Cartia d'Asero, Mirja 47–9
cause/sense of purpose 238–9
change, constant 60–1

change *vs.* transition 161–2
chaos 59
Chekov, Anton 127
Choucair, Sabine 130–1
Christensen, Clayton M. 264
climate emergency, global and personal impact of the 30–2
cognitive workload (CWL) formula, Hinsta Performance 237–8
collaboration and connection 22, 132–7, 138–, 239–40, 253–4
competition, nature of 137, 138
complexity 59–60
   tackling complex problems 66–7, 240
Confucius 147, 247–8
confusion and ambiguity 60
congruence and congruence scale 163
consolidation, knowledge 220
conspiracy 46–7
contextual intelligence 9–10, 13, 22, 145
control system *vs.* trust ecosystem 88
convener networkers 142
Convey, Steve 221
Cook-Greuter, Susanne R. 11
Corrado, Francesca 123–5
Covid-19 global pandemic 57–8, 60, 80, 86
creativity and innovation 132–3, 138–41, 240–1
credibility *vs.* visibility 71–2
crisis and opportunity - Crisis Game 18, 23, 59, 91, 247
   author's experience 148–51
   barnacle *vs.* lobster characteristics 159–61
   change *vs.* transition 161–2
   midlife changes 151–6
   question/photograph exercise 160–1
   restlessness and typical responses 156–9
   as a rite of passage 175–6
   speed of transition and growth 171–5
   transitional process - Autumn, Winter and Spring 162–71
critical creativity 241
critical thinking 46, 47
Csikszentmihalyi, Mihaly 262
curiosity/active engagement 219, 221–2, 227

Dalton-Smith, Sandra 235
Dan, Dilbert 183
Dante 151, 265
dating ideas 171–2
de Bono, Edward 75–6
de Botton, Alain 158–9
decision making 46, 60–1
deficiency motivators 90, 153
Degsell, Tobias 133–6
Dehaene, Stanislas 216–17
delayed gratification 97–8
demographics 35–8
dependability 83

development
  author's teenage 98–104
  developing from, to 259–61
  Game Two – the Better Game 18, 117–26, 147, 246
  impact of megatrends 31–2
  of intelligence 76–7
  Jung's stages of human 89–90
  lateral, vertical and actual 11
  personal 10, 11, 46, 89–91, 147, 259–61, 262–3
  professional 11, 18, 91–3, 147, 246, 259–61
  realising potential 9–10, 23
  Spiral Development Framework 248
  see also Seven Games
diamond thought pattern 6–7
digital transformation 43–6
disenchanted vs. disillusioned 164
disruption, appetite for 18
diversity, importance of 38–9, 134, 231
Donne, John 135
dream jobs, creating 187–9
Drucker, Peter 20, 113
du Sautoy, Marcus 141
Duke, Annie 207
Dunbar, Robin 143
Dweck, Carol 76–7
Dylan, Bob 166
dysfunctional teams 78–9

Eco, Umberto 240–1
Edwards Deming, W. 24
effective teams 81–2
  dependability 83
  impact 84
  meaning/sense of purpose 84
  psychological safety 82–3
  structure and clarity 83
ego 89–90, 98, 153–4, 246, 247, 248
Einstein, Albert 22
emotional involvement 217–18, 246
empathy and connection 130–1, 246, 247, 253–4
employed vs. employable 85–6
Enron 227–8
error feedback 219–20
expansionist networkers 142
expectations, inner and outer 107–8
'extra mile', going the 235–7

failures and learning 220, 222
  see also mistakes, learning from
Faithful Soldier response to crisis 156–7
fake news 46–7
Fauci, Dr Anthony 248
Fear Of Missing Out (FOMO) 201–2, 247, 261–2, 263
Federer, Roger 114–15, 138, 152–3
feedback and self-awareness 112–13
Festina Lente 27–8
First World War 232–3
'Five Cs' of the 'new context' 58–62
  another 'Five Cs' to deal with the 'new context' 231–42
'flow' state 154, 262
Focus On Meaningful and Essential (FOME) 262–3
Frankl, Viktor 28–9
freedom of choice 28–9
freelance job market 54

French Revolution 128
future mindedness 88
Fyre Festival (2017) 71

Gallwey, Timothy 114
Galton, Sir Francis 73
games defined 17
Gardner, Howard 74–5
Garnett, Kevin 257–8
geopolitics 49–51
'George Gray' (E.L. Masters) 165–6
George, Gunnar 255–6
ghost teams 80–1
ghosts vs. ancestors 258–9
Gini Coefficient 33
globalization 50–1
Goethe, Johann Wolfgang von 182–3
Golgi, Camillo 239
Google 81–2
Gravitas 56, 57
Great Resignation 12
Greece and Greek mythology, ancient 56, 90, 94–5, 169
Greenberg, Sandy 218
growth mindset vs. fixed mindset 76–7
guidance and advice, seeking 119–20

Harari, Yuval Noah 85–6, 216
Harvard Business Review (HBR) 113, 153 234–5
healing and forgiveness 18, 202–3
Health of Munitions Workers Committee (HMWC) 232–3
helping people 23, 246–7, 253–4
  see also caring and responsibility – Caring Game; revolutionary hero – Revolution Game, becoming a
Hemingway, Ernest 135
Henley, William Ernest 147
Hobbes, Thomas 127, 128–9
Hoffer, Eric 25
human nature, Hobbes' and Rousseau's competing views on 127–8

idiotes 90
Il Sole 24 Ore Group 47–9
immigration 37–8
impact, team 84
improvement see development; Seven Games
in-person vs. digital 87
inequality 32–5, 51, 128
infodemic and reputation 46–9
inner voice 18, 113–14, 149–50
  mastering 114–15
intellectual honesty 68–9
intelligence, types of 74–5
IQ tests 73–4
Isaacson, Walter 120
Ise Grand Shrine, Japan 177–9

Jacques, Elliott 151–2
Janus, Roman god 56–7, 245
job market, future of the global 51–2
  interview with Riccardo Barberis 53–5
Jobs, Steve 221–2, 241
Johnson, Spencer 60
Jung, Carl 89–90, 154, 246
Juventus 56–7

Kahneman, Daniel 136–7
Kazantzakis, Nikos 215
King, Marissa 141–2
Kline, Nancy 262
Kuhn, Thomas 62–3

Lagom, concept of 19, 255–6
lateral thinking 75
Latin America, inequality in 33–5
leadership 54–5
  courage in 241–2
  lessons from CEOs 242–4
  and self-care 238
  sense of purpose 238–9
  toxic 230
  trust and integrity 22
learning/knowledge 216–21, 239
  four pillars of 219–20
  life-long 23, 222–3
  rules for learning 221–3
  sources of 20
legacy 91, 198, 210–13, 247
letting go – Game Seven 18, 198, 208–10, 247–8
  Fear Of Missing Out (FOMO) 201–2
  importance of legacy 91, 198, 210–13, 247
  learning from losses 203–5
  letter to basketball from Kobe Bryant 199–200
  time for healing and forgiveness 202–3
  when to quit 204–8
Leviathans 127
Lievegoed, Bernard 91–2
life-long learning 23, 222–3
life quakes vs. life decisions 181–2
listening and co-operation 20, 227
losses, learning from 203–5
love 13

management roles, caring in 129–30
Mandela, Nelson 257
Maslow, Abraham H. 98
McCollum, Oswald and Margaret 87
McCullen, Aidan 179–81
McFarland, Billy 71
'meaning at work' 84
megatrends 10 17–18, 22, 29–30, 143, 145
  climate emergency 30–2
  demographics and diversity 35–9
  geopolitics 49–51
  inequality and trust 32–5
  infodemic and reputation 46–9
  technology, AI and digital transformation 39–46
  visualization 29
memories 217–18
Mersch, Danielle 180
Messinger, Ruth 190
Michelangelo 23
midlife crises see crisis and opportunity – Crisis Game
Miller, Henry 209
'Mind the Gap' announcement, TFL 87
MindGeek Holdings 68–9
mindset, power of 76–7
Minutolo, Gianfranco 225
mistakes, learning from 122–5, 246
Moore, Gordon 59
Morrison, Van 202
motivation 108–9
Mozart, Wolfgang Amadeus 137

Muir, John 20
Museum of the Future, Dubai 179

Nadella, Satya 132
Narayan, Lux 197–8
negativity and cynicism 95–6
net-zero economy 31
networks/networking 141–3, 224–7
neuroplasticity 239
'new context' and the 'Five Cs' 62–3
  another 'Five Cs' to deal with 231–42
'new normal' 58–62
New York Times 69, 196
newspapers, national 47–9
Nobel, Alfred Bernhard 210–13
Nobel Prizes/Nobel laureates 132–7, 166, 183

Obama, Michelle 24
obituaries 197–8, 211–13
'Ode to Joy' exercise 104–7
Ogun 132–3
Olympic basketball team (2004), US 118–19
Othman, Walter 23–4
Outer Game 143–5, 148

paradigm shifts 62–3
passions, your 77–8
passive vs. active learning 223
Pedulla, Salvatore 49–51
Pellegrini, Federica 118
Pencavel, John 232
Peter Pan response to crisis 158
Peterson, Jordan B. 233–4
Pfeffer, Jeffrey 230
Philippe, Patek 59
Picasso, Pablo 141, 245
Pittis, Riccardo 203–5
Polleri, Silvia 193
populism 241–2
Pornhub 69
problem solving skills 240
professional value calculation 229–30
psychological safety 82–3, 88
psychometric test, Red Bull 110–12
purpose, goals and a wish, comparison of 72–3
Putin, Vladimir 69

questioning and life choices 93–7, 104–13, 169
quitting 18, 204–8
  see also losses, learning from

raison d'être/purpose, finding our 95–6, 104–13
  see also self-awareness and the Inner Game
Ramon y Cajal, Santiago 239
reciprocity, cultivating 227
Red Ball response to crises 157–8
reinvention – Game Five 18, 170–5, 177–9, 205, 247
  creating your dream job 187–9
  how should we do it? – managing change 185
  life quakes vs. life decisions 181–2
  mindset of permanent reinvention 179–81
  need for self-knowledge 185–6
  role of perception – seeing the invisible 186–7
  when is the right time? 184–5
  why should we change? 182–3
relationships, importance of meaningful 91, 142–3,
  171, 175, 223–7, 246–7, 257

remembrance 258–9, 262–3
remote working 86–7
reputation and credibility 18, 227–30
response-ability 13, 29
responsibility, levels of 253–4
Ress, Maria 230
rest, importance of 235, 237
retirement 248
revolutionary hero – Revolution Game, becoming a 253–4
  heroes *vs.* revolutionaries 190–1
  learning from obituaries and legacy 197–8
  stories from revolutionaries 191–7
Rivers, Doc 256–8
role specialization 180
Roman Empire/Romans 27, 56–7, 258
Roosevelt, Theodore 122, 126, 130
Rousseau, Jean-Jacques 127–9
Rubin, Gretchen 108
Russell, Bertrand 136
Russia 69–70

sabotage/backstabbing 137
Salieri, Antonio 137–8
Scartascini, Carlos 33–5
Second World War 186–7
self-awareness and the Inner Game 104–5, 147, 154, 185–6
  asking for feedback 112–13
  author's experience 98–104
  Ode to Joy exercise 104–7
  recognizing your talents 109–11
  recognizing your weaknesses 111–12
  response to inner and outer expectations 107–9
self-care 29, 155, 223, 231–8
self-discipline 97–8
self-improvement and the Better Game 117–19, 138, 147, 246
  adopting atomic habits 119–20
  advice and guidance 120–1
  learning from mistakes 122–4, 125–6
  what we learn from ugly characters 120–1
Senge, Peter 60
Seuss, Dr 232
Seven Games 7, 11–12, 18–19, 93, 249–52, 265–6
  Game One – Inner Game 18, 89–116, 147, 245–6
  Game Two – Better Game 18, 117–26, 147, 246
  Game Three – Caring and Outer Game 18, 126–45, 148, 246–7
  Game Four – Crisis Game 18, 148–, 247
  Game Five – Reinvention 18, 177–90, 247
  Game Six – The Revolution 18, 190–8, 247
  Game Seven – Letting Go 18, 198–209, 247–8
Shaw, George Bernard 177, 263
sleep and knowledge consolidation 220
Smith, Adam 88
social cohesion 34
Socrates 169
soft skills/internal competencies 54
'The Sound of Silence' (Simon and Garfunkel) 217–18
Soyinka, Wole 132–3
Spiral Development Framework 19, 248
Spirit stage of development, Jung's 91
Springsteen, Bruce 224, 258–9
Statement stage of development, Jung's 91
stem cells 180–1

Stevenson, Gary 35
Stigliano, Giuseppe 43–5
strengths and talents, your 10, 77–8
strong State, Hobbes' 127
structure and clarity, team 83
success, defining 6–7, 70–1
surrender state 209–10
survivor bias 187
system thinking and awareness 13, 22, 144–5

talents and strengths, your 77–8, 109–11
team types 78–82
teams/team work, importance of 224, 256–8
'thinking hats' 75–6
This I Believe CBS Radio Network show 21–2
Tomlin, Lily 109–10
toxic people and environments 24, 175–6
transformation and adaptation, your 23–4, 162, 179, 247
transformation for others 247
transition 18, 56–7
  Autumn: the ending 162–5
  Spring: reinvention 170–1
  Winter: the neutral zone 165–8
  managing speed and growth 171–5
  see also reinvention - Game Five
Triebl, Sandra-Stella 38–9
Trump Administration 85–6
trust 22, 88, 127, 134–5, 225, 227
  and inequality 34–5
Tutu, Archbishop Desmond 257
Tversky, Amos 136–7
Twain, Mark 94

Ubuntu, concept of 19, 256–8
Ukraine, war in (2022–current) 69–70
Ulrich, Dave 6–8
United Nations 49–50

Valentina typewriter, Olivetti 241
Vanham, Peter 194
Velasca 43–5
value systems 18
Viorst, Judith 162–3
von Humboldt, Alexander 59
von Oech, Roger 76
Wald, Abraham 186–7

Warrior stage of development, Jung's 89–90, 246
Washington, Denzel 46
weaknesses, recognizing your 111–12
wealth *vs.* health of nations 88–9
Werner, Fred 39–43
Williams, Danny 205–7
words, language and phrasing, importance of 68–70, 245
working hours, assumptions about 87–8
World Bank 20–1, 65–6, 112, 136, 150, 178, 239
'WTF moments', destabilizing 13, 143–4, 245
  applying *Festina Lente* and freedom of choice 27–9
  defining components 26–7

Yoruban mythology 132–3
Young, Margaret 103–4

Zander, Ben 24, 65, 103